FIVE REMARKABLE ENGLISHMEN

★★★★★

FIVE
REMARKABLE ENGLISHMEN

A New Look at the Lives and Times of

Walter Ralegh

Captain John Smith

John Winthrop

William Penn

James Oglethorpe

by DENIS MEADOWS

illustrated

The Devin-Adair Company
New York 1961

to my wife

Canadian Agent: Thomas Nelson & Sons, Toronto
Library of Congress Catalog card number: 61–17792

designed by Robin Fox
Manufactured in the United States of America
by H. Wolff, New York

Contents

A NOTE ON NAMES

Sir Walter Ralegh's family name seems in its time to have had as many spelling variants as Shakespeare's. He himself used several of the variants, but never the one in very general modern use—Raleigh. I have used the form, Ralegh, which he adopted about the time of his marriage and used consistently thereafter for the rest of his life.

All of Walter Ralegh's attempts at colonization, through deputies, on the North American continent, took place in what is now North Carolina. The term *Virginia,* which he and his contemporaries used, was loosely applied to all English territory on the eastern seaboard below Canada. The term *Florida* was used in a similar way by the Spaniards for the area which they claimed as their own. In theory the whole country was theirs, in virtue of Pope Alexander VI's Bull. We know that actually they exercised authority at times as far north as the Carolinas. The drama of the French Huguenot settlers who were massacred by the Spaniards under Menendez near Mayport had its beginnings in what is now North Carolina.

The *Guiana* of Ralegh's travels and writings is the region watered by the Orinoco River. His own travels were in what is the modern Republic of Venezuela.

Preface

Here are five remarkable Englishmen who in various ways had some part in establishing the English-speaking dominion, an empire they called it, in North America. Of all the territory they colonized, or tried to colonize, not a single acre is any longer subject to the crown which held their allegiance. Each one of them is connected in history with one of the States of the American Union. Nevertheless, in virtue of their personalities and of the traditions that bind their past to our present, both Americans and Britons feel that these men are part of a common inheritance.

Sir Walter Ralegh, last of Elizabethans or first of modern Europeans, towers over all his contemporaries who had anything to do with North America. Although his Lost Colony seemed to end in failure, it was actually the beginning, not the end, of a great achievement. Two of our quintet were conspicuously religious men, although anyone who associates "Puritan" and "Quaker" with what is fanatical, narrow and dour should revise his mental picture of John Winthrop and William Penn. Captain John Smith, whose name is inextricably and often erroneously tangled up with that of Mrs. John Rolfe, née Pocahontas, is one of the early Americans whom the chroniclers and historians have been fighting over since his death. His greatness is admitted nowadays. At one time, however, there were critics who would have had us believe that he was merely a great liar and impostor. Modern research has not, indeed, put him on a pedestal, for pedestals have been out of fashion since Lytton Strachey wrote biography, but now we can see the foibles without losing sight of the virtues.

The fifth member of our quintet is General James Edward Oglethorpe, who founded Georgia. An energetic, forceful, slightly pompous but good-hearted soldier, he was an early example on American soil of a class of men, philanthropists, in which the United States has long held a worthy preeminence.

DENIS MEADOWS

FIVE REMARKABLE ENGLISHMEN

1

★★★★★

Sir Walter Ralegh
AND THE LOST COLONY

British and American schoolboys who grew up before tele-
vision and the epidemic of "reading difficulties" ousted
books from their lives will recall a picture that often served
as frontispiece to volumes of sea stories and exploration.
The picture, in its photographic realism that pleases a cal-
low mind, was called *The Boyhood of Sir Walter Ralegh.*
The future knight has with him a younger boy, one of the
various cousins, perhaps, or a Gilbert half-brother. The two
are listening entranced to an old sailor who tells of his adventures on the Spanish Main, of the wonders and the incredible wealth of those vast lands which the Spanish king
jealously claimed as his own in virtue of a papal Bull. Probably young Ralegh did not look so well-groomed and decorous as the boy in the picture and perhaps he was already
too sceptical to be thrilled by an ancient mariner's yarns.

Nevertheless the Victorian artist has recorded a historic fact on his canvas. The many-faceted Walter Ralegh directed his thoughts and his aspirations westward during most of his adult years and it is not unreasonable to suppose that what became a ruling passion in the grown man had its roots in adolescent dreams.

More has been written about Ralegh than about any other Elizabethan—understandably, in view of his many-sided genius—and it would be ludicrous to deal with his entire career in a brief essay. For our purpose we shall consider him as the pioneer of English-speaking colonization. All his dreams, labours and expenditure of money ended, it is true, in failure, if we assess material achievement, but he set a pattern and started a movement in which John Smith, Winthrop, the Calverts, Penn and all the other American founders are his followers and associates. Fittingly the State of North Carolina decided, a few years after the Revolutionary War, to name its capital city after the Elizabethan Englishman whose colonizing ventures justify us in calling him the pioneer of English-speaking North America.

Of the childhood and schooling of the Elizabethan boy in the romantic picture we know almost nothing. His parents were not wealthy, but they were related by blood and by marriage to old and respected families in their native Devonshire, the English county that was and is so prolific in seafaring men. Although the Raleghs had no coat of arms until Walter was knighted, he was not the "upstart" envious fellow-courtiers branded him. His parents seem to have been earnest Protestants, but what impact religion, old or new, had on their son we do not know. His mother, a Champernown by birth and a Gilbert by her first marriage, brought her second husband three stepsons. To the two nearest him in years, Humphrey and Adrian, young Walter Ralegh, born about 1552, became much attached and later both were associated with him in colonial enterprise.

Ralegh was sent to Oxford to study and the record of him as an undergraduate of Oriel College remains, but he did not stay to take a degree, nor do we know how long he was actually in residence. At an age when modern youths, English or American, are beginning to get ready for the university, Ralegh was over in France as a volunteer soldier in the ferocious wars of religion—on the side of the Huguenots. Of his part in the battles of Jarnac and Moncontour and in the gruesome "smoking out" of Catholics seeking refuge in caves in Languedoc we know only a few details mentioned in the course of his *History of the World*.

His interest in the New World and his country's challenge to Spain's monopoly across the Atlantic may have faded while he was at Oxford, but it is very likely it was revived while he was serving with the Huguenots. A party of Protestant colonists from France had attempted a settlement on the "Florida" coast (that is, they were in North Carolina), but a Spanish force overwhelmed them and left their corpses hanging from trees or gibbets with notices about their necks to say they had been slain as pirates, not as Frenchmen. The French duly took their revenge. Seizing and killing the Spanish successors to the French colonists, they left the bodies placarded with a statement that they had been executed as murderers, not as Spaniards. All this had taken place when Walter Ralegh was growing up in Devonshire, but Huguenot refugees in London kept the memory of it fresh in English minds and it is likely that it figured in camp-fire talk when the English volunteer was among his French comrades-in-arms.

When Ralegh went back to England after five or six years of campaigning in France he stayed in London for a time, taking rooms among the law students in the Temple. This did not of necessity imply serious law study, although remarks he made in later years suggest that law had at one time interested him. We have hints of a good deal of riotous conduct, possibly the aftermath of years of soldiering in a war notorious for ruthlessness and sporadic atrocity. The young ex-soldier was no mere swashbuckler. An alert and vigorous mind like his was affected by the ferment of interest, discussion and speculative business connected with North America. American colonization, combined with active hostility to Spain, was a main point in the foreign policy of Sir Francis Walsingham, Elizabeth's Principal Secretary, or Foreign Secretary as we should call him.

Ralegh's half-brother, Sir Humphrey Gilbert, some dozen years his senior, was already immersed in schemes for establishing colonies across the Atlantic. Soon after Ralegh took up residence in London, possibly interrupted by a short spell of active service in Flanders, Gilbert drafted a prospectus to attract investors and he appealed to Queen Elizabeth for leave "to discover and inhabit some strange place." To forestall objections caused by fear of an all-out war with Spain, Gilbert specified territories not in possession of any "Christian prince or people." The wishes of mere barbarians, who might consider themselves the owners of such territories, did not enter into the calculations of most sixteenth century colonizers, English or Spanish. Anyhow, it was justification enough that the souls of the poor savages, red-skinned or brown, would be redeemed by baptism and the Christian religion, whether the Old Faith of Catholic Spain or the new Anglican variety of Tudor England.

That Ralegh, despite the binding-over for breach of the peace of two of his servants, and his own readiness to quarrel and issue challenges to his enemies, was no mere man about town, we know from his intellectual interests at this time. Among the young men who graduated from Oxford colleges in 1580 was Thomas Hariot, a twenty-year-old student known for his keen, analytical mind and his brilliance as mathematician and scientist. Ralegh became friendly with him and offered him the post of mathematical tutor, which he could now afford to do, for he had made his way among the go-getting courtiers jockeying for favour in the eyes of the Virgin Queen, then nearing her fifties. The Devonshire country gentleman who had fought alongside the Huguenots was an impressive figure, the cynosure of all eyes, mostly jealous and spiteful eyes, in London. He was over six feet tall, lean and athletic, of swarthy complexion, with black hair and beard, naturally curling, and keen, grey eyes. He never lost his broad Devon accent, but that was no drawback in those days, and, anyhow, it amused the queen.

Ralegh had begun to outshine his rivals as claimant to be considered England's best-dressed man in an age of fantastic display and extravagance in male attire. With all this there was nothing soft about Walter Ralegh, either physically or morally. He could put up with the hardships of a soldier's life without being sorry for himself and there was discernible in him a touch of almost Puritan moralism which was to come out more strongly in his later years. We see it in his lifelong abhorrence of drunkenness, which of all vices, perhaps, was the one most readily condoned by the Englishmen of Ralegh's or any other era until very recent times.

Sir Humphrey Gilbert's first attempt at a colonizing expedition across the North Atlantic, in which his half-brother was associated with him, took place in 1578. It was a dismal failure. Sir Humphrey seems always to have had bad luck in his enterprises. He is an enigmatic character in the history of his time. Intellectual, good-looking—a claim to royal notice in Elizabeth I's time—tenacious in hardship and misfortune, loyal to friends and family, he appears to have been harsh and ruthless in command, always the advocate of "tough" policies in Ireland.

An interesting feature of Gilbert's plan is the suggested inclusion of a party of English Catholics among the would-be colonists. They desired a new home overseas, where they could practise their religion unhampered by the severe penal laws, yet living under English rule as loyal subjects of Queen Elizabeth. Catholics suspicious of the arrangement denounced it as a Machiavellian scheme of Walsingham designed to split up the Catholic body in England, while the Spanish ambassador appealed to the consciences of the prospective colonists by saying the Pope disapproved of the plan. He buttressed this religious appeal with a reminder of what had happened to the French Huguenot settlers on territory which Spain said was hers. Conscientious scruples or Spanish threats did their work; the Catholics dropped out of the venture.

The 1578 expedition failed for a variety of reasons. There was an initial delay due to government interference in connection with a dispute about a captured Spanish vessel, and this at a time when the autumnal storms were nearing their worst point. Walsingham had craftily enticed one of Philip II of Spain's pilots into English pay for the voyage, but Philip had contrived to include a spy of his own, a renegade Englishman, among the "adventurers." Finally, the enterprise was hamstrung by the childish quarrelsomeness which recurs so often among the Elizabethans. As soon as the contrary winds which held the ships in harbour died down, one of the subordinate commanders, son of Elizabeth's cousin Sir Francis Knollys, began to squabble with Gilbert. Young Knollys seems to have been a snob who despised Sir Humphrey's knighthood, given some years earlier for service in Ireland, and he insulted the commander at his own table.

Possibly, too, he resented his chief's half-brother, who, as captain of the *Falcon*, was subordinate only to Gilbert. Anyhow, when the little fleet was battling with head winds in the Bay of Biscay, Knollys and a party of malcontents deserted for some privateering on their own.

Further misfortune came quickly. The expedition was attacked by well-armed Spanish ships, one English vessel was lost and there were many casualties, especially on Ralegh's *Falcon*, which for a time was in peril of capture or destruction. At length the crippled remnants of the English expedition were driven by westerly winds into Plymouth just as winter was coming on. Gilbert, Ralegh and their officers went before the mayor of that city to present their complaint against the deserter Knollys; we do not know the outcome, if any.

Gilbert and his half-brother Walter Ralegh had at least one trait in common, a robust determination to go on with what they had begun. Perhaps the quality came through their mother from the sea-going Champernowns. After some minor activities in home waters, privateering against the Spaniards (a euphemism for piracy winked at by queen and Council), in which Ralegh may have had a part, Sir Humphrey set to work on another colonizing venture before his six years patent ran out. While he was busy scraping together enough capital, Ralegh was soldiering once more, this time in Ireland. Of his personal courage and efficiency as an officer in that unhappy country there is no question. Regrettably there is no question either of his harshness and cruelty in dealing with the Irish "rebels." Their hostility to England was now augmented by religious bitterness, for English Protestant penal legislation was being applied to a country wholly Catholic except for a tiny enclave of English "planters" and officials.

Ralegh's policy, suggested contrary to and over the head

of his superior, Lord Grey of Wilton, a more temperate man, was that of Sir Humphrey Gilbert during his time in Ireland —wholesale hanging and the quick, non-judicial extinction of the leaders. Of Ralegh's doings in Ireland, the pleasantest thing to record is the beginning of his friendship with Edmund Spenser, who was acting as secretary to the Lord-Deputy. Ralegh and the poet were contemporaries, but Spenser was as yet poor and unknown, Ralegh on the way up in official favour at home and with rosy prospects before him. One of the endearing qualities of Walter Ralegh, even in the early days when his arrogance and ambition aroused enmity on all sides, was his loyalty to his friends and his anxiety to help them. We shall see it later in his attitude to his colonists. The acquaintanceship between Ralegh and Spenser developed into a genuine friendship later and Ralegh did all he could to win both prestige and material reward for the poet.

When Ralegh left Ireland with dispatches and arrived in London in the winter of 1581, he found his half-brother Sir Humphrey Gilbert busy with the preparations for his new colonizing venture. He had managed to get together five small ships, one of them, the best one, contributed by Ralegh, and he had enlisted in all about two hundred and sixty men, including, he says, masons, shipwrights, carpenters and other skilled workers. There were also musicians and morris dancers, "to delight the savage people." Unfortunately the crews were largely recruited from the dregs of the seafaring population, the unemployed or the unemployable. The queen would not allow Ralegh to go. She liked his looks, his courtly manners, his well-stocked mind and quick wit, and his Devonshire accent. He was well started on the upward climb which made him one of the best-hated men in England, despised by the old aristocracy and regarded with jealousy by the "new" men who had their own climbing to do.

The queen would have kept Sir Humphrey at home also, for she said, truly enough, that he was a man "of not good hap by sea," but he had mortgaged all he possessed for the enterprise, to the point, as he put it, of selling the clothes off his wife's back. Aided probably by his half-brother, he talked the queen into allowing him to go; by Ralegh's hand she sent him a charm as mascot, "an anchor and a lady."

The story of this second attempt at North American colonization belongs rather to the history of Gilbert than of Ralegh. The latter lost only money, Gilbert all his possessions and his life. Amid the usual vicissitudes of ocean storms, disease and insubordination due to Sir Humphrey's unpredictable temper and intermittently harsh discipline, the party reached Newfoundland, annexed it for the queen, collected samples of alleged silver ore and then set a southerly course in search of a milder climate and fertile soil on the mainland. The ship supplied by Ralegh had deserted the expedition on the way out and now another, the *Swallow*, was sent homewards with the sick.

Calamity fell on Sir Humphrey again. The *Delight* was blown on to a shoal, broke up and was lost, although one boatload of her people managed to get back to Newfoundland. The fleet was now reduced to the *Golden Hinde*, named after Drake's famous ship, and the tiny *Squirrel* of ten tons (perhaps twenty by modern reckoning). On this perilous craft, crowded with people and top-heavy with her artillery, sailed Sir Humphrey Gilbert. Both ships were carried to the north-eastwards of the Azores by storms until the commander's *Squirrel* foundered under huge waves. The story of the gallant, if often unlovable, Sir Humphrey's end is the record of one of those grand Elizabethan gestures.

When within hailing distance his officers on the more sea-worthy *Golden Hinde* saw him sitting astern with a book. They urged him to come alongside and transfer to the larger ship. "I will not forsake my little company with whom I have passed through so many perils," he shouted, and then, a few hours before the end, "Be of good heart, my friends. We are as near to heaven by sea as by land."

The *Golden Hinde* reached Falmouth at last with the sad news of Gilbert's final failure. We see the Elizabethan resiliency and optimism in Ralegh's action after the loss of his half-brother and the money he had invested in the expedition. Despite the medieval legacy of meditations on death, the grave, worms and decay which the sixteenth and seventeenth centuries cherished, the will to live and to do invariably triumphed. Walter Ralegh was busy making his way in the fiercely competitive world of Elizabeth's court. It is said that about this time took place the incident of the expensive cloak thrown over a mud puddle as the queen approached. The incident may be mythical, but it may have been planned and the opportunity awaited. The gesture was an accepted one in continental chivalry and Ralegh may have had the idea while in France. The thought needed for strengthening his position with the queen as a preliminary to winning substantial rewards from her did not distract him from the dream he had shared with his half-brother. Where Sir Humphrey had left off, he would carry on, or start again if need be.

Ralegh was fortunate in his friends. England's leading geographer and chronicler of her seamen's voyages, Richard Hakluyt, and his young cousin, another Richard Hakluyt, were enthusiasts for American colonizing schemes. Sir Francis Walsingham, the "English Machiavel" in international affairs, was wholly in sympathy and, as Elizabeth's Principal Secretary, that is, her minister for foreign affairs, was willing to help such schemes to offset Spanish influence in the New World.

Early in the year following Gilbert's death Ralegh had received new letters-patent to go on with the colonial venture. We may note that the document authorized him to seize and discover barbarous countries—where the English could get in before the Spaniards and other "Christian princes"—and also to "occupy and enjoy" them for ever. Hitherto Englishmen had not dreamed of "occupying" such lands; their object had been to loot them, to seize all that was valuable and movable, whether the precious metals of the west or the spices and fabrics of the east, and then return to the homeland to enjoy an honorable and, it might be, armigerous leisure.

A month after he had received his letters-patent, which he had confirmed by Parliament, Ralegh sent out his first expedition. The queen would not allow him to go in person, so he chose two able sea-captains and an expert pilot. The captains were Philip Amadas and Arthur Barlow, the pilot was Simon Fernandez, a Portuguese, whom Walsingham had cozened away from the Spanish king's service. This first voyage was planned as a reconnaissance only, which suggests that Ralegh planned more wisely than his adventurous but impulsive and unpractical half-brother.

Fernandez set his course for the West Indies and from thence to the North American mainland. The two little ships probably made their first landfall at some point in the area claimed by Spain and worked their way northwards to avoid friction with Christian princes. In mid-July they found an entrance, possibly New Inlet, beyond Cape Lookout, and were soon riding at anchor in the calm waters of Pamlico Sound, with North Carolina's seaward rampart of narrow islands on one side of them, and on the other an unbroken line of mysterious forest as far as they could see.

Ralegh had instructed the two captains to seek out local inhabitants and make friends with them. At first there were no natives to be seen. There were, however, other novelties on which the English sailors gazed in astonishment—the great oaks and cedars of the virgin forest as it was before civilized men took steel tools to it, the vast flocks of birds that rose from the water when a shot was fired from an arquebus or a musket, the abundance of fish visible from the ship's rail and the wealth of wild grapes on the vines which trailed down almost to the line of the high tide. These men, and others who made the same landfall on later voyages, were enchanted by the perfumed air that the land breezes carried out from that still unravaged forest, but above all they seem to have been fascinated by the grapes, a rare delight after weeks of salt meat and mouldy, weevil-infested biscuit.

The first contact with human beings in this western paradise was encouraging. The local Indians, copper-coloured men and women of good physique, with ebony-black hair, brown, friendly eyes, and a minimum of clothing, were courteous and hospitable, lavish in their gifts of food and drink, enchanted by the objects bestowed as presents or payment in kind by the white men. The Indians and the Englishmen had no word of language in common, but the English sailors seem always to have felt that if you asked a "native" a question patiently, loudly and repeatedly, he would understand in time. Thus a request for the name of the country received the answer, *"Wingandacoa,"* but this, it was found later, meant, "What fine clothes you wear!"

The two ships, under their able and very observant commanders, were back in England in the fall of 1584, carrying as passengers two young Indians, Manteo and Wanchese, persuaded to accompany the English as evidence of all that was to be reported about the new country. Amadas and Barlow passed on the information they had collected to Ralegh, probably *Sir* Walter by this time, although the date of his knighthood is somewhat uncertain. He in turn told the queen of the wonderful fertility and the wholesome climate of this new land added to her dominions. It now received its name, Virginia, in honour of England's Virgin Queen. Possibly the name was Ralegh's own tactful suggestion, although it has been said that the queen herself insisted on it.

The satisfaction felt by the queen and her enterprising courtier was not shared by the Spaniards. The meddlesome Bernardino de Mendoza, Philip's former ambassador to England, had been expelled by the Council for his alleged intrigues with disaffected English subjects, and he was now in Paris, but he had his spies in England. They gave him news of the forthcoming expedition, although they were misinformed about its size. He passed on to Philip II the current rumours about Ralegh's scheme. The English queen, declared a bastard and deposed by Pope St. Pius V fourteen years earlier, naturally was unimpressed by the fact that long before that date Pope Alexander VI had assigned to Spain all newly discovered western lands.

Ralegh decided the time was opportune for a serious colonizing venture and he set to work accordingly. Early in 1585 he was ready—with two ships of about a hundred and a hundred and fifty tons burden and five smaller vessels. Prospective settlers had been recruited, largely among Ralegh's own people, the men of the West Country.

The list of competent men to accompany the colonists testifies to the wisdom of Ralegh's choice and to his good fortune in finding the men available. Ralph Lane, one of Queen Elizabeth's equerries, who had seen service in Ireland, was to be governor of the new colony. John White, artist and cartographer, and Thomas Hariot, the mathematician, were chosen for their artistic and scientific gifts respectively, and to them we are indebted for our knowledge of the North Carolina coast and its hinterland as first seen by trained observers. One of the "gentlemen," impoverished and so content to go in a less exalted capacity, was Thomas Cavendish. He was not one of Ralegh's fellow Devonshire-men, but a man from Suffolk, the strongly Puritan county that thirty-five years later would provide New England's earliest colonists. Already, in his early thirties, if as old as that, a skilful and experienced seaman, he was destined to follow Drake's course as one of the earliest Englishmen to circumnavigate the world. Simon Fernandez again was the pilot.

Of supreme importance was the leadership of such an expedition. Sir Walter Ralegh had planned to command the enterprise himself and was full of enthusiasm for the task. The hardships, dangers and discomforts of such a voyage in the sixteenth century make a stern demand on our reading and our imagination if we are to picture them. From certain clues in his writings we gather that Ralegh was a man of acute physical sensibilities and was repelled by the dirt and vermin, the filth and stench of Tudor city life, the gross habits of eating and drinking—especially the drinking—which the average well-born Englishman of the period accepted as the natural order of things. Nevertheless, Sir Walter, newly knighted, latest of the royal favourites, and the most splendidly as well as the most expensively dressed man in an age of peacock display, was all ready for the arduous Atlantic voyage—the sort of voyage that would make a record for health and safety if not more than twenty-five per cent of the passengers and crew had perished on the way.

Had Ralegh sailed as admiral of the little colonizing fleet in May, 1585, England's North American empire might well have had a different beginning and a happier infancy. Sir

Walter was arrogant and scornful towards equals and rivals, including fellow-climbers at the Court, and he was hated by a populace that knew him only by rumour and hearsay for his tight grip on certain monopolies awarded him by the queen. She liked to reward her faithful servants generously, but not from her own exchequer. On the other hand, he had a knack of winning the loyalty and devotion of those social inferiors who had direct contact with him—sailors and soldiers under him, his personal servants and the hard-bitten tin miners of Cornwall when, later in his career, he presided at their local "Parliament" as Lord Warden of the Stannaries. Moreover, of all the Elizabethan men of action, he was most fitted to win the friendship and co-operation of the Indian tribes who, in the event, became the bitter enemies of all white men. Thirty years after the Virginia experiment he gave proof of this gift for friendship with primitive peoples in his dealings with the aboriginal Indians of his Guiana, present-day Venezuela. Clearly he had no colour prejudice, for one of his suggestions for drawing Indians and Englishmen together in a common fealty to England's queen was intermarriage and the education of selected Guiana natives in England.

Unfortunately this was not to be. The fifty-two-year-old queen could not bear to part with her latest acquisition, the tall, ornately dressed man of Devon, about thirty-five years old, strikingly handsome in a rather exotic way, more Celtic than Anglo-Saxon, and with a turn for the flattery Elizabeth demanded. Nor should we attribute her action solely to an aging woman's attempt to halt the passage of time with a pretence of youth. She had too good a brain to fool herself to that extent. We may dismiss the scabrous assertions of some of the Catholic exiles about the Virgin Queen. Sad to relate, even the saintly Cardinal Allen does not hesitate to attribute to the queen, in the relative obscurity of scholarly Latin, sexual aberrations in which he couples her name with that of Ralegh. Elizabeth's vanity and her love of pseudo-chivalric devotion were inexhaustible, while her harping on "that long preserved virginity" had become rather ridiculous as she drew near her status as the lady whom time had overtaken. There was an element of flirtatiousness in her attitude to Ralegh and other good-looking men, perhaps a measure of vague and diffused sexuality about it and, as she grew older, and chose younger favourites—Essex for example—almost a maternal solicitude.

So Sir Walter, the *Water* of her puns and coquettish passes, was not allowed to risk his life and his looks on the treacherous Atlantic or among the barbarians whom Christian princes had not yet tamed and exploited. We may ask why he did not, as second best choice, call on one of the professional and seasoned navigators Amadas and Barlow, who knew the site of the projected colony and its seaward approaches, or, indeed, any one of many worthy sea captains of his acquaintance. The answer is—social hierarchy and family solidarity. In those days gentlemen and, still more, non-gentlemen, demanded that a gentleman govern them. Moreover, with members of the Devonshire clan related among themselves by blood and marriage available for command, it was unthinkable that a leader should be chosen from outside. Accordingly Ralegh offered the command to his cousin Sir Richard Grenville. This man was, in both his virtues and defects, a typical Elizabethan Englishman of his class—personally courageous, almost insanely so, magnanimous to a defeated enemy, but hot-tempered, arbitrary and tyrannical in command. He was quite incapable of a balanced judgment once his prejudices were aroused. Further, like most of the Elizabethan sea dogs, whatever their social rank, when he was on the high seas and Spanish shipping was at hand, he was undisguisedly a pirate.

While Spanish and English ambassadors were observing protocol in London and Madrid, the seamen of the two nations, especially in the Caribbean, were virtually at war. The absurdity of things was increased by the fact that Spanish settlers and planters in the West Indies were glad to trade amicably with the English freebooters, often for goods that had been on the way to them in Spanish ships. Grenville's readiness to forget everything else and chase a Spanish merchantman was an unhelpful trait in the commander of a colonizing expedition.

Friction arose between Grenville and Ralph Lane, the governor-designate of the colony, long before the ships reached their destination, Roanoke Island, which had been decided on as the scene of the first "planting." Lane, of course, wished to land his men and stores as soon as possible. Grenville, however, was in supreme command at sea and decided on sailing into the Caribbean for the double purpose of seeking Spanish vessels to plunder and of "playing the Merchant," that is, trading with the Spanish colonists. Lane, meanwhile, had to see valuable food supplies used up, his men discouraged and weakened, physically and morally, by the continued discomforts of shipboard life, and the season passing when they might have cleared land and sown grain in readiness for the first winter ashore. Not until the end of July did the ships come to anchor off the coast of North Carolina. Afterwards Lane placed the whole blame for the failure of the 1585 venture on Grenville. This, perhaps, was not entirely just. Lane and his men, unlike their master Ralegh, gave little thought to organizing agriculture and a food supply, establishing good relations with the Indians and, in general, setting up that overseas England of which Ralegh dreamed. English colonists, as much as the Spaniards, were obsessed with the idea of gold.

Then there was trouble with the pilot, Simon Fernandez.

He was charged with nearly wrecking Grenville's own ship and with actually running another ship on a reef, the implication being that this was deliberate treason and deserved, in Sir Richard's words, "a halter for hire." It is possible that the Portuguese navigator, harassed and insulted by Grenville, had been driven to sabotage, but without any thought of treason to his English masters, who had won him over to English service. Walsingham had evidently looked on him as a useful acquisition.

The hope of a lasting friendship with the Indians, a point that Ralegh kept in mind throughout his colonial schemes, was soon lost through Grenville's truculence. A silver goblet disappeared, stolen perhaps by an Indian when the English were on a visit to a native village. Unable to recover the goblet, even by the threat of an armed escort with which he went ashore again, Grenville "burnt and spoyled their Towne and corne." Probably he saw nothing reprehensible about this, for his attitude to all "Salvages" was very much that of Sir John Hawkins to the West African negroes he captured and sold as merchandise—a very different state of mind from that revealed in Ralegh's book on "Guiana." Relations with the Indians at Roanoke Island went from bad to worse. A conspiracy, suspected but not proved, led to open fighting, and a too-zealous Irishman among the settlers chased a wounded Indian chief and returned with his head as a trophy.

In spite of these ominous events, a dwindling supply of stores and the uncertainty of food for the winter, Lane wrote enthusiastically, after Grenville's departure, to Walsingham and Sir Philip Sidney about the fertility of the land, the wholesome climate and the future of the colony. Perhaps, as governor, he felt called upon to put a better face on things than the facts justified. Anyhow, Sir Francis Drake, on his way home from one of his marauding expeditions against the Spaniards, put in at the new colony and offered the settlers provisions and a boat. Grenville had promised to return, but was overdue.

A storm that made Drake resolve on immediate departure entirely demoralized the already wavering colonists. They begged Drake to take them home, abandoned their island and left North America, only a short time before a fast supply ship, sent out by Ralegh, reached the coast. Two weeks later Grenville arrived, with supplies and new recruits for the colony. He had kept his promise, but missed the opportunity of forestalling the flight of the settlers because he was looking for Spanish vessels to loot. The best he could do was to leave fifteen men on Roanoke Island as a temporary garrison and colony to hold the bridgehead in Queen Elizabeth's name until a fresh "planting" could be made. Despite his glaring faults as a colonial administrator Grenville shared his cousin's enthusiasm to see North America an "English empire" and both men were deeply disappointed at the initial failure. Ralegh, moreover, along with some other speculators, had lost a great deal of money and would find it increasingly hard to raise capital for future attempts. The queen was happy to know of new territories added to her dominions and took pleasure in seeing *Virginia* on the new maps in London. She was unwilling to contribute directly from the royal purse, nor would she allow her favourite to leave her side. Ralegh's presence in "Virginia" might, perhaps, have made an early success of the enterprise.

About this time the phrase *British Empire* was first used. The credit for inventing it is given to Dr. Dee, the queen's astrologer so-called, who mingled a hocus-pocus of horoscope-casting and communicating with the spirit world with genuinely scientific work in physics and geography. He was well regarded by Ralegh, the Gilberts and Sir Francis Walsingham and they all looked on him as a strong sympathizer with their colonial aspirations.

Two of nature's American gifts to European man are allegedly connected with Ralegh's first colonial experiment. The potato, originally a migrant from South America, was grown by the Indians of Ralegh's Virginia and *may* have made its way to England at the time, although we lack evidence of its presence there until the time, some ten years later, when it was growing in Lord Burghley's (William Cecil's) garden and is described by Gerard in his *Herball*. The Irish, who on other counts have no reason to love Ralegh, may recall in his favour that he started the cultivation of the potato on his estate near Youghal. Ralegh's detractors sought to deny him any credit as regards the potato by pointing out that Sir John Hawkins had introduced potatoes into England twenty years earlier (1565), but Sir John's vegetable was the sweet potato, no relation, botanically, of its namesake.

The vegetable product more popularly associated with Ralegh is tobacco. At the time of the 1585 voyage under Grenville's command the plant was known to the Spaniards and the Portuguese, but there is no evidence that the English knew or used it. Thomas Hariot, an indefatigable observer with the same mental curiosity as his friend and employer, Sir Walter, had watched the Indians smoking tobacco, decided that it was a very healthful practice and made up his mind that his master and his countrymen generally would benefit by it. Whether Ralegh's fondness for tobacco began as early as Hariot's return from the deserted colony is uncertain; but the silver tobacco pipe became as well known as the knight's silver armour when he was captain of the guard. Even the queen deigned on one occasion to try a puff at the famous pipe, but was not pleased with it.

We are told she coughed, spat, and swore one of her irreverant oaths.

The returning colonists had to find a scapegoat for their failure to carry out the plans of Ralegh, Secretary Walsingham and all who had put money into the enterprise. They were unwilling to admit that they had squabbled among themselves, antagonized the Indians and wasted time looking for gold and pearls when they should have been clearing and tilling the land, according to instructions. They blamed the land itself—the fertile, virgin soil, the wholesome North Carolina climate! Ralegh, by nature disinclined to bear fools gladly, was grateful for the testimony of one trained observer who was honest as well as loyal. Thomas Hariot spoke and wrote with enthusiam, but also with scientific accuracy, about the natural resources of "Virginia." The elder Richard Hakluyt, who apparently combined great industry in collecting travellers' records with his duties as an Anglican clergyman, remained steadfast in his belief that there was a future for an English settlement in North America. Ralegh set Hariot to work on a detailed report, but, as *A Briefe and true report of the new found land of Virginia,* it was not printed and published until Armada year (1588), when Ralegh's most ambitious venture, the famous "Lost Colony," was already a mystery of the North American forests, while most Englishmen's minds were too preoccupied with the threat of invasion to spare thought for a handful of adventurers across the Atlantic.

By this time Ralegh had climbed quickly to royal favour and to wealth, but the North American expeditions were making serious inroads into his resources. Undismayed, however, by the anticlimax of Drake's landing in England with the returning colonists, he set to work at once to prepare a new expedition. That his ideas of colonization were ahead of those held by his contemporaries, who thought almost wholly in terms of gold and other treasure, chiefly to be cozened out of the Indians or seized from the Spaniards, is shown by the fact that the party was to include women and children. The ships' cargoes were to contain, besides the food supplies needed for the first winter, farm equipment and agricultural tools. It may be pointed out that even the Virginia Council in London, years later, when Ralegh was a prisoner in the Tower, in legislating for the Jamestown settlement saw it chiefly as a trading post to supply marketable commodities for the shareholders at home.

For the new contingent of prospective North American settlers Ralegh recruited a hundred and fifty persons. This included seventeen women and some children, how many we do not know. A group of men, who either shared Ralegh's dream of an authentic colony or else hoped for a quick return on their investment, joined him in the scheme. It was given legal status by incorporation as "the governor and assistants of the city of Ralegh in Virginia." This implied at least a measure of colonial self-government, wherein again Ralegh shows himself ahead of most sixteenth-century thought. Mr. John White was to be governor, with twelve assistants. It may be said that Ralegh's, and Dr. Dee's, "British Empire" was a federal rather than an imperialistic concept. Having in mind Cousin Grenville's buccaneering sidelines, Ralegh directed that the Spaniards should not be molested. Philip II's invasion plans were no secret, but an uneasy peace still existed and the queen, an intelligent woman, loathed war for its futility and wastefulness.

The John White whom Ralegh chose to govern the colony is generally taken to be, although complete proof is lacking, the John White who was on the previous expedition and whose drawings and water-colours of the native people, the fauna and the flora of "Virginia" touched the English imagination with a sense of wonder. When Hariot's report on the country appeared in a Frankfurt edition put out by de Bry, it was illustrated with etchings based on White's pictures.*

If Governor White *was* John White the naturalist and artist, the colony had over it a man of sensitive and cultivated mind. The extant evidence, anyhow, suggests a person of generous spirit and a conscientious administrator.

The expedition set sail in the spring of 1587. This was not a propitious time for such a journey; all serviceable shipping was being held at home to repel the Spanish attempt at invasion which might begin at any moment and England's fighting seamen were needed for naval warfare. Ralegh had to content himself with the *Lion*, an unarmed merchantman that was almost ready to be broken up for her timbers and equipment, and two very small vessels. In command at sea was the Portuguese pilot Simon Fernandez, who had aroused Grenville's suspicions of treason. On this voyage there was more trouble with Fernandez, said White bitterly, for "He forsooke our fly-boate" (one of the smaller vessels) "leaving her distressed in the Bay of Portugal." The little craft ultimately made her own way to Roanoke Island and rejoined the other two ships.

The original plan called for a visit to Roanoke Island to pick up Grenville's fifteen men and then the establishment of a permanent colony on Chesapeake Bay. The choice of location for the projected city of Ralegh was largely due to

---

* White, already a travelled man, was official draughtsman to Ralegh's expedition, as well as the colony's future governor. He took with him his box of water-colours and made a number of beautifully painted pictures of North American people, animals and plants. His art medium was a new one in England and his pioneer work as a water-colourist has won him the title of father of English water-colour painting in histories of art. For the benefit and delight of present-day readers it may be pointed out that his pictures have been splendidly reproduced in *The New World*, edited by Stefan Lorant, New York, 1946.

the younger Richard Hakluyt, the parson, who had studied every available map, chart and piece of writing about North America.

Fernandez, whatever else he had learned from his English associates, had a truly Elizabethan tendency to self-will and disobedience to orders. He did, indeed, look for Grenville's men, but found only the bones of one of them. Apparently all had been murdered by hostile Indians. The fort had been razed, although the houses were still more or less intact, overgrown with melon plants, on which deer were grazing.

The new arrivals met Manteo, one of the Indians who had been in England and remained loyal to the English. As a gesture to conciliate the former "loving" but now suspicious Indian tribes of the coast, Manteo was baptized and solemnly installed as "king" and overlord of Roanoke Island, but a suzerain of the Virgin Queen, whom he may have met during his sojourn in her country.

Governor White set to work with a will. He assigned the colonists, some of whom were farmers and trained craftsmen, to useful tasks. He definitely had a stake in the country, for his daughter Eleanor was married to one of the settlers, Ananias Dare, one of the governor's twelve assistants. The site of the earlier settlement was cleared of the intrusive plant life, the fort restored and the houses made habitable again. The task of clearing the virgin soil of its lush growth and making it ready for food crops was more formidable than farmers used to conditions in an old and settled country had imagined.

Obviously someone must go to England to present the facts to the London "adventurers," that is, the investors, and bring back supplies to tide the colony over its first winter. White was very loth to leave the settlement. His daughter had just given birth to a baby girl, christened Virginia. The governor was deeply attached to his daughter and his grand-child, but the colonists begged him to go; probably they dis-trusted the ability of anyone less than their governor to loosen purse-strings among the shareholders. Reluctantly he sailed away from America and reached England towards the close of the year. He had planned that the colonists should, when possible, leave Roanoke Island for a site among the friendly Croaton Indians and near a safer an-chorage for sea-going vessels. If they moved before his re-turn, they were to inscribe the name of their new location on a tree or post, with a cross incised underneath the name if they were in trouble.

Except in the case of Ralegh and, to his credit, Sir Rich-ard Grenville, Governor White's pleas fell on deaf ears. In-vasion by Spain was imminent; the country was agog with rumours of Philip II's enormous naval forces being got ready, and everyone knew the high quality of the well-trained in-fantry who would be put ashore. In every tavern and ale-house one heard blood-curdling stories of hosts of Inquisi-tors equipped with instruments of torture. People had no time or patience for reports about North America.

Grenville made a noble effort to help his cousin Walter Ralegh and got a first-class fleet fitted out and ready to sail from Bideford, but it was requisitioned for the queen's serv-ice against Spain. Ralegh managed to have two of the smaller vessels released for his use and Grenville agreed to sail them, but was forbidden to do so. Ultimately, when the Spanish invasion fleet had already been sighted, the two ships, with scanty stores and a few new colonists, headed west across the Atlantic.

White was nominally in charge, but the sea captains, with the indiscipline of their time, flouted his authority and went on a privateering rampage. They fell in with some French pirates, were ignominiously beaten and fled back to England. White could do nothing more for his people at the time and had to wait a whole year before again attempting to help them.

The coming of the Spanish Armada kept Ralegh fully occupied in the defence of the south-western tip of England, Cornwall and Devon, and possibly he was serving at sea in part of the running fight up the English Channel when westerly gales and the more manoeuvrable English ships forced Philip II's great battleships on their disastrous course into the North Sea.

Next year (1589) Ralegh turned over the management of his "Virginia" to a company of adventurers (speculators). He has been blamed for this, as showing a callous attitude towards his countrymen stranded among the savages of the New World. His critics overlook two points—the crisis that overhung England, a small kingdom threatened by the most powerful nation in Europe, with the moral force of the Papacy behind King Philip's effort, and, secondly, that even Ralegh's sizable income was beginning to feel the strain. He had, he tells us, already spent some £40,000 on his colonial project. Multiplying by 5, for the old par value of the U.S. dollar, we have $200,000, and multiplying this, very conservatively, by 4 or 5 to take account of purchasing power then and now, we have about a million dollars in modern currency. Many authorities are inclined to put Ralegh's outlay at about two million dollars. As the elder Hakluyt said at the time, "It would have required a prince's purse to have followed it out." When the transfer was made, Ralegh kept his patent and his title as proprietary lord, not, as some hostile critics suggest, out of mere vanity, but because he could thus continue to help the settlement in the future.

The unhappy Governor White, ignorant of the fate of his colonists, including his daughter and son-in-law and their child, could not find passage to America until the summer of 1590. Then, only at considerable expense and with the prestige of Sir Walter Ralegh to help him, he managed to obtain a place as passenger on a merchant ship sailing with two others for a London man of business. The captains, unconcerned about White's anxieties, did some Caribbean cruising at first; with the advantage of three to one they hoped to waylay lonely Spanish ships. Finally, when the summer was nearly over, White saw again the sandy shore where the wild grapevines grew down to the water's edge.

Hope revived in his mind when he and the men aboard the ship saw a column of smoke rising above the trees. Two of the ship's guns were fired as a signal, but there was no reply. White went ashore with a party of sailors sent to fill the ship's water casks. A palisade around the site of the settlement was still in place. On a log or tree trunk from which the bark had been removed there had been carved the letters CRO, for Croaton, but without the cross which had been agreed on as a distress signal. Buried chests, among them three which had held White's own papers, maps, drawings and other things, had been dug up and the contents scattered, the papers stained and decayed, the armour eaten away by rust.

All things pointed to looting after the colonists had left. Nevertheless, White comforted himself, deluded himself it may be, by the absence of the danger signal, the incised cross on the tree. "Although it grieved me to see such spoyle of my goods yet I greatly joyed that I had found a certaine token of their safe being at Croaton, which is the place of Manteo and the Savages our friends." Unhappily for John White and for posterity he had no chance to go in search of the Lost Colony. Bad weather descended on the ships at their perilous offshore moorings so that even the filled water casks could not be taken aboard. The captains put to sea with a good deal of trouble, promising to return later, a promise they broke in order to do some more privateering.

American colonial history has not so far yielded up the secret of Sir Walter Ralegh's Lost Colony. John White consoled himself with the thought that all the colonists lived securely in friendly Croaton Indian villages under the protection of Manteo, the baptized chief who was a friend to the English. This belief claimed confirmation in later generations from travellers' stories of Croaton Indians with undeniable Caucasian traits, fair hair and complexion, blue eyes, even, some said, recognizably English mannerisms of gait and gesture. More gloomy is the judgment of historians who think the whole contingent, weakened in health and reduced in numbers, perhaps out of ammunition, fled from superior forces of hostile Indians and was massacred on the way.

Throughout all the vicissitudes of his later life and under the crushing blows of loss of fortune, royal injustice, imprisonment, personal tragedy, Ralegh never lost his interest in American colonization and the foundation of English dominions across the Atlantic. For several years after the disappearance of John White's settlement, Ralegh was in the good graces of Queen Elizabeth and was able to make good his losses on colonial ventures. Then, some time in 1592, he made the mistake, from the point of view of retaining royal favour, of a secret marriage.

Rumours put about by his enemies, repeated by Camden the antiquary and, in a later age, in the scabrous anecdotage of John Aubrey, maintain that he seduced one of the queen's beautiful maids-of-honour, the tall, fair-haired and blue-eyed Elizabeth Throgmorton. When and where the two were married we do not know, nor are we sure that the queen believed the story of seduction. She was, rightly enough, as watchful over the chastity and honour of her young ladies as any Victorian dowager and she may have

affected a belief in Elizabeth Throgmorton's lapse as a pretext for venting her jealousy. We know how unforgiving she
was when her favourites married without her permission;
there is the case of Sir Philip Sidney's wife, the charming
daughter of Sir Francis Walsingham. After her husband's
death from his wound received at Zutphen she married the
young Earl of Essex and thereafter was treated as an out-
cast by the queen.

Rather unchivalrously, Ralegh at first denied the marriage
in a letter to Robert Cecil, old Burghley's son. It was, he says,
"a malicious report." One suspects that he repented of this
later, for the love between him and Lady Ralegh was a deep
and lasting one. Whatever she truly believed about the affair, Queen Elizabeth promptly clapped both of them in
the Tower, whence Ralegh sought to move the queen to
pity by a ludicrously fulsome letter to Robert Cecil about
his royal and quasi-divine mistress. He knew well, of
course, that it would be brought to her attention. So far as
we know, it had little effect. A fortunate accident got him
out of prison. A Spanish prize, the great carrack *Madre de
Dios*, full of treasure, had been brought into harbour at
Dartmouth. Her cargo was disappearing piecemeal in an
orgy of looting by the English sailors, whom the local officials were unable to control. Ralegh, it was pointed out to
the queen, was the only person to bring these turbulent
men of Devon to order. He was sent down hastily as a paroled
prisoner under guard. The mission was successful, Ralegh
welcomed with joy and ready obedience by the hitherto uncontrollable sailors, and the Spanish treasure was saved.
Ralegh was still in disfavour with the queen, but he had regained his liberty and he received £30,000 as his share of
the prize—a beggarly return in his judgment, only £2,500
more than his investment. He had, however, a charming
and devoted wife, the Dorset manor of Sherborne and his

various interests, among them the improvement and landscaping of his estate. Various North American trees and shrubs may have owed their introduction or their popularity to him, for instance, sumach for use in tanning leather, "saxafras" (sassafras) for its imagined medicinal properties, as a cure for ague and, more remarkably, for what the Elizabethans called the disease of France or the French pox (syphilis).

Altogether the years of domesticity at Sherborne were probably the happiest in Ralegh's life. He was in his early forties, intensely vigorous in body and mind, happily married, in possession of plenty of money and a beautiful home. Ralegh himself calls this period "the winter of my life," but that is Tudor hyperbole. He had a restless temperament and a mind that was both sceptical and speculative. His friendship with Christopher Marlowe, the dramatist, and Thomas Hariot, the scientist, was cause for widespread suspicion. Both the men were what the age called "atheists," but this was a blanket term for all degrees of scepticism and intellectual doubt. A Dorset supper party led to an enquiry held at Cerne Abbas, near Ralegh's country home at Sherborne, to look into charges of agnostic questioning of a clerical guest. The affair seems to have faded away, but the popular belief in some kind of heterodox association was reinforced by the description of "Sir Walter Rawley's School of Atheism" in a book published under a pseudonym by the redoubtable English Jesuit, Father Robert Persons.

This mental restlessness was paralleled by an equal urge to outward activity. The improvement of the Sherborne estate, details of local government, visits to London to sit in Parliament, the charms of his "dear Bess" and the interest in their first-born son, who turned out to be a veritable problem child—all was insufficient for Sir Walter's energy and ambition. Colonial enterprise had not ceased to hold an important place among his many interests. This time he thought out a scheme to achieve a twofold objective—the establishment of an English dominion beyond the seas and the recovery of royal favour by procuring gold for Elizabeth's coffers. The sexagenarian queen still demanded and received the incessant flattery of her courtiers, but she was too percipient to be fooled by it. A substantial addition to her revenue and, therefore, in the national structure of those days, to England's welfare, was the surest way to gratitude. Once again Ralegh's thoughts were concentrated on the New World, not North America this time, but the southern continent where the Spaniards had tapped, as it appeared, an unfailing reservoir of treasure. Actually, of course, the stream of precious metals into Europe was raising prices all the time in all countries, but it is unlikely the economics of inflation were widely understood four centuries ago. In South America there was enough gold for everybody; why, in virtue of a Bull of Pope Alexander VI, should Spain act as dog in the manger?

Lady Ralegh, the loving wife, content with the amenities of family life in Dorset, was troubled in mind. She did what many a woman has done in such circumstances—appealed to her husband's best friend, shrewdly relying on the innate sex snobbery of males. If only her man could be diverted from the perils of the dreaded western ocean, the risk of armed conflict with the Spaniards and all the vaguely-imagined hazards of a continent full of cannibals, Amazons and wild beasts! A letter she wrote in 1594 to Sir Robert Cecil, whose friendship for the Raleghs had not yet betrayed its flaws, is touching in its sentiment and a gem of epistolary prose unique even in those days of casual orthography.

"Now Sur," she writes, "for the rest I hope for my sake you will rather draw Sur Water towardes the est, then heulp hyme forward toward the soonsett, if any respecke to me or love to him be not forgotten. But everi monthe hath its flower and everi season his contentment, and you greate counselares are so full of new counsels, as you are steddi in nothing, but we poore soules that hath bought sorrow at a high price desiar, and can be pleased with the sam misfortun wee hold, fering allterracions will but mulltiply misseri, of which we have all redi felt sufficient . . . . . . therfore I humbelle besiech you rathar stay hyme then furdar hyme. By the wich you shall bind me for ever."

We are not told that Lady Ralegh's appeal had any effect. The younger Cecil, like his father, Lord Burghley, knew how greatly the addition of territory to her realm and gold to her exchequer would please the queen. The lure was a dream that obsessed both Spanish and English minds, of a country of untold wealth somewhere in the interior of "Guiana" (Venezuela) ruled by *El Dorado,* that is, the Gilded One, descendant of an Inca prince from Peru. The name was based on a story of the king's covering his body with gold dust for ceremonial occasions. From time to time wanderers, with minds upset by fevers and hardship, made their way from the virgin forests on the Brazilian hinterland and told marvellous stories of gold in such abundance that the Gilded One's subjects used it as Europeans used iron and tin.

Ralegh set to work as he had done in the days of the Lost Colony, sending a subordinate on reconnaissance while he carried out his preparations for the main expedition. His scout now (1594) was one Jacob Whiddon, an experienced sea captain whom he liked and trusted, but, unfortunately, a simple soul easily taken in by a man of the world. Captain Whiddon called at Trinidad on his way to the mouth of the Orinoco. The Spanish governor of the island, Berreo, treated the bluff English sailor with great kindness and much hospitality—and easily learned from him all about his master's plans.

When, the following year, Ralegh reached Trinidad, he used tactics similar to Berreo's. He treated the poor, homesick soldiers of the Spanish garrison with lavish hospitality and loosened their tongues with wine, thereby acquiring a good deal of information about the land watered by the Orinoco, as well as further alluring stories about the kingdom of *El Dorado*.

From Indians who came to him secretly Ralegh learned of Berreo's atrocious treatment of the aborigines and, what moved the English to greater anger, that the Spanish governor had treacherously murdered eight of Captain Whiddon's men the year before. Ralegh's response to this was immediate and brutal. He had the governor's bodyguard ambushed and massacred—he does not tell us the number of victims—captured and burned the town of St. Joseph and made Berreo a prisoner, treating him, however, with great courtesy and consideration. The Indians were then assembled and, with their late master present, told of the Englishmen's great Virgin Queen and her wish to deal with them in all friendship and humanity. Berreo seems to have been very philosophical about it all, returning his captor's courtesy with Spanish punctilio, sharing meals and conversation with him and telling him what he could about the fabled city of Manoa, *El Dorado's* capital. He sought, however, to deter Ralegh from the expedition by dwelling on the dangers and hardship and the risk of friction with Spain.

The details of the party's journey in small boats up the great Orinoco River are recorded in the Elizabethan travel classic, Ralegh's *The Discoverie of the Large, Rich and Beautiful Empire of Guiana*. There were unspeakable discomforts from tropical heat, torrential rain, and backbreaking work at the oars. An unfortunate negro servant was de-

voured by an alligator. Ralegh, interested in new sensa-
tions, was agreeably surprised by the delicious quality of
armadillo meat and voted the pineapple the "princess of
fruits." The travellers did not return with the treasure they
had dreamed of nor did they set eyes on Manoa. The autumn rains, the terrifying rise of the Orinoco and the onset
of the flood waters, which every year inundated untold
square miles of tropical rain forest, forced a hurried retreat
to the ships anchored at the river's mouth. There were stories of rocks, of whole mountains veined with gold, but no
mining tools or even assaying equipment had been taken up
the river. To convince a cautious and thrifty queen and
hard-headed London business men to consider a fresh "venture" the only tangible evidence was a sample of ore which,
assayed in England, yielded a moderately encouraging percentage of gold.

The empire of *El Dorado* was a will o' the wisp. Of more
interest to us are Ralegh's ideas about colonization as set
out in his book, especially his insistence on winning the
friendship and support of the native peoples. The Spaniards
had, indeed, won enormous wealth and built a great colonial
empire in Mexico, Peru and all the upper part of the South
American continent by harsh methods that often degener-
ated into fiendish cruelty which shocked normal consciences.
Against such things humane churchmen like the great
bishop Las Casas protested, usually in vain. The methods
of the *Conquistadores* had earned them fear and hatred
from the Indians, emotions which Ralegh shrewdly utilized
in seeking to win them to his side by dwelling on his queen's
readiness to use her power in their defence. An impartial
estimate of treasure seekers, Spanish and English, compels
one to admit that Indian fortunes might have been little
better had Spanish gold-hunters been replaced by English
ones. Of this Ralegh was well aware and he makes it an argu-

ment for Queen Elizabeth to take over the new territory and garrison it with adequate forces. Thus the royal treasury would benefit, a motive highly acceptable to the queen, and the native peoples would be protected. The subsequent history of colonial expansion may make this seem rather unduly sanguine.

Ralegh's character has fascinated later generations by its complexity and its paradoxes. The ruthless slaughter of disarmed soldiers by Captain Ralegh at Smerwick during the Irish fighting—under military orders and in accordance with the brutal convention of surrender "not on terms"—and the surprise attack on Berreo's men are repulsive incidents. Nevertheless we must account for the wholehearted devotion to Ralegh of the Cornish tin miners, proletarians who would have no love for the "knave Ralegh" of popular rumour, the arrogant upstart, the go-getter made rich by monopolies at the expense of the common man. And the tough-minded sailors at Dartmouth who welcomed the "queen's poor prisoner" with shouts of joy and meekly forebore their looting of the *Madre de Dios?* In the honest, forthright Tudor sense of the word, they *loved* their swaggering, insolent captain.

So it was with the Indians of the Orinoco, simple, unvindictive and naturally hospitable people until embittered by the cruelties of those who wanted to wrest their gold from them. Everywhere their suspicions of the white man, born of stories about the Spaniards, quickly gave way to trust and friendliness when they met Ralegh. For many years after his imprisonment and his death, we are told, they handed down to their children the story of this messenger from the great *Cacique*, the queen of England, and later generations of dwellers along the Orinoco still hoped for his return and their liberation from their Spanish masters.

We must take account of two features of Ralegh's conduct

during those weeks of hardship, labour and discomfort of all kinds while the travellers were making their way for four hundred miles into the Venezuelan forests. Both points concern his handling of his subordinates. He strictly forbade any looting of Indian property; whatever he and his men asked of the Indians they paid for in the only way known to those primitive people—barter. Secondly, even more impressive in Indian eyes, was the behaviour of the English towards the native women. The Indians had unhappy memories of the treatment of their women-folk by Spanish soldiers and adventurers and marvelled at the godlike chastity, as they regarded it, of the white men sent by the Virgin Queen. Probably the simple Indians did not suspect that English virtue was in this case enforced by the stern discipline of a strong-willed commander. For a man of Ralegh's personality to have his way with the ordinary sailors and servants was understandable in those days of social hierarchy, but we must bear in mind that his party included "gentlemen-adventurers" who thought themselves, socially, as good as their leader and who regarded women of lower social status as fair prey. Ralegh himself appears to have been surprised by the self-restraint or the prudence of his followers, the more so, he remarks, as many of the women were very beautiful and went about almost completely nude.

When it was obvious that a return to the ships was urgent, two volunteers were left with the Indians to learn their language and to gather more data about *El Dorado* and the approaches to the golden kingdom. Ralegh was firmly set on going back later to fulfill his promises to the Indians, to tap the natural resources of the country, including the gold that would justify him in the eyes of English statesmen and speculators and, above all, to establish a permanent English colony in his "Guiana." He hoped to make a north-westerly detour on the way home to see whether his Virginian colonists were safe and to encourage them with his presence and with stores from his ships. Clearly he did not at the time regard his settlement as a "lost colony." Strong, westerly winds made the journey impossible, but our knowledge of his intention refutes the charge that he was indifferent to the fate of his settlers. Even when his rise in power and wealth was over and a doubtful future lay ahead of him his hopes for his "Virginia" were unwavering. "I shall yet live to see it an English empire," he said.

Ralegh was destined to set foot in "Guiana" again, but not until twenty-two years had passed, twelve of them as a prisoner in the Tower of London. The year (1596) following his return to England he sent his friend and trusted subordinate Captain Lawrence Keymis to South America with the idea of continuing exploration and consolidating the English position in the Orinoco River valley. Also, Keymis would survey for gold, the necessary bait to lure investors. Keymis found that the Spaniards, alarmed by Ralegh's incursion into the area and his claim that it had been annexed to the English crown, had reinforced their garrisons and were ready to repel further English activity. Ralegh's captain, however, took home an optimistic report of an accessible and immensely rich gold mine, but there was nothing more tangible to show for the expense and trouble of the voyage.

Ralegh had gone back to his Dorset home, Sherborne, after returning to England and was busy with Parliamentary affairs and with local defence against an expected second attempt at invasion by Spain. In 1597 he took a brilliant part in an English attack on Cadiz. He had by this time recovered something of his former place in the queen's good graces and was allowed to resume his position as captain of the guard, although his wife remained an exile from the court. In the late summer after the Cadiz raid he was again in action against the Spaniards, in the so-called Islands Voyage, an attack on the Spanish colony in the Azores planned as preliminary to waylaying Spanish treasure ships from South America. A dashing and successful raid on one of the islands led by Ralegh in the absence of the supreme commander, the Earl of Essex, revived in the young nobleman his smouldering dislike of the "upstart" who was his vice-admiral. For a short time Ralegh's career and his life were in danger of being ended by execution for disobedience, but older and wiser men calmed the young earl and peace between the two men was patched up.

When the expedition was over, having proved financially unsuccessful, Essex having missed the treasure ships, Ralegh was glad enough to go back to Sherborne and recover from the fatigue and bodily strain of active service. He had been wounded in the leg at Cadiz and was still lame when he sailed to the Azores. The company of his wife and his four-year-old son, the ebullient Wat, and further improvements on the Dorset estate, gave him another interlude of tranquil happiness in a stormy life. The queen smiled on him now, enjoyed his conversation and his wit, and consulted him on matters of defence. The Earl of Essex now enjoyed her more sentimental regard, but he was presuming too much on it and his tragic fall was drawing near. Elizabeth's long reign and her life were nearing their end also. When her death occurred, the fate of her favourites still on the scene would depend on the judgment or the whims of her successor.

The brilliance of the Renaissance had already faded before Elizabeth passed away in her seventieth year. We may see a dramatic fitness in the shortness of the interval, under four months, between her death (March 24, 1603) and the day, July 17, when Ralegh, the most versatile genius of the English Renaissance, was sent to the Tower on a charge of treason. The mind of the Stuart king, James VI of Scotland

and I of England, had been subtly worked upon for Ralegh's undoing by his false friend, Sir Robert Cecil, and by numerous enemies eager to pull down one of the late queen's favourites. The trial which followed, the details of which do not concern us in a study of Ralegh as a colonizer, is one of the most notorious miscarriages of justice in English legal history. Anglo-Saxon traditions of presumed innocence until guilt is proved exerted little force in a charge of treason. The accused would need almost unattainable proofs of non-complicity to win his acquittal, but Ralegh's conviction, based wholly on the assertions of one admittedly perjured witness, the weak, shifty, vacillating Cobham, set a record in unjust legal procedure. The mass of the English people, who had hated Ralegh before his trial, were shocked by the unfairness of the Lord Chief Justice, John Popham, by the blatant prejudice of the court, and by the uncontrolled vituperation of Sir Edward Coke, the attorney-general, who prosecuted. The insults which that truculent jurist hurled at the defendant included such terms as, "thou viper" and "spider of hell" and the use of the second person singular to show contempt—"for I thou thee, *thou* traitor." From being the best-hated man in England Ralegh became a popular hero, a symbol of English patriotism and English hatred of Spain.

To satisfy some vague urge to inflict mental torture or, it may be, to make a vainglorious display of royal power and royal clemency, the king allowed the death sentence to remain operative until the last possible moment. The execution of the sentence was then postponed, not cancelled or commuted, and Ralegh was sent back to imprisonment in the Tower of London, the trial having been held at Winchester because of the plague raging in the capital. He remained in the Tower for the next dozen years. Helplessly he had to see much of his property confiscated, his wife and child impoverished. The years in the Tower, however, were not without their consolations. The governor of the Tower showed himself more humane than Ralegh's prosecutor and judges. A small shed or hen house was fitted up as a chemical laboratory, there was little or no restriction on books and visitors and for part of the time Lady Ralegh and young Wat were allowed to live with Sir Walter. During this period his younger son, Carew, was born. The heir to the throne, Prince Henry, virtuous, intelligent, athletic, beloved of the English people, in fact a complete contrast to his father, was a good friend to Raleigh. So was Anne of Denmark, James I's pretty, blonde but feather-brained queen.

We know that English colonization across the Atlantic remained a ruling passion with Ralegh all the rest of his life. His assertion that he would yet see it (North America) an English nation, was already being justified a few years later, when the Jamestown settlement was started in 1607. For years Ralegh begged Queen Anne to intercede with her husband for release, so that he might do something overseas, in "Virginia" or down in South America, "that I may rather die in serving the Kinge in Virginia than to perish here in idlenesse." Anne did her best, but without success, for her husband had no love for her; only male beauty touched James' affections. Anyhow, Ralegh's presence in America, North or South, would have been counter to James' appeasement policy towards Spain, a policy the more despicable that Spain had so clearly passed her zenith and was now in decline.

In 1612 the young Prince of Wales died of typhoid in his nineteenth year. Speaking of his friend Ralegh's imprisonment he had said, "Only my father would keep such a bird in a cage." Prince Henry had determined that one of his first acts when he came to the throne would be to release the distinguished prisoner. The young prince's early death was the prelude to the final tragedy of Ralegh's life.

His wife's and his son's intercession could not influence the king, but Ralegh dangled the thought of gold before his eyes and worked on him through the current favourite, the Duke of Buckingham. Even James' fear of offending Spain and his subservience to the Spanish ambassador, Count Gondomar, seemed for a time to be in abeyance. Ralegh set forth a scheme for a second expedition to "Guiana," which, he said, had a mine containing vast amounts of gold, easily accessible and workable, nor need its exploitation impinge on Spanish rights. Doubtless Ralegh was counting on the accepted policy in the late queen's time—that final success was its own justification, and previous warnings against friction with Spain a mere façade. James, poltroon that he was, hedged his bets by betraying the details of Ralegh's plans to the Spanish ambassador, who promptly related them to King Philip III. Moreover, Ralegh's head was promised as satisfaction for any violation of Spanish colonial sovereignty.

When Ralegh was getting ready for his conditional release and this last adventure (1616), the Indian princess Pocahontas, with her husband John Rolfe and their infant son, was on a visit to England. It is unlikely that Ralegh saw Pocahontas, whose exotic beauty and romantic legend made her the talk of the town, but he undoubtedly heard a great deal about her. She was staying at Brentford, some ten miles up the River Thames from London, and there also, as a guest and dependent of the Earl of Northumberland in Syon Park House, lived Ralegh's friend and old-time mathematical tutor, Thomas Hariot. Hariot paid constant visits to the Tower and we may be sure that he carried to Ralegh all the news of the Christianized princess from Virginia.

Ralegh's last journey across the Atlantic was a desperate

gamble in which he staked all that was left of his fortune and his wife's inheritance, as well as his reputation and his life itself. To achieve his object and yet avoid friction with the Spaniards would, he knew, be impossible. Years earlier Keymis had reported the new vigilance of Spain to safeguard her monopoly in South America. Only a spectacular harvest of gold could outweigh the suspended death sentence and James I's craven fear of Spain. What Ralegh did not know at first was that his king had already betrayed him to the Spaniards, whether his journey was a success or failure. Later he was to learn that James had confided to the Spanish ambassador the number and tonnage of the ships, the armed forces being carried and the route to be followed. The king had even promised, under the spell of Count Gondomar's flattery conveyed in excellent Latin, that Ralegh should be handed over to the Spaniards so that they could have the pleasure of hanging him in Madrid.

From its beginning the story of the voyage is a chapter of mounting calamities. Ralegh's ships, especially his flagship, the *Destiny*, of his own design, were good vessels, but they were poorly manned. The conditions of a journey more than likely to end in disaster had forced Ralegh to recruit the scum of England's ports for his crews. Many of the gentlemen-volunteers and investors who joined him, and whom he could not afford to refuse, were ne'er-do-wells their relations were glad to be rid of at a small expense. Trouble began when the fleet of seven ships reached the Azores. One of Ralegh's captains promptly deserted, sailed his ship to England and carried home false stories of aggression against unoffending Spaniards on the islands.

Sickness broke out on the way to South America and the casualty rate was terrifying. By the time the ships anchored off Trinidad and had been cleansed and their stores replenished, the men under Ralegh, gentlemen-volunteers, sailors and soldiers, were in a sullen and mutinous state of mind. Ralegh himself, now in his sixties, had nearly died of fever and was exhausted by illness, fatigue and worry. Finally, to avoid a mutiny he could not have quelled, he was forced to remain in command at the base off Trinidad and put the river expedition under his friend Keymis, who was accompanied by Sir Walter's elder son, the irrespressible Wat, whose wildness had always amused him, but disturbed Lady Ralegh.

Sick and anxious, Ralegh waited for over a month between Trindad and the Orinoco delta. Then the tragic news made its way to him and at length Keymis, overcome with remorse and despair, rejoined his command and met Ralegh on the *Destiny*. The Spaniards had moved their settlement to a position that cut off access to the gold mine and made a clash inevitable. In the fighting, under Ralegh's cousin George, young Walter Ralegh, headstrong and rash, had been killed. His dead body now lay buried before the high altar of a church abandoned by the Spaniards. A desultory search for the gold mine was given up when it was seen that further lingering in the area, subject to Spanish ambuscade, meant the piecemeal destruction of the whole party of survivors.

In his bitterness at the loss of his son and with his own life forfeit, Ralegh upbraided his faithful but ill-starred subordinate. "You have undone us both," Ralegh said to him. Later the unhappy Keymis committed suicide, by stabbing himself in the heart when a pistol shot had failed to kill him.

Two of Ralegh's other captains deserted him about this time, taking their ships to the open seas for piracy. From the West Indies Ralegh wrote a despairing letter to his "dear Besse," telling her of the death of their elder son, and he sent a trustworthy captain, one of his cousins, ahead with the letter, while he followed more slowly to England. Some of his associates urged him to stay at sea as a freebooter or to sell his services to France, but Ralegh had given hostages to fortune. His wife and his younger son, Carew, were now dependent on the king's goodwill to save them from penury. Further, the two friendly noblemen, the earls of Arundel and Pembroke, were standing surety for his return to England. The many flaws of character in the last of the great Elizabethans did not include the betrayal of friends.

After the eastward voyage across the Atlantic, in the course of which he was in danger of mutiny and murder and had no rest by night or day, Ralegh made his landfall in the south of Ireland. There many of his men, fearful for their own necks in England, now deserted the ship. Finally he brought the *Destiny* into harbour at Plymouth some time in June and awaited a doubtful future, for although he was a doomed man he seems to have cherished some hope of a royal pardon.

The Spanish ambassador, playing on King James' fears, vanity and his anxiety to secure the betrothal of his son Charles to the Spanish Infanta, was striving for the fulfilment of the king's promise that the Spaniards themselves should be Ralegh's judges and executioners. This was too much even for Ralegh's enemies on the Council. Gondomar, due for leave of absence, had to sail to Spain with the assurance that his country's enemy would die the bitter death for high treason decreed more than a dozen years earlier (1603), since no other pretext for execution could be devised. There was a good deal of legalistic make-believe, directed by Coke, to give a semblance of justice to what was being done. By the end of October all the hocus-pocus had been completed and Ralegh was told he must die. Pathetic appeals to the king from Lady Ralegh and young Carew, now a twelve-year-old schoolboy, were disregarded; the king had retired to the country to dodge such appeals and to avoid witnessing the evidence of his subjects' anger. One concession to humanity had been made; Ralegh was to die by the axe, not to endure the statutory penalty for high treason in the case of one of his status, that is, semi-strangulation, followed by castration and disembowelling while still alive.

The final curtain of the drama fell on October 29, 1618, in the Palace Yard at Westminster. Lady Ralegh had been granted a farewell visit to her husband in the Gatehouse the night before, but young Carew was left at home; his father felt that the boy's visit would be more than he could bear.

The memory of Ralegh's faults, his arrogance, acquisitiveness, his later frenzied appeals to James I, was wiped out by the resigned, even playful composure of his last public appearance. It was a dignified end, and a Christian one. The Anglican Dean of Westminster gave him communion and attended him in his last hours. After his death his body was buried beneath the floor of St. Margaret's church, where, in a spot unknown, it still lies. On the fly-leaf of the Bible he had read the day before his death were the verses, possibly composed earlier and then revised, which begin *"Even such is time!"* and end with his expression of faith and hope:

> "But from that earth, that grave and dust,
> The Lord shall raise me up, I trust."

Did Ralegh, in the last hours after he had taken leave of his "dear Besse," think again of his colonizing efforts and his dream of another England across the Atlantic? If he did, he may have been cheered by the thought that Virginia, thanks to Captain Smith and, later to Sir Thomas Dale, another of young Prince Henry's friends, was now in a fair way to survive as an English colony. Although Ralegh, in the last hours in the Gatehouse, may not have known it, there was in London that night, probably sleeping the sleep of a tranquil, moderate Puritan, a successful and well-born youngish lawyer, John Winthrop, who would set out twelve years later and establish another "English empire" in the northern part of "Virginia," as Ralegh and his contemporaries interpreted the name.

2

★★★★★

Captain John Smith

AND HIS VIRGINIA

Captain John Smith and *his* Virginia; note the possessive *his*. Whatever be our final verdict on this controversial figure in colonial history, we cannot deny his love for the wild and perilous territory, as it then was, which is associated with his name. "That industrious Gentleman Captaine John Smith, still breathing Virginia" his friend, the Reverend Samuel Purchas, called him. We do well to establish this point at once, for, when all has been said against him, John Smith remains the founder of a great tradition—the patriotism of Virginians to the Old Dominion, the first of those colonies whose rise began a new era in the history of western man.

Long before Lytton Strachey started the modern craze for debunking historical figures, not always without a lapse from historical accuracy, the iconoclasts had been busy with

Captain John Smith. They attacked him as a braggart and a liar, a mischief-maker and an incompetent colonizer. Above all, they took a sneering delight in taking from us the legend, as they called it, of Smith's rescue from death by Pocahontas. More thorough research and, it must be admitted, more cogent and logical handling of the evidence have restored the Pocahontas incident to valid history, while at the same time making it readily intelligible. Captain Smith himself is indeed no longer the romantic, story-book character of the myth-makers, but he still is greater and more admirable than the iconoclasts would have us believe.

The family background and circumstances of John Smith's childhood and adolescence are exactly the kind for the European equivalent of a "Log Cabin to White House" epic, but such epics were not in vogue in the sixteenth and seventeenth centuries. We know how Walter Ralegh was labelled "upstart," "jack" and "knave" by contemporaries and they probably exaggerated the record of his insolence and arrogance. The genuine aristocrats resented his success; the "new" men, his fellow climbers, were jealous of him. John Smith was born less than thirty years after Ralegh and so, with vastly fewer advantages of birth, education and worldly experience, he had to make his way in that hierarchically stratified society of Elizabethan and Jacobean England.

Smith was a north countryman and that is a fact which should be taken into account. The self-assurance, the no-nonsense attitude of northerners are a tradition, often an irritant, among the English of the southern counties. John's father was a Lincolnshire farmer, reasonably prosperous, it seems; when in his will he refers to himself as the lord of the manor's "poor tenant" that is conventional humility in the presence of death and the aristocracy. George Smith was a more mellow type than the property-conscious Northern Farmer of Tennyson's poem, for we hear of his love of horses and falconry, his fondness for a game of bowls, and his popularity with gentry and commoners alike. John, one of a small family, for those days, was born in 1580, which means that he was eight years of age in Armada year, old enough to share in the excitement and the fears of imminent invasion and the subsequent rejoicing when English seamanship and the autumnal gales defeated Philip II's great fleet and drove it northwards on its calamitous course around Scotland and Ireland.

John's schooling was as thorough as that of most boys of his social class at the end of the sixteenth century. He attended two reputable grammar schools, first of all the one at Alford which held its sessions over the porch of St. Wilfrid's church, perhaps in what had been the priest's room in the days of a celibate clergy. Later young Smith was at school, as a boarder because of the distance from his home in Willoughby, in the market town of Louth. He had started as an "A-B-C-darian," in the contemporary slang, at Alford with a good deal of emphasis on religion—orthodox Anglican—and "manners," which comprised such diverse ethical items as the due respect for one's betters and the avoidance of blasphemy and "filthy talk."

In the more advanced grades at Louth the boys acquired a smattering of Latin, enough anyhow for the more receptive of them to garnish their correspondence with a phrase here and there. John Smith did not take kindly to the ancient classics and he never adorns his rough-hewn but vigorous prose with gems from Caesar and "Tully." The emphasis on "manners" was continued in the grammar school at Louth; perhaps it was needed, for Louth had a reputation for much drunkenness, despite the church census of "1400 communicants." It is interesting to note that Smith, like Ralegh, had an intense and lifelong hatred for drunkenness.

During his adolescent years John Smith seems to have dwelt much on ideas of adventure, chivalric romance and heroic deeds in foreign lands. That he was always religious, in a moderate, Anglican fashion, is undeniable and, amid the licentiousness of camp life on active service, he seems always to have been a chaste man. His mental picture of a soldier's career, formed in those school days at Louth, was partly based on the military career in Flanders of the local nobleman Peregrine Bertie, Lord Willoughby, for whom the schoolboy and his father both had affection as well as respect.

School ended for John when he was fifteen, that is in 1595, and he had already thought of running away to sea, but "his father's death stayed him," he says, erroneously fixing the date in the year after he left Louth. His father died in the following year, after apprenticing the boy to Thomas Sendall, a prosperous merchant with shipping interests at King's Lynn. Sendall, according to Smith himself, was "the greatest merchant of all those parts." He was a solid citizen of Lynn, one of its aldermen and three times its mayor. John, as an industrious apprentice, might have gone a long way under Alderman Sendall's aegis, but we should never have heard of Captain John Smith of Virginia.

If his father's death "stayed" him in the uncongenial apprenticeship for a year, his mother's early remarriage, to one Martin Johnson, caused the emotional crisis that made a runaway of him. He never got over it and he tells us that the year of his mother's remarriage as a recent widow was for him as the year of her death. This, perhaps, is the key to much that is singular in his career and his character—the blamelessness, in a sense the immaturity, of all his relations with women, as well as the lifelong bachelorhood, which was the celibacy of a knight-templar or a monk rather than the freedom of a libertine. In women, of various types and races, Smith sought always the mother he had lost, never the lover, mistress or wife other men were seeking. Only in the case of Pocahontas shall we find this pattern changed and then it was, with sexes and ages reversed, a cognate pattern. With the Red Indian maiden it was a father-daughter substitute, a military Lewis Carroll and a wild and very un-Victorian Alice.

An apprentice who ran away from his legal master faced serious consequences, physically painful ones if he were recaptured. Smith apparently broached the subject of a transfer to some job aboard a merchant ship in which Thomas Sendall had interests, but did not get a satisfactory response, so he slipped away without leave and did not again set eyes on the Lynn merchant and civic leader for eight years. Before the days of conscription and national armies, soldiering was an obvious job for a runaway apprentice if, like Smith, he was physically fit, not too softly nurtured and not too fussy about whom he fought or for what cause. In his book of *True Travels* Smith speaks of three or four years campaigning in the Low Countries under a Captain Duxbury, presumably an English volunteer with the Dutch fighting against the Spaniards.

At the age of nineteen (1599) John Smith was home again, experienced as well as interested in soldiering as a profession and with a working knowledge of one or two foreign languages, for he appears to have had a knack for such things. Perhaps his service in Flanders had made a good impression on the aristocratic Bertie family in his part of Lincolnshire, for his next employment was as "servant," something between companion and gentleman's gentleman, to young Peregrine Bertie, who at the age of fifteen or sixteen was going on the Grand Tour which had become part of a gentleman's education. The teen-age nobleman, with his tutor and the two "servants," Smith and another young man, travelled about France.

Smith does not make it clear whether he completed the tour with the party, but he tells us of being sent to Scotland as a courier and then making his way down to Lincolnshire. Then, in 1600, comes an interlude which seems to take us back from the opening of the seventeenth century to some date in the Middle Ages. We see the young ex-soldier and gentleman's attendant transformed into a hermit. He "retired himself," he relates, "into a little woodie pasture" and lived in a hut or shack built of branches and standing beside a brook. It was a flimsy kind of shelter, for its occupant "lay only in his cloathes." None of this had any religious significance, but Smith was "glutted with too much company." He tells us of two books to which he gave serious study at this time, Machiavelli on the *Art of War* and a translation of Marcus Aurelius. The meditations of the virtuous Stoic emperor appealed to the strain of Puritan earnestness that comes out in Smith from time to time—his abhorrence of drunkenness, his dislike of tobacco just when "drinking tobacco" was becoming fashionable and the habitual absence from his thoughts of women except as mother-substitutes.

The hermitage intermission was ended by another of the offers which came his way from the local nobility. Henry, Earl of Lincoln, master of Tattershall Castle, the great building of red brick that is still one of the tourist sights of Lincolnshire, had in his employ Polaloga, a master of horsemanship or "manage" in the fashionable Italian style. Smith, who like his father before him knew and loved horses, was invited to join the nobleman's household and receive instruction from the Italian master in return for some kind of service or as an addition to the earl's retinue. This training under an expert in horsemanship, which in those days would

include the management of weapons on horseback, is part
of the answer to the sceptics who have sought to discount
Smith's autobiographical account of his later deeds as a
fighter on horseback.

The period of three to four years (1600-1604) that follows
his sojourn at Tattershall Castle while he was being trained
by Polaloga is the portion of Smith's career about which
his veracity has been most bitterly attacked. The onslaught
may be said to have started in 1662, when Fuller, in his
Worthies, points out, with an implied questioning of Smith's
truthfulness, that we have no witness for Smith's achievements except Smith himself. The attack was renewed a hundred years ago by Charles Deane of Boston, Massachusetts,
but since then so much proof of Smith's reliability in other
matters than his own deeds has come to light that his nar-
ratives of his own actions can no longer be dismissed as
mere fabrication. This is especially true of his account of
events in central Europe when he was serving in the Hungarian forces. The happy conjunction of access to newly
opened archives and the work of a research scholar able to
deal with the Magyar language have done much to restore
confidence in Smith as a fundamentally truthful writer.*
Perhaps Smith gilded his exploits somewhat when he recorded them. We must remember that he was a farmer's
son seeking to make his way, like Ralegh, in a station above
that to which it had pleased God to call him. To such traits
as the insolence and arrogance—towards his equals only—
of Sir Walter Ralegh, and the occasional domineering truculence of Captain John Smith we may assign as cause the
insecurity of a "new" man in a class-conscious society.

* See *Captain John Smith; his Life and Legend,* by Bradford Smith (Ap-
pendix I—*Captain John Smith's Hungary and Transylvania.* By Laura
Polany Stricker, Ph.D.), Philadelphia and New York, J. B. Lippincott Co.,
1953.

In the first year of the seventeenth century John Smith had not yet started looking westward to find an outlet for his energies. He was a soldier, a well-trained professional at the age of twenty, and he turned with a certain disgust from the thought of settling down to cultivate the land, as his ancestors had done, in rural Lincolnshire. Warfare was always going on in some part of Europe. Somewhere on the continent there must be a niche for a young cavalryman, broad-shouldered, hard-muscled, sober in his mode of life and well versed in his profession. Perhaps Smith's first idea was to seek a post in the country of his earlier term of soldiering, for he went direct to the Netherlands. There, however, he fell in with four Frenchmen who said they were on their way to join the Hungarians who were at war with the invading Turks. This impressed the young Englishman, perhaps with its suggestion of a crusading vocation, for there was in him a touch of what later ages would call romanticism. Anyhow, he went along with the Frenchmen, who were about to make their way to northern France by sea. At the port of arrival they robbed the Englishman of everything but the clothes he wore by carrying his baggage ashore and leaving him to await the boat's immediate return. Once on land, of course, they disappeared. For the good name of the French it is pleasant to record that the robbers' countrymen took pity on the victim, lodged and fed him and sent him happily on his way again.

At Marseilles he was able to get a passage on a ship taking pilgrims to Italy, but this led to another misadventure. Bad weather imperilled the vessel, and the devout pilgrims concluded they had a Jonah aboard. It was of course the English heretic, the "Lutheran" as they called him, apparently their generic term for all Protestants. Without further ado they tossed the English passenger overboard, happily for the future colony of Virginia near a small, deserted is-

Sir Walter Ralegh, 1552?–1618. By an unknown artist. Shown standing beside his son, Watt, who was killed as a young officer on Ralegh's expedition to the Orinoco. *courtesy of National Portrait Gallery, London*

Ralegh, probably some years later, in characteristic velvet, brocade and gold. Artist unknown. *courtesy of National Portrait Gallery, London*

THE PORTRAICTVER OF CAPTAYNE IOHN SMITH ADMIRALL OF NEW ENGLAND

These are the Lines that shew thy Face; but those
That shew thy Grace and Glory, brighter bee:
Thy Faire-Discoueries and Fowle-Overthrowes
Of Salvages, much Civilliz'd by thee
Best shew thy Spirit; and to it Glory Wyn;
So; thou art Brasse without, but Golde Within.

CAPTAYNE IOHN SMITH

Captain John Smith, 1580–1631. Wearing the armor of the period. From an engraving by Simon de Passe in the British Museum.

John Winthrop, 1588–1649. From an original painting in the State House, Boston, of Winthrop as Puritan Governor of Massachusetts. Artist unknown.

William Penn, 1644–1718. This portrait of a young man in 17th century armor is often presented as representing William Penn. Some experts are doubtful. *courtesy of N. Y. Public Library*

An older William Penn, from a portrait which has not been
fully authenticated. *courtesy of N. Y. Public Library*

James Oglethorpe, 1696–1785. Believed to be in his late twenties in this portrait. *courtesy of N. Y. Public Library*

James Oglethorpe, founder of Georgia, in later years, from a panel by Alfred E. Dyer, after the William Verelst portrait. *courtesy of National Portrait Gallery, London*

land off the coast of Savoy. Smith swam ashore and hoped for the best. Next day he was rescued by a skipper from northern France. Perhaps the man was a Huguenot; anyhow, he was kind and hospitable and a man of integrity after his fashion, for when he had done a bit of privateering at the expense of a foreign merchant ship he gave Smith his fair percentage of the spoils. Moreover, Smith adds piously, God sent him a little box containing as much again as the prize money.

The surmise that John Smith had a romantic soul under the bluff soldierly exterior is confirmed by the fact that, although a hard-headed north countryman, he surrendered to the magic of Italy as Anglo-Saxons have done all through the ages. He met again the aristocratic Bertie brothers, Robert and young Peregrine, at Siena and then made his way to Rome.

In Rome, surprisingly, he called on Father Robert Persons, the famous English Jesuit who had been in charge of the "mission," consisting of himself and the martyr Edmund Campion, sent to England in 1580. Once again we hear of Smith's making a point of meeting Jesuits, an English and an Irish one, when he had reached Austria. In Rome he saw the Aldobrandini Pope Clement VIII with some of his entourage making the painful ascent—on one's knees—of the *Santa Scala*, held by tradition to be the steps up which Christ had been taken to Pontius Pilate. There is no evidence that all this meant any dawning interest in the old religion of Smith's ancestors. He was always a sincere, somewhat Puritanical, Christian believer and at any time would have drawn his sword in defence of the Church of England, but without any great interest in the details of its doctrines. Unlike one of his successors in the government of Virginia he was not an amateur theologian. The ceremonies in Rome were, as they still are, items in a touristic programme, while the visit to Father Persons may have been to obtain an introduction to Catholic commanders in the war with the Turks. The great English Jesuit, whose name was anathema to his Protestant fellow countrymen and many of his co-religionists, had a finger in several political pies and would gladly have helped an Englishman going to fight the Turks.

If Smith made his way to Hungary bearing with him a romantic dream of a good, old-fashioned Crusade, a tussle of Christian devotion with the Saracen anti-Christ—"God wills it" the Crusaders' battle cry—he must have been disillusioned when he reached headquarters and presented himself to the Austrian archduke. He would soon have learned that the internal squabbles of the Christian rulers were at times more virulent than their quarrel with the Moslem enemy. Part of Hungary was already under Moslem control, administered by Christian collaborationists. In other areas the German Hapsburgs were busy gobbling up the territory of their Hungarian Christian neighbours. Many of the Hungarian units were aggressively Protestant, in opposition to German Catholic rivals, while Catholic regiments would not accept Protestant volunteers lest their presence should dim the glory of an exclusively Catholic victory.

Smith, of course, was attached to a Protestant regiment of Hungarians and quickly proved his value as an alert and quick-witted professional soldier. He introduced a system of signalling to besieged allies by means of lights and successfully misled the enemy as to an intended attack. This he did by means of a display of burning "match" in the dark to simulate the presence of a large unit. He also invented a form of primitive incendiary bomb for launching against enemy positions. He was soon rewarded with an independent cavalry command of two hundred and fifty men.

The exploit which the sceptical critics of his *True Travels* have treated with the greatest scorn is his defeat in single combat and the decapitation of three Turkish warriors outside the walls of "Regall." To start with, say the critics, there is no such town as Regall. There is, however, one called Drigall; a foreigner listening to one of the most difficult of all European languages might well have transformed Drigall to Regall, and Smith consistently spells words as he thinks he has heard them. An alternative explanation is that he heard some reference to the *urbem regalem* (royal city). He had already told us of his small enthusiasm for Latin in the Louth grammar school, so he may well have been tripped up by the Latin accusative, tumbled out in a spate of unintellgible Magyar.

The story of the combat is well known. There still lingered the medieval practice of a temporary truce while two mounted warriors, armed with appropriate weapons, met in tournament, with both armies as spectators. The winner was entitled to behead his opponent and carry off the head as a trophy. One Turbashaw, a formidable fighter, challenged the Christian besiegers. Captain Smith was allowed to accept the challenge, unhorsed the Moslem, cut off his head and carried it to the Hungarian commanding officer. A friend of the dead man, wishing to avenge Turbashaw's defeat, lost his own head in similar fashion and then the English officer issued his own challenge. It was taken up by a Moslem warrior with the improbable name of Bonny Mulgro, but that was what the Turkish names sounded like to Smith and so they appear in his book. Bonny Mulgro met the same fate as his two colleagues.

Apparently what most disturbs the critics is the threefold victory of the English champion. One man killed in single combat—perhaps, but the sceptics draw the line at three in succession. Actually the objection seems to have its roots in a predisposition to think John Smith a liar. There is no inherent difficulty about the achievement; if the English soldier overcame the Turks' champion, Turbashaw, by superior skill and strength, why not the other two men, who were presumably less skilled than their leader? Smith, still in his twenties, broad-shouldered, rather stocky and muscular, with health unimpaired by drink, tobacco or sexual excess, seasoned by years of active service, was probably a match for anyone from a city that had already stood a month's siege.

An answer to those who deny Smith's veracity is the grant to him by Sigismund Báthory, Prince of Transylvania, of a coat of arms commemorating the incident—three Turks' heads on a shield. Surely no prince, not even one sometimes touched with madness, as was Sigismund, would, without enquiry, issue his patent for a coat of arms to a foreign charlatan. We may be sure there would have been onlookers in plenty to have given Smith the lie had he tried to fool the prince. Of course it has been suggested that the alleged patent from the prince is a forgery. Nevertheless it satisfied the College of Heralds. In those days of new knighthoods—James I sold them in large numbers to help his exchequer—the heralds would have had plenty of experience to enable them to detect a forgery.

Smith's good luck deserted him a few months later. At the battle of Rotenthurn (November, 1602) he was wounded and lay on the battlefield helpless, weakened by loss of blood and wondering what his fate would be when the looters came prowling. They carried him off and sold him in a slave market. His purchaser, a Turk, sent him to Adrianople and then to Constantinople, where he was given to a young woman, Charitza Tragabigzanda. Smith speaks of her as a lady of aristocratic family; evidently she was educated, for she spoke Italian and she called in people to converse with Smith in French and English. After a time he was sent to Asia Minor to be in her brother's care, to learn Turkish and, perhaps, to become a Moslem. Had the lady fallen in love with him? We do not know, although the brother's harshness suggests it. It is certain her affection would not have been reciprocated, for if ever a man, neither monk nor ascetic, kept himself unspotted from the world where women were concerned, it was Captain John Smith.

The brother acted barbarously. He humilated the captive, bullied him and drove him to desperation. One day, when threshing grain at a remote spot, Smith turned on his tormentor, killed him with the threshing tool, hid the corpse under the straw and fled, wearing the dead man's clothes and riding his horse. After various vicissitudes he made his way to Russian territory, where he was able to rid himself of the slave's iron collar about his neck. He passed through Germany and France and went by sea to northern Spain. A trip to Morocco, with the idea that a soldier of fortune might hire himself out there, led to nothing and in 1604 he was back in England.

With his new coat of arms and a sizable bonus from the grateful Prince of Transylvania the young cavalry officer went to London, at all times the Mecca of Englishmen back from overseas. One would like to see an authentic portrait of the twenty-four year old Smith at this time. The cast of his features later in life we know from a portrait in one of his books—an intelligent, rather broad, face, with high forehead and full cheeks, attractive but definitely not aristocratic. The expression is alert yet good-natured, almost quizzical. The full beard and impressive moustache extending horizontally out beyond his cheeks were perhaps not cultivated until his sojourn in Virginia.

Smith has not told us exactly when he turned his thoughts towards North America. London, in the early years of

James I's reign, was a stimulating place for a young man like Smith, with good health, an active mind, a knighthood, albeit a foreign one, and a purse full of ducats. The city taverns and ordinaries were full of gossip about adventure in distant lands, the wonders of the Americas, North and South, and the exploits of English seamen in the region which Spain claimed as her monopoly in virtue of Alexander VI's Bull. Through all the talk and argument ran the *leit-motif* of gold—so abundant that the aborigines in Manoa, El Dorado's capital, used it, says a contemporary playwright, for their skillets and chamber pots.

The obsession of gold was more often than not a deadly snare, for it lured men to starve or die of disease in regions where no gold was and where they might have saved their lives and enriched themselves in the end by a colonization based on agriculture. Even when the dream of gold in rocks, mountains and river beds had lost some of its potency, the stay-at-home investors thought of trading posts rather than of genuine settlements. A few forward-looking men, Ralegh and his Gilbert half-brothers and Sir Francis Walsingham and, most insistently, Dr. Dee the scientist, had indeed thought and talked of a "British Empire," an overseas England where white men from Europe and brown or red men in the Americas would live as equals and subjects of Queen Elizabeth under a *Pax Britannica* that would revive the best features of Rome at her zenith. Those men, however, were the great Elizabethans. The London business magnates under James I were a diffrent breed.

John Smith at this time was moved by two forces which were to dictate most of his future actions. In the first place, he needed money. He never became a rich man; all that he ever had he earned by his sword and, later, by his pen and, in minor ways, was helped by a few generous patrons.

More insistent as well as more constant than the economic motive was his passion for adventure. In this respect he was, like so many of his countrymen, an eccentric, in biological language a "sport." By all the rules of ancestry and tradition he should have lived and died an obscure north country farmer, his career just another unexciting line in the short and simple annals of the near-poor. His mother's remarriage and his own aversion from a farmer's or a merchant's life had combined with thoughts of travel and adventure to lead him to Flanders, Hungary, Morocco. Now these same influences would make him one of a small band of colonists who set out for Virginia in 1606. He was a relatively unimportant member of the party at its inception, for he can have had very little money to invest. His supply of ducats was running low and he had no mind to stay in London and earn a living there. Jacobean London probably made small appeal to him except as a jumping-off place. There was nothing of the soldier on leave about him, the man freed from discipline and seeking solace for past hardship in the illicit pleasures of the town.

His first plan had been to join Charles Leigh's colony on the Wiapoco (Oyapock) River, which is now a boundary between Brazil and French Guiana. What would have happened had he done so, we cannot tell. Perhaps he would have perished in that adventure or perhaps he would have been its saviour. The chance to go to Virginia came his way and he embraced it.

The king signed the charter for the Virginian enterprise in the spring of 1606. What followed is typical of the impracticality that is mingled with the energy of that era. Had preparations been speedy and efficient the colonizing fleet could have taken advantage of summer weather on the Atlantic. Failing that, wisdom counselled postponement until the next spring. Neither course was followed; the ships set sail just before Christmas in the teeth of bad weather and contrary winds.

There were three ships, the *Sarah Constant*, the *Goodspeed*, the *Destiny*. The first-named, largest of the three, was only 100 tons burden, the other two forty and twenty respectively. Into these were packed a hundred and five people, Smith tells us; "six score" says the official record. For six weeks the ships lay in the Downs, off the Kentish coast— within a few miles of the English mainland—using up their stores of food, subjecting crews and colonists to unspeakable misery. It seems unjust to blame, as some have done, the able navigators in charge: they had their orders and did what they could. In supreme command was Captain Christopher Newport, one of "Ralegh's men," who had taken the captured *Madre de Dios* into port in 1592. He was assisted by another Elizabethan veteran of the sea, Bartholomew Gosnold, who several years earlier had discovered and named Cape Cod and Martha's Vineyard. He, too, was one of "Ralegh's men." Smith admired both these seamen, although he did not always see eye to eye with Newport.

The composition of the party that was to grow into the "English nation" in North America, of which Ralegh and the other Elizabethans had dreamed, is interesting. Nearly a quarter of these people were officially "gentlemen." The word had a very precise and, from the standpoint of good colonizing, sinister meaning at that time. A "gentleman," like the lilies of the field, toiled not neither did he spin. More often than not he was a man of courage and fortitude, skilled with weapons and horses, inured to hardship, but he must not soil his hands or tarnish his honour with menial work.

These gentlemen Virginians-to-be were a mixed bag. The most authentic, as a gentleman, was George Percy, a younger son of the Earl of Northumberland—and conscious of it. Edward Maria Wingfield was the only charter member who was also a practising colonist. His middle name gave him trouble; people took him for a Catholic, as he would have been had his family not slipped. Smith disliked him, not on religious grounds, and the antipathy was mutual. The party had to have its "recorder," whatever else was lacking, so the post was given to Captain (courtesy title) Gabriel Archer, who had studied law in Gray's Inn. He and Smith were destined by their temperaments to be enemies, Archer was fussy, legalistic, devious, while Smith was the forthright man of action. Another with whom he fell out, although friendly at first, was Captain John Ratcliffe. At one time this man adopted the alias of Sicklemore (or Sickelmore), but as he did it openly and for no evil purpose, perhaps Smith's hostility made him read too much into the change of name. Going by the record, the most admirable of all the party was the clergyman, Robert Hunt, whom the Archbishop of Canterbury had appointed to be the settlers' first Anglican chaplain. He was one of those lovable clerics, gentle, modest, physically frail, yet of great fortitude and unbreakable will. He was vicar of Reculver in Kent, so during those dreadful weeks in the Downs he was within a few miles of his home. Extreme and continuous sea sickness had brought him to the verge of death, but he refused to be taken ashore. His genuinely Christian character did much to preserve a semblance of peace among the demoralized colonists and the sailors. Smith became and remained his fervent admirer.

In February (1607) the ships managed to get out of the English Channel, to everyone's relief. Newport, although a good sailor and a dashing privateer, was a conservative. The extreme danger of calms on the short northern route to the west was an article of faith at the time, so he took the lengthy route by way of the Canaries and the West Indies. It had its advantages. Fresh water and wholesome food, above all, fruit as a preventative against scurvy, could be taken aboard. The Spanish settlers were glad to trade with anyone, including English privateers. When the ships reached Dominica the travellers exchanged English gew-gaws for fruit with the naked savages, fierce-looking but peaceable, who came swarming out in their canoes.

John Smith was in trouble at this time and had no share in the fun. He was in irons in whatever served as a ship's prison on a charge of mutiny. This is all we know of the affair. The term "mutiny" was undoubtedly excessive and unjust, but Newport sounds a touchy commander; Smith's good qualities at no time included tact or diplomacy; he was a real north countryman in that. There were many envious and unscrupulous fellow-gentlemen to do a bit of backbit-ing. That the Lincolnshire farm boy and soldier of fortune had become a gentleman was itself a cause of offence. Anyhow, when the fleet reached the island of Nevis a gal-lows was set up, but, says the intended victim, "Captaine Smith, for whom they were intended, could not be per-swaded to use them." We have no extant evidence of a trial or a formal verdict, so perhaps the gallows is a bit of fiction. Smith liked to indulge himself in the saturnine humour which appears in his writings and some of his recorded sayings. And there was the gentle but inflexible Reverend Robert Hunt to exercise a calming influence on people.

An irony of the situation, which was not revealed until an American landfall was made, was that in a sealed box which Captain Newport held, and which on strict orders from the London Council for Virginia might not be opened on the voyage, was a list of names of those who were to

form an administrative council to run the colony—and one
of the seven names was that of Captain John Smith.

The ships left the West Indies on a northward course towards the middle of April, but an error in reckoning left
them still without sight of land three days after a landfall
should have been made. Faint hearts were for an immediate return to England, but Captain Newport kept going
and towards the end of the month he sighted land. As the
ships sailed into Chesapeake Bay and dropped anchor the
travellers, like Ralegh's people in Pamlico and Albemarle
Sounds, were cheered by the green vegetation, the perfume
of flowers and spicy shrubs and the sight of noble trees in
the still unravished forests.

A landing party was arranged, but John Smith, fuming
with impatience, was still under duress. That may have been
his good luck, for the boat's crew and passengers were received by suspicious Indians with a volley of arrows. One
of the colonists was wounded in the hand, a sailor more
seriously.

In the evening the sealed box was opened. One of the
seven names was now seen to be Captain Smith's. The other
councillors refused to accept him, an action dictated possibly by the aristocratic Wingfield, who may have despised
Smith's plebeian origin and, more pardonably, resented a
certain bumptiousness in him. Edward Maria Wingfield was
not an ignoble character; he was a fine soldier and a man of
honour, but pompous, inclined to take himself too seriously;
perhaps the whole affair was a case of the mote and the
beam. Before Wingfield left Virginia, under humiliating
circumstances, the antagonism between the two men had
gone so far that Smith sued the other for slander, won
his case and was given heavy damages. Meanwhile they
had to endure each other's company. The fantastic mutiny

charge had been allowed to lapse and doubtless Captain Newport was glad to use the services of an experienced soldier who, whatever his faults, had courage, fortitude and energy.

The hostile Indian reception of the first landing party did not discourage the commander. He ordered the collapsible boat (shallop) designed for river travel to be put together and he then began the exploration of Chesapeake Bay. For a time there was trouble with the many shoals in the estuary until a good navigable channel was found—to the great comfort of the party, hence the Point Comfort on our maps. A couple of days later a cross was put up near the scene of the first landfall; Cape Henry was named in honour of the young Prince of Wales, Captain Newport's patron. On the last day of April another landing was made and this time the Indians were friendly, impressed perhaps by the dignified and courageous bearing of Captain Newport, who advanced at the head of his party, his hand on his heart in token of peaceful intentions. The Indians conducted the visitors to the village of Kecoughtan and regaled them with food, drink and tobacco, entertaining them with dances and singing, "like so many Wolves and Devils," says the chronicler ungratefully.

During the early part of May the councillors, with Smith still barred from their meetings, were at work on plans for the "city" they had to build. Their London masters, in happy ignorance of North American conditions, had made various rules to guide the planners. They were to choose a site on a navigable river or estuary practicable for vessels of fifty tons, yet far enough inland to be safe from attack by sea. They must consider ease of defence, wholesome climate and the absence of "natives" between themselves and the sea. What they should do if they could not find this ideal site the London magnates did not tell them. Newport and the others did the best they could, which was to settle on a small cape in the river having the strategic features demanded. Unfortunately it failed in the matter of salubrious climate; it was marshy, low-lying and infested with mosquitoes. The settlers would soon have worries enough on their minds, so it may have been as well they did not know of the connection between the mosquitoes and malaria.

The ships were moved up to the chosen site and moored to tree trunks. Then colonists and their stores were landed, tents set up for temporary shelter, the outline and rough plan of a fort decided on and a name bestowed on the city-to-be, Jamestown in honour of the king, whose name was given to the river also. History does not tell us how the land was acquired. The local Indians, whose headquarters were a village on the Chickahominy River, were amiable enough, so possibly they received some kind of payment.

Although excluded from the Council, Smith was by this time accepted otherwise on the same footing as the other gentlemen-adventurers. Captain Newport and others not blinded by prejudice saw that the chief difference between him and the others lay in his superior ability and his readiness to work at whatever was necessary. He was chosen to be a member of an exploring party got together in the latter part of May. Among the objectives laid down by the Council in London were gold and the search for survivors of Ralegh's lost colony on Roanoke Island. This should be kept in mind by those who have blamed the councillors and Smith in particular for losing time and energy that should have been given to agriculture.

The addition of the newly released "mutineer" to the party was probably dictated by the idea that a trained army officer would be useful in dealing with the Indians. There had already been some trouble when a friendly meet-

ing ended in friction over the attempted theft of a hatchet.
Fighting and bloodshed were averted only by the Indians'
fear of the white men's firearms, a novel and disturbing
means of inflicting death by remote control. The visiting
warriors left in a sulky mood and that ended the incident
for the time.

All went smoothly at first on the exploring trip. The
shallop made her way up the river, some Indians in a canoe
proved to be friendly and one of them acted as guide and
interpreter. The explorers started downstream again after
coming to waterfalls near the site of the future city of
Richmond. More Indians were met and they too were
friendly. The travellers visited the "queen" of one tribe, a
large, mannish woman wearing only a deerskin and copper jewellery. She was not very forthcoming until Captain
Newport cheered her up with various gifts.

At Jamestown the situation had, as soldiers say, deterio-
rated. An Indian attack in force had been repelled by the
use of the ships' guns; of the settlers one, a boy, had been
killed and another fatally wounded. Wingfield had a narrow
escape when an arrow passed through his beard, but without even grazing him. As the shallop drew in to the shore
the occupants found the fort alerted, a hastily constructed
palisade going up, the guns mounted for action and the
men being drilled in the use of arms.

Smith's status was still a matter of contention. Some of
the Council members wished to send him home, but others
insisted on his rights in virtue of the London Council's
nomination. Finally, when the dispute had continued into
June, he was admitted to the Council and duly took the
oath of office. For this outcome of the affair he was indebted to Captain Newport's good sense and the efforts as
arbitrator of the well-loved chaplain, Mr. Hunt. The wisdom
of the decision was made clear when Smith at once set to

work on the crude fortifications, drawing on his military experience in Flanders and Hungary.

The time had now come for Captain Newport to return to England and one is puzzled by the London Council's inclusion of his name as one of those chosen to govern Virginia. That, however, is less absurd than the London sponsors' town-planning, the demand that a model English county town should at once spring into being amid the forests and swamps of tidewater Virginia.

Captain Newport's departure was celebrated with becoming gravity, Mr. Hunt holding a communion service on the Sunday morning and the captain giving a supper party aboard his ship in the evening. When the *Sarah Constant* made her way to the Atlantic she carried a letter to the Council in London. In her hold was a consignment of the local timber, but most of the cargo space was filled with what the gold-hungry colonists had thought was valuable ore. In London only the lumber was marketable, for the first Virginians had yet to learn that all that glitters is not gold.

As Captain Newport sailed down the James River he must have wondered what the future held in store for Jamestown. Of those left behind a few optimists, including Captain John Smith, may have dreamed of the "English nation" to be born of the quarrelsome, dispirited and disunited group of men within the fort. The summer heats were beginning, the stocks of food were inadequate in quantity and beginning to deteriorate in quality, and the drinking water, whose chief source was the river, was muddy and probably typhoidal. The population at the time was wholly a male one, made up of involuntary celibates, with all the angularities and touchiness that implies. In command of them was the self-conscious aristocrat, Edward Maria Wingfield, antipathetic to most of his colleagues, including Smith, who was the most energetic and competent of the Council members. As much of the settlement was made up of "gentlemen," unwilling to lose prestige by working with their hands, the burden of manual tasks fell on the remainder. Smith was free from this inhibition, but then his early life on a Lincolnshire farm had preceded his rise to a gentleman's standing.

The first summer in Virginia was a calamitous one. Soon after the *Sarah Constant* was on the high seas disease swept through the settlement. The "summer sickness" the colonists called it, giving as its cause the mists on the river and miasma from the nearby swamps. No doubt the true destroyer was malaria, but the settlers were ignorant of the part played in their tragedy by mosquitoes, which they regarded only as a source of minor discomfort. Typhoid also claimed its quota of deaths. The surgeon who had stayed in the colony was, like the chaplain, a man of sterling character and he worked hard under hopeless conditions, but the number of deaths grew from day to day and by the autumn half the population had perished. One of the victims was Captain Bartholomew Gosnold, a seaman of the old Elizabethan breed, whom the colony could ill spare. The food situation went from bad to worse. The daily ration of grain had to be reduced and part of it, the barley which had been taken to America loose in the ships' holds, was full of maggots. Actual starvation would have overtaken the settlers but for the fish, sturgeon, caught in the river.

As though all these bodily ills were not enough to try the fortitude of the people, quarrels and intrigues weakened their capability of united and sustained effort. Their president, Wingfield, was deposed by his fellow-councillors, the three left alive, and was held prisoner aboard the pinnace Captain Newport had left behind. The unfortunate man decided to appeal his case to the crown and was, therefore, kept as the king's prisoner until he could be sent back to England.

At this point the settlement may be said to have reached the nadir in its history so far as administration goes, although the terrible crisis of the "Starving Time" was yet to come. With the deposition and arrest of Wingfield began the rise of Captain John Smith to the position of command which has been belittled by his enemies but in whch his advocates see him as the saviour of the Jamestown venture. Even if we discount some of his own story as self-glorification, it is undeniable, on the evidence of other witnesses, that he set to work on the two most urgent needs of the colony.

He succeeded in getting from the Indians supplies of corn (maize) sufficient to ward off the famine that had seemed almost inevitable. In the second place, he took in hand the matter of house-building. Trees had been felled and crude fortifications set up, but so far the settlers had been living under canvas. The material of the tents was decaying rapidly; adequate shelter was, next to food, the most urgent essential if the colonists were to survive the winter ahead. Force of character, enhanced by an army officer's experience, enabled Smith to exact obedience from all the people. He made the "gentlemen" take their share of all the work that had to be done and he himself set the example by showing that his Transylvanian knighthood and his coat of arms were no obstacle to a job of work with mattock, axe or saw. Wooden houses were built of clapboard and roofed with thatch, English style, or the bark of trees in the Indian manner. The log cabins in some artists' pictures of early Jamestown and her sister colony up north a decade later are unhistorical. The English settlers did not adopt this form of building until later immigrants, Finns and Swedes, brought it from their own countries.

In this early period of John Smith's ascendency occurred the incident which was to become a well-loved portion of the American story and which has been attacked by sceptical critics in later times. The chief argument against the truth of the Pocahontas story, if we disregard the prejudice of those who are bent on seeing Smith as an out-and-out liar, is a simple one and, at first sight, plausible. It was first brought forward nearly a hundred years ago and, later, was taken up by Henry Adams.

There was published in London in 1608, *A True Relation of Virginia,* written by Captain Smith and containing an account of certain events that had taken place the year before. This narrative differs in a few minor points and one important particular from *The Generall Historie of Virginia, New England and the Summer Isles,* published in 1624. The minor points are only such as are explicable by the lapse of time and, to this writer, appear no more destructive of credibility than the differences in detail to be found in the four gospels of the New Testament. The important particular is that of the omission in 1608 of the story of Pocahontas and its inclusion in 1624.

One naturally asks, with the critics, "Why the omission in the earlier narrative of so outstanding and interesting an event?" History provides us with an answer to this question. One of the orders given the settlers by their masters and financial backers in London was, "No friction with the natives." Smith's narrow escape from being clubbed to death on the orders of a chieftain with whose men he had been fighting certainly would not suggest amicable relations with the Red Men, whatever the subsequent state of affairs. The *True Relation* came out in London so early in the colony's career that it does not seem at all remarkable that its writers, Smith and others, should have kept quiet about the spot of trouble with Powhatan and his braves. By 1624, when the

Generall Historie was published, Smith had long since left
Virginia and severed his connection with the Council in
London. Two other points in his favour may be noted. He
had plenty of enemies, both because of his personal idio-
syncrasies and because of the snobbish jealousy of some of
his rivals. These enemies by no means pulled their punches
when they attacked his character or his deeds. Not until
modern times, however, did anyone seek to throw doubt on
the substantial accuracy of Smith's account of his rescue by
the Indian girl.

A false glamour has tarnished the story of Smith and
Pocahontas when romantic writers have overlooked the relative ages of the two and, also, are ignorant of what seems
to have been an accepted code of the Indians in cases
like this. As Smith himself tells the story, it has a simple
charm as well as a convincing appearance of veracity.

When Smith became the virtual dictator of the colony he
at once tackled the problem of food. He has been criticized
for setting out on voyages of exploration when he should
have been fostering agriculture, but the criticism is neither
just nor logical. Winter was drawing near by the time he
had the authority to impose his will and a semblance of
order on the colonists. No corn could be sown that year, so
he set to work to buy, borrow or beg or even squeeze from
unwilling Indian traders enough grain to keep his people
alive through the winter months. Foraging expeditions were,
therefore, essential if starvation was to be held off.

On one of these expeditions Smith ran into trouble with
the Indians. He *may* have been ambushed by a party of
braves or his guide *may* have been treacherous, although
this does not seem to have been the case. It is possible that
Smith, suspicious of the fickle and enigmatic Red Men, may
have precipitated an outbreak of violence. He admits that he
killed two, or possibly three, Indians before his position was

hopeless and he threw away his weapons and surrendered. When death seemed inevitable he distracted his captors' volatile minds by the gift of a pocket compass to their chief, a brother of the great Powhatan. To the latter Smith was sent as a captive. In Powhatan's quarters Smith was well treated, washed, warmed and fed, but all this, he knew, might be preliminary to a cruel death.

Powhatan, an elderly man and no fool, asked searching questions about the presence of the English in territory which he claimed as his own. The prisoner improvised a story of a hurried and desperate escape from Spanish pursuers, but Powhatan, himself something of an expert in diplomatic finesse, was not deceived. When the conference was over, the chief ordered the execution of his prisoner.

Two large stones were laid on the ground and then some of the warriors held Smith down with his head on the stones, while others, armed with clubs, stood by, awaiting orders to beat out the captive's brains. Before Powhatan could give the order, there was a stir in the crowd of attendant braves and squaws, a young girl rushed forward, threw herself down so as to protect the intended victim and held his head in her arms, resting her own upon it. The king's dearest daughter, as Smith calls her, was thirteen or fourteen years old, more mature than a white girl of the same age. She would have been wearing the modest apron of deerskin or leather which succeeded the very exiguous garment of a girl who had not yet reached puberty. Her father at once gave way and Smith's life was spared so that he could remain with the Indians to make weapons for the chief and trinkets for his daughter. Apparently the remission of a death sentence at the pleading of a favourite child was common practice among the Indians. The young Indian girl, the delight of her elderly father, had seen the white-skinned prisoner, with his fair hair and curly beard, as a desirable playmate, as a modern child might plead for a kitten, a puppy or a rabbit. There is nothing incredible about Powhatan's concession to his daughter. Indian custom apart, she was used to cajoling her father so as to get what she wanted. Her true name was Matoaka; the *Pocahontas* by which we know her is a nickname meaning something like "Madcap" or "Little Wanton," understanding the latter term in an innocent sense. The relation between the English captain nearing his thirties and the Indian girl only on the threshold of womanhood was that of uncle and niece or godfather and child. One of the sentences Smith put into a phrase book of her people's language, a dialect of Algonquin, he thus translates, "Bid Pocahontas bring hither two little baskets, and I will give her white beads to make her a chain." This was many years before he published the story of her rescuing him.

Her intercession seems to have been very effective. Not only was Smith's life spared; he was accepted in friendship by the chief and went through an initiation making him an honorary member of the tribe. Then he was sent back to Jamestown with an escort and a request for gifts. Powhatan asked for a grindstone and two cannons. Smith's impish sense of humour comes into his account of the return to the settlement. Smith was welcomed by his friends, who had despaired of his life, but his enemies sought to have him condemned to death because of the English lives that had been lost before his capture, and as no precedent in English law could be quoted they based their claim on a text in Leviticus. The timely arrival of Captain Newport from England saved Smith from these machinations of his enemies. Meanwhile Powhatan's braves who had escorted Smith back safely had to be given presents they could carry back through the forest to their master. Perhaps they brought up the question of the cannons. Smith pointed to a couple of the demi-culverins which were mounted on the fortifications, but the Indian warriors were nonplussed, for, as he tells us, "They found them somewhat heavie."

There were at that time less than forty survivors of the original group of settlers, but Newport had brought new recruits with him along with greatly needed supplies. Things seemed to be going well and then a new catastrophe overwhelmed the colony. A fire destroyed the flimsy wooden buildings and the fortifications and the place was for a time without shelter or defence. Possibly the Indians, Smith's connection with the chief and his daughter notwithstanding, would have exterminated the English settlers but for the presence of Newport and his crew. Even the armed ship and its complement of sailors, however, did not prove an unmixed blessing. The newcomers traded with the Indians, carelessly and extravagantly, as sailors will, and up went the price of corn: the Indians saw they had a sellers' market. Meanwhile, too, the presence of all the visitors meant an increase in the consumption of food stocks. Diplomatic amenities as between Indians and English were kept up by the bestowal of more gifts on Powhatan and the formal introduction to him of Captain Newport, whom he insisted on referring to as Smith's father, understanding the word, perhaps, in a metaphorical sense.

Shortly thereafter Newport set out for home again in his ship the *Francis and John*. Less than two weeks after she had sailed, the companion vessel, the *Phoenix*, long since given up for lost, turned up safely in the James River. She had become separated from Newport's ship in a storm and had put in to a West Indies port for repairs and fresh supplies. When the time came for her to sail for England, some of the colonists as well as members of the ship's crew wished to fill her hold with the glittering mineral which had been stowed away in the *Sarah Constant* to no purpose. It was hard to exorcize that obsession of gold from the minds of the people. This time Smith's common sense prevailed and the ship sailed with a cargo of cedar.

Trouble with the Indians broke out again. Either they were naturally light-fingered or their own lives were run on such communistic lines that the English sense of private property meant nothing to them. On one occasion four Indians made their way into the settlement and were apparently about to attack Captain Smith. He had the gates closed, arrested the four intruders and held them as hostages for the return of things that had been stolen. Powhatan shrewdly sent Pocahontas, the little charmer, to act as ambassador and mollify the English. Whatever Smith and his countrymen thought of her father and whatever their distrust of his good faith, they always welcomed his daughter and applauded the scantily clad child dancing and turning cartwheels with unselfconscious grace in the open space within the fort. Smith speaks of her as outstanding among her people both for looks and mind and calls her the only Nonpareil of Powhatan's kingdom.

During the summer that followed the departure of the *Phoenix*, Smith continued his voyages of exploration and trading. His adventures included a painful encounter with a sting ray while he was fishing and for a time his sufferings were so intense that he thought he would die, but the doctor treated him with an emollient oil and he soon recovered. His return from this journey was followed in September (1608) by his formal election to be "president" of Jamestown. His predecessor in office was held a prisoner, charged by his fellow councillors with "mutiny."

The year Smith spent as "president" or governor—the terms were loosely used and his own occasional use of the second one has no significance—has been a subject of controversy. Was he the man whose leadership and strength of will saved the struggling colony from extinction or was he merely the "vayne glorious" braggart his enemies called him? Briefly, we may say that his reputation has suffered the vicissitudes of many historical reputations. There was the phase of uncritical admiration which in turn called forth scepticism and iconoclasm, but now in recent years we have seen the prevalence of a more balanced judgement of his character and his deeds.

Captain Smith, we must remember, was a soldier trained to receiving orders and to giving them and having them obeyed. Possibly under the conditions of a prosperous colony at peace and with an organized civil government he would not have been an ideal president. Early Jamestown existed under anything but these ideal conditions. Disease, food shortage, perils from the Indians, and disharmony among the settlers produced something akin to the state of things when the ancient Romans suspended normal government and called one man to rule the state for them. Captain Smith's sergeant-major attitude was just what those first Virginians needed at the time.

He tackled first things first, safety from Indian surprise attack and the provision of a food supply when winter was coming on. The rough-and-ready fortifications were extended and reinforced, the original triangular palisaded enclosure being made into a five-sided fort, which gave greater defensive strength and also made more room for dwelling houses. A weekly parade was organized so as to train a garrison ready for defence. The Indians were always an uncertain quantity and there was the possibility that Spain would exert herself to enforce the monopoly given her by Pope Alexander VI.

Trading and fishing expeditions were sent out as a means of dealing with the threat of famine. Those who have criticized the captain for his neglect of agriculture overlook the fact that he did make a start by ordering land to be cleared and ploughed and sown with Indian corn. In everything he initiated he had to cope with the imported "gentleman" shibboleth, which, had he been a weaker autocrat, would have withdrawn from the available working force a large proportion of the colonists. He made them all work, himself setting the example. No doubt his air of command, his occasional flashes of temper, and the fact he was a plebeian giving orders to "gentlemen" account for much bitterness and even slander. No one, however, ever accused him of asking of others what he would not do himself or of claiming special privileges in food and lodging.

Some time during the autumn of Smith's term of office Captain Newport again arrived from England with more settlers, including Dutchmen and Poles to manufacture naval stores, but unfortunately the planners at home had not sent food supplies adequate to the increase in population. The usual orders of the Council were repeated—to find gold, to discover survivors of Ralegh's lost colony, and to locate the passage to the great South Sea, for as yet no one had any idea of the breadth of the North American continent. Furthermore, Powhatan was to be solemnly invested with a copper crown, to establish his position as a sovereign in alliance with James I of England. The Indian chief proudly declined to go to Jamestown for the coronation, so a deputation, headed by Captain Newport, went to his dwelling and, more or less forcibly, placed the crown on his head. He stoutly refused to kneel for the ceremony.

When Captain Newport sailed for England he took as cargo a token supply of naval stores—tar and pitch—demanded by the Council and also a very forthright letter from John Smith, pointing out the absurdity of diverting men and labour to getting products so much more cheaply and easily obtained from Sweden and Russia. The trouble-maker Ratcliffe was sent home at the same time.

One of the consolations of Smith's life during the trou-blous year when he ruled the colony was the friendship of Pocahontas. Certain winning traits in his personality or the dramatic circumstances that first brought them together evoked in the Red Indian girl deep affection and loyalty. The affection and the loyalty were reciprocated. The record shows a side of Smith's character less familiar to the colo-nists, who often chafed under his rather domineering man-ner and a north country cocksureness which they resented. With the girl he was fatherly, kind and solicitous, admiring in her the qualities a soldier admires, fidelity and courage.

Powhatan, despite his pledges of friendship and his oc-casionally lavish hospitality, seems to have been something of a Machiavelli of the American forest, so Smith never wholly trusted him. On at least one occasion, when Smith was on a trading expedition, the chieftain had laid plans to ambush and kill the man who had come to expropriate the Indians around Jamestown. Pocahontas slipped away from her father's dwelling at night, made her way through the woods and warned the English of their peril. With tears she refused the gifts her friend wished to press upon her, for they would have made her father suspicious and in his anger he might not have spared even his favourite child. There was a nonchalant impudence about the old chief that is amusing in retrospect, although it called for constant vigi-lance on Smith's part. When the murder plot failed and Pow-hatan found himself out-generalled by the bearded white man from across the Great Water he promptly became the brother and good friend again and the more or less honest broker in the trading of corn and deer fat for copper and English trinkets.

The winter following Smith's election as president was a trying one, but he contrived to keep the people from starvation. Fish and shellfish eked out a meagre diet and the colonists were put to gathering some roots capable of being ground up for flour. This they called "tuckahoe," their version of the Indian name they had heard. At some other time in this early phase of Virginian settlement the Jamestown colonists discovered a stimulant and intoxicant in the *datura* plant, the Jamestown or Jimson weed, so potent that more than a very small quantity produced a temporary insanity.

With summer came relief for the suffering colony when four ships under Captain Samuel Argall arrived at Jamestown. Unhappily for Captain Smith two of his worst enemies had come back as passengers, Ratcliffe and Archer, who had been busy in London poisoning the minds of the Council members against him. Captain Argall brought the news of a fresh charter and of new appointments for the government of Virginia—a lieutenant-governor and an "admiral." The first of these was to precede Lord De La Warr as governor. Unfortunately the *Sea Venture*, carrying the two officials and all their commissions and other papers, had become separated from Argall's other ships in a storm and was thought to have been lost. This left Smith in a quandary. There was no person to whom he could legitimately resign his commission and he had no authority to appoint other councillors in Jamestown. Ratcliffe and Archer sought to make trouble, but were quickly, Smith tells us, "laid by the heels," probably his phrase for protective custody. All he could do was to continue the government of the colony, grappling single-handed with its problems—food, the Indians, intrigue and discord among the settlers, the chance of Spanish attack.

In September a serious accident befell Smith and he was forced to abandon any hope, for the time being, of giving further service to the colony. On someone else's shoulders must now rest the responsibility of saving the people of Jamestown from anarchy among themselves or massacre by hostile Indians. Smith had sent one of his subordinates up the James River to trade with the Indians as a way to improve the food supply. This man, Francis West, seems to have little in his favour beyond the fact that he was a brother of the governor-to-be, Lord De La Warr. He soon got into trouble and Smith travelled up the river to deal with the situation. Neither gratitude nor cooperation was forthcoming so far as West was concerned. Even Smith's resilient spirit seems to have wilted; weary and discouraged he started on the journey back to Jamestown. While he was alseep in the boat there was a sudden explosion of gunpowder. Someone may have dropped a spark into the powder from the "match" used for firearms or been careless in the tobacco-smoking learned from the Indians. Smith was awakened by the noise and by the agonizing pain in his leg. Horribly wounded and with his clothing on fire he jumped overboard to extinguish the flames and was then pulled in by his men, who did their best for him, little enough in the absence of a doctor and any medicaments.

Back in the settlement Smith resolved to sail for England, for crippled and in constant pain he could do no more for Jamestown. Now arose the question of a successor, even if only a temporary one. He would not place authority in the hands of Ratcliffe, Archer and their clique and so he prevailed on George Percy to take over the presidency. Smith's enemies were callous and vindictive. Although the ship on which he hoped to sail was due for immediate departure, they contrived to delay its sailing for three weeks, time they employed in fabricating a list of charges against him to be read by the Council in London.

John Smith was not given to brooding and introspection,

so we have no record of his thoughts as he saw the American coastline disappear from view on the horizon. From the evidence of his life and writings after his return to England we know he was always an enthusiast for English colonization of the northern continent. It is no exaggeration to say that his heart was in Virginia, a name which he understood as applying to the whole eastern region from French Canada to Spanish Florida.

The ship in which he travelled reached London about Christmas time, 1609. We hear nothing more of the effects of the explosion that had ripped a large piece of flesh from his thigh, so it is likely that a strong constitution and sober living had enabled him to recover in the course of the voyage. When he stepped ashore in London he was still a comparatively young man—just within sight of his thirtieth birthday. There were more than twenty years of active life still before him, filled with attempts at colonizing, adventures at sea, and much work with his pen. Throughout there was the dream he shared with Ralegh, a prisoner in the Tower when Smith landed and for another eight years after that time—to make North America an "English nation." In spite of everything, however, we are left with a sense of anticlimax and of frustration. We do not know how thoroughly the minds of the London councillors had been prejudiced against Smith. He was eager for an opportunity to be heard in his own defence and was granted a "trial" or hearing before the Virginia Company. Whether a verdict was given and, if so, what it was, we do not know. He was never called upon to go back and serve the colony despite his earnest petition that he might do so. It would have been in a subordinate position, for which he was quite prepared. The ship carrying Virginia's lieutenant-governor and her "admiral" had indeed been wrecked on the way—on the coast of Bermuda, but Sir Thomas Gates and Sir George Somers, the two officers in question, had shown remarkable energy and initiative. They built another ship from the wreckage and from local products and made their way to Jamestown. It is interesting to speculate on the course of events had Smith been sent back to aid them with his experience and his training as a soldier. Perhaps he could have forestalled the horrors of the "Starving Time," when the colony was on the eve of being abandoned, and it may be that his military knowledge would have prevented the appalling massacre of settlers by the Indians in 1622.

We have only scanty and disjointed scraps of information about Smith's doings in London at this time. He formed a friendship with Samuel Purchas, the Anglican clergyman a few years his senior who was carrying on the work of another cleric, Richard Hakluyt, as chronicler of English seamanship, travel and adventure. Smith heard, about this time, that the Virginians were giving up their dreams of gold to be picked up on the seashore or scooped out of rocks and streams. They had found what was to become the source of the colony's prosperity in the future—the culture and curing of tobacco. The industry owes its beginnings to John Rolfe, a serious young widower who had gone out to America the year after Smith's return to England, and who was destined to become the husband of Pocahontas after her conversion to Christianity. With great business acumen Rolfe set to work to make a practical success of the crop for which the Virginian climate and soil were suited. Probably John Smith was not enthusiastic about this development. He was a non-smoker and may have shared the prejudice of his sovereign, James I, who wrote a scathing denunciation of what he regarded as a filthy and unwholesome habit—"drinking tobacco," as it was called.

Smith's reflections on the vicissitudes of the Jamestown settlement certainly took note of two of its great weaknesses.

One of these was the poor morale of the colonists, against which he waged a wearisome uphill fight all the time he had authority to do so. The second was the attempt to control a colony three thousand miles away by a body of men ignorant of its living conditions, climate, natural resources and its problems of contact with aboriginal people. Moreover, all these London magnates were under the spell of the old dream of gold, of a kingdom of El Dorado in Virginia to match the southern one in Ralegh's "Guiana."

There were two other faults in the colonizing plan of which Smith, trained to a soldier's life of barracks and camp, may not have been fully conscious. Jamestown in its early years was wholly a male community; without wives, children and settled homes, men do not normally put forth roots and make a home of a new and savage region. Another weakness which a professional soldier might easily overlook was the absence of incentive for the individual settler. The Jamestown colonists of the first phase of the colony's history were, willy nilly, communists. However hard and conscientiously a man worked, he received as much, or as little, as his less active neighbour. He did not own his house, his tools or his land; what he produced went into the common fund. It is true that Smith was driven to impose a Stalinist rule of "No work, no ration card," and he had to drive the unwilling gentry to do their share of jobs, but beyond that there was no motive for seeking to make a fortune—except the vain hope of picking up gold nuggets if one were lucky. A later administrator brought in a policy of private enterprise and private gain and, with John Rolfe as pioneer of the tobacco industry, a new era of colonial expansion began in Virginia.

Captain John Smith's temperament did not lead him to sit down and cry over spilt milk. When the members of the Virginia Company would not employ him, he turned his eyes northward. If Southern Virginia, as it was called, would not use him, then he would seek scope for his energy in Northern Virginia—the region known since his time, and thanks to him, as New England. The name itself had been inspired by the fact that Sir Francis Drake, one of Smith's great heroes, had given the name *Nova Albion* to the land, now part of California, which he had annexed for Queen Elizabeth I in the course of his voyage round the world. Smith had already become interested in this northern part of the continent when Captain Bartholomew Gosnold discovered and named Cape Cod and Martha's Vineyard and he was a personal friend of Henry Hudson. It is not surprising that by 1614 Smith had managed to find sponsors and the necessary capital to provide a couple of ships for a new venture across the Atlantic.

He was to be in command of one of the ships, although with a professional sea captain as navigator. The second vessel was commanded by one Thomas Hunt, who turned out to be a scoundrel who enticed friendly Indians aboard his ship and then, deserting the expedition, sailed to Spain as a slave-trader. Smith's humanity and his sense of honour were revolted by his vile conduct. The hope of paying for the voyage by whaling proved an illusion, but Smith was happy enough as explorer, cartographer and as student of the Indians, with whom on this occasion he got on remarkably well. He was struck with their friendliness in the territory of Massachusetts, a part of the country which he regarded and described as something nearly an earthly paradise.

Back in England, in August of the same year, he found a sympathetic patron in Sir Ferdinando Gorges, who shared his interest in colonization, although he had not been to North America. In March, 1615, the new expedition, of two ships, set out to establish a colony on the coast of Maine. Smith knew a friendly Indian chief who would be helpful and the abundance of fish in the area seemed to ensure food for the settlers and perhaps a source of future wealth. Almost at once disaster overtook the venture. The ships became separated in a violent storm, the larger one, in which Smith travelled, being dismasted and having her timbers so badly sprung that only incessant pumping kept her afloat. Finally, under a jury mast and with the pumps going night and day she managed to get back to Plymouth.

Smith's backers stood by him in spite of his misadventure and loss of money. They found another ship for him, although one of sixty tons only this time, and they gave him a hopeful send-off in the middle of June. He had not yet come to the end of his misfortunes. He fell in with pirates and thought that all was lost, but, suprisingly, they turned out to be old comrades-in-arms of his soldiering days. They urged him to join them, he refused, and both went their own ways, parting on good terms. Perhaps he wished he had gone with them, for he was soon captured by French privateers and, with no choice in the matter, joined them in harrying the Spaniards. The French promised him his share of prize money and he filed his claim in Rochelle, but we do not know that he was paid. By the end of the year he managed to get back to Plymouth and told his story to Sir Ferdinando, who held him blameless but held out no hopes of further colonial ventures.

That was the end of the captain's career as an active colonizer. He made numerous attempts to get support for a new venture, but without success. To the end of his life, however, he was advocate and propagandist for his Virginia.

The year 1616 was marked for him by two notable events. Early in June his book, *The Description of New England,* was entered at Stationers' Hall and when it was printed his friend and former patron, Lord Willoughby, arranged for him to present a copy to the royal heir, young Prince

Henry. From now on we do not hear of "Northern Virginia," for the term "New England," accepted by the popular young prince, passed into general use.

The second outstanding event of the same year was the first meeting in about seven years with Pocahontas. The Indian child he had known as a semi-nude wench turning cartwheels in the fort at Jamestown was now a dignified young Christian wife and mother, the Lady Rebecca by baptism, Mrs. John Rolfe by marriage. She was lionized in London, received by its bishop and presented at court, although the Stuart King James apparently disapproved of Rolfe, a simple English gentleman, marrying "royalty." For years Pocahontas had heard nothing of her friend and had even been told he was dead. Now they met again at Brentford, where she was lodged with her husband and little son. There was at first a certain constraint between Smith and Pocahontas. Perhaps he was too conscious of her position as a cossetted visiting "princess" and of his own standing as a simple and not too prosperous private citizen, no longer the president of a colony. She was grieved by his formality and seeming coldness and at length reminded him that he used to call her playmate and she thought of him as another father.

The ice was broken after a period of silence on her part; Smith forgot the contrast in their new positions in society and the old, affectionate friendship was renewed. They were able to laugh together at the simplicity of the Indian brave who had travelled with the Rolfes across the ocean, commissioned by Powhatan to meet the king of England, to see the Englishmen's God and to make a census of the population of England by cutting a notch in a stick each time he saw one of the people. The Indian soon gave up the census-taking, failed to make any contact with the English God, and did not think much of James I, who did not give him a single present.

Early in the new year (1617) came the final tragedy. The Rolfe family had embarked on a ship lying at anchor in the Thames ready for the voyage to Virginia. The young woman was taken ill and grew worse so rapidly that she had to be taken ashore at Gravesend. There she died and her body was buried beneath the chancel of St. George's Church, whose register contains the entry, "1616,* May 2j, Rebecca Wrothe, wyff of Thomas (*sic*) Wrothe, gent., a Virginia lady borne, here was buried in ye chauncell." We are told that she died piously, faithful to the Christianity of her baptism in the Jamestown church. The broken-hearted widower left his infant son with an uncle in England and set out on the long Atlantic journey back to Virginia.

The fourteen years of life that remained to John Smith were full of activity but also of hope frustrated. At one time it looked as though he would again be able to sail for North America, but the proposed expedition petered out into a fishing trip off Newfoundland. His plea that at least one ship might be released for a genuine colonizing voyage fell on deaf ears. He was given the empty title of Admiral of New England, which appears on the title pages of his books. The honour may have been some slight consolation for the neglect of his offers to help in overseas work, but he had lost much of the zest of life and he settled down to do what he could by his writing. The "Pilgrims" of 1620 were glad enough to use his maps and the carefully gleaned geographical and other information he had collected, but they did not

---

* Presumably an error of a parish clerk vague about the time of year Old Style; the new year (O.S.) would have started on March 25, but as Pocahontas was taken ill in March, there may have been confusion in the writer's mind.

deign to accept his offer of service when they set out on their
journey to New England.

The last two decades of his life were chiefly filled with
his activity as an author. His *True Relation* had been written when he was under a cloud and was intended to justify
his work in Jamestown to his masters in London. Four years
later, that is in 1612, he published his *Map of Virginia; With
a Description of the Country,* and in 1616 *A Description of
New England.* This was followed by *New England's Trials*
(1620 and 1622), then in 1624 by the *Generall Historie of
Virginia, New England and the Summer Isles.* This is an
imposing catalogue of writings for a country farmer's son,
with no education beyond the forms of a couple of provin-
cial grammar schools and an early departure to the continent of Europe to take up the life of a mercenary soldier.
We see his versatility in the next two books, both well regarded in their day and for many years widely used by
English seamen. These were *An Accidence or the Pathway
to Experience* (1626) and, in the following year, *The Seaman's Grammar.* Those competent to judge consider that he
was as efficient at sea as when soldiering ashore. Most con-
troverted of all his books, *The True Travels, Adventures
and Observations of Captaine John Smith,* appeared in 1630.
It told of the military campaigns in central Europe and is
the book that was formerly most quoted by those who
sought to prove Smith an impostor. Finally, in the last
year of his life, 1631, he brought out a handbook for intending settlers overseas. Having, perhaps, by this time finally
given up hope of again standing on a ship's deck as she
sailed to the New World he may have wished to do his best
to help others to start a hopeful life in the new-found country across the Atlantic. He called his little book *Advertise-
ments For the Unexperienced Planters of New England, or
any where* and dedicated it to the two archbishops (Can-

terbury and York) of the Church of England. There is much
advice for English colonists, some of it reprinted from his
earlier books, and it was intended largely for the people now
sailing in increasing numbers to the Massachusetts settlements.

John Smith's latter years would have been lonely and
comfortless but for the hospitality of Sir Humphrey Mild-
may, an Essex country gentleman with an estate, Danbury
Place, near Chelmsford. Sir Humphrey was a kindly, expan-
sive country squire, easy-going in his home, interested in
his land and his cattle and glad of a companion who could
talk about such things over a tankard of wine or beer. It was
not, however, in the rural peace of Danbury Place that death
came to Captain John Smith. He died, still only fifty-one
years of age, in the noisy, fetid city that was seventeenth-
century London. His body was buried in the old city church
of St. Sepulchre. Enough people still knew and respected
him to put up a memorial tablet commemorating in verse
his life and doings. The Great Fire of 1666 damaged the
church badly and the tablet was lost, but a replica was put
up to replace it.

"To overcome is to live," John Smith had adopted as his
motto in his early life. Could he revisit the Virginia and the
New England of our day he might well be happy to find his
name still living in the traditions of the English-speaking
peoples.

3

★ ★ ★ ★ ★

John Winthrop,
THE FIRST BOSTONIAN

To be a Bostonian means more than to have been born in New England's premier city. The word has a wider connotation than the merely geographical one; it is the name of a genus, a type, genuinely American no doubt, but more different from, say, a Virginian or a mid-Westerner than is a southern Englishman from a northern Frenchman. In this sense we may regard John Winthrop as the spiritual ancestor of all authentic Bostonians.

Were one asked to conjure up, from history and literature, a composite picture of a Bostonian, certain traits would suggest themselves and the completed picture would be remarkably like a portrait of the founder of Boston. To start with, he must be a man with what used to be called a gentleman's education—like Winthrop's in Cambridge University and the Inner Temple. Old Hickory, with his muddy boots on the upholstered chairs in the White House, or young Lincoln splitting rails and "wrastling" with the boys of the village, however admirable in other ways, would not fit into the Boston picture frame. Your Bostonian, moreover, combines the strength of his convictions with a certain moderation in expressing them and a temperate attitude towards those who disagree with them. In the great controversies with Roger Williams and Anne Hutchinson the temper of Winthrop's mind was in strong contrast with the inspissated bitterness of most seventeenth century ideology.

Lastly, we may assign to our ideal Bostonian an undemonstrative self-respect shown in an equally modest outward dignity. One cannot picture John Winthrop, born again in our age and speaking our idiom, indulging in the electioneering buffoonery of some of our politicians or presiding, as governor of his state, at a bathing beauty contest.

By the time John Winthrop was born, on January 12, 1588 (Armada year), at the village of Edwardston, in the county of Suffolk, the family was definitely aristocratic, but, like so many Tudor families, it was "new" aristocracy. It owed its rise from yeoman class to the status of gentry to Adam Winthrop, John's grandfather. Adam, who was born at the end of the fifteenth century, lived through the Reformation and profited by that upheaval to hoist his family to a higher level in the social hierarchy. He was a prosperous clothier* in Lavenham, then East Anglia's wool centre and now an exquisite museum piece, the most perfectly preserved of English medieval villages. Adam Winthrop, early in his business career, extended his operations beyond his native

* Not, as we might interpret the term, a manufacturer of clothes or a dealer in them, but a middleman who bought raw wool and farmed it out for cleaning and weaving to artisans who did the work in their own cottages. The clothier was thus the forerunner of the mill owners of the Industrial Revolution.

Suffolk, for in 1626 he received the freedom of the City of London.

It is probable that Adam Winthrop, like most of the people of England, took as a matter of course, best not questioned, Henry VIII's religious changes—the suppression of the monastic houses, the break with the Papacy, the equally cruel persecution of the old "Papists" and the new Protestants. In the breaking-up and the distribution of monastic property a choice morsel came Adam's way and he seized it. The manor of Groton, until then an outlying possession of the great Benedictine abbey of Bury St. Edmund's, became Winthrop's by royal grant. Four years later, when the sickly boy king Edward VI was on the throne and his uncle the Duke of Somerset actually ruled the country, Adam Winthrop became "armiger" and could enjoy for the remaining fourteen years of his life the ownership of a coat of arms and the knowledge that he was now gentry.

He had seven children by two marriages; his third son, another Adam, was the father of John Winthrop. This second Adam Winthrop was sent to Cambridge University, studied law and married the sister of an Anglican bishop, then, when she died, the daughter of a well-to-do business man. Adam had intellectual interests outside his law books, for when a married sister gave birth to a son her brother sent her a set of commemorative verses to be set to music. He seems also to have been a connoisseur of religious oratory, for he recorded that in one year he had heard nearly three dozen different preachers in the parish churches at Groton, Edwardston and Boxford, the last-named still noted for its locked font—to prevent evil-doers stealing the baptismal water for the purposes of witchcraft.

By his second marriage Adam Winthrop had four daughters and one son, John, the future Bostonian. Of John's infancy and boyhood we know little beyond the fact that his father paid a local clergyman to teach the child, but whether this "scholinge" was private tuition or lessons in a small, private school we are not told. The choice of Cambridge as the youth's university was a matter of course; it was the intellectual hub of East Anglia, its faculty normally committed to the left wing, theologically speaking, of the new Church of England. Add to this the fact that the second Adam Winthrop, competent in accountancy as well as law, was auditor for Trinity and St. John's Colleges and that his first wife had been a sister of the Master of Trinity. When John was fifteen his father took him along on the annual accounting visit and entered him at Trinity. This college was then rising to first place in the university as the breeding ground of intellect and erudition.

Young Winthrop doubtless worked hard at his books, but his own memories of university life are chiefly concerned with moral issues, seen by a serious youth as religious problems. Early adolescence is a trying time of life in which to be thrown into the hurly-burly of college freedom, especially after a sheltered boyhood with a clerical teacher in a quiet Suffolk manor. Loneliness and homesickness were added to the young fellow's spiritual teething pains. His "lusts," he tells us, "were so masterly as no good could fasten upon mee," a rather hyperbolic expression of a sensitive boy's worry about the often obsessive nature of sex in early youth. He speaks also of being "neglected and despised," which we may interpret as the result of his unwillingness to share the coarse fun and perhaps the licence of his contemporaries. He did not stay in Cambridge to take a degree; a couple of years in one of England's two ancient universities was enough to safeguard the reputation of a gentleman's son. Three and a half centuries ago people generally lived fewer years than we, matured earlier and started their adult life at an age when we are still in our mental puppy-hood. Soon after his seventeenth birthday John left Cambridge, became engaged to an Essex gentleman's daughter and, in the spring of 1605, married her. The use of the passive voice would be more correct; he *was married*. It was one of the marriages on the accepted pattern of the times, arranged by the respective fathers with an alert eye on jointure, dowry, real estate and so on. In the late winter following his marriage his first son, named John, was born at Great Stanbridge, Essex, the bride's home. In the ten years of her married life Mary Winthrop, née Forth, gave her husband three sons and two daughters. She died in the summer of 1615 and was buried at Groton.

Six months later John married, or was married, a second time, but in the interval an influence had come into his life which would, with some modifications, continue to the end. This was his friendship, which was also a discipleship, with an Anglican clergyman, one of the Puritan left wing of the national church. Ezekiel Culverwell's Calvinistic piety quickly and deeply impressed the twenty-seven-year-old widower, earnest, religious, but somewhat at sea about his beliefs, responsive to affection and, on indisputable evidence, inclined to scrupulosity. For a time John seriously considered taking holy orders, but gave up the idea or was talked out of it by friends he consulted.

The scruples which marred his religious earnestness and disturbed his peace of mind would seem rather comical to the average worldling of any era, yet a substratum of common sense underlay all his broodings and self-accusations. He enjoyed a pipe of tobacco—for the fashion set by Sir Walter Ralegh survived all James I's vituperation. Winthrop was sociable and liked a draught of wine or beer with other country gentlemen. He loved to wander, fowling piece in hand, about the fields and coppices for what later sportsmen

1 call rough shooting. Sometimes, having a discerning
te and a good digestion, he ate too much at dinner and
n found, like all the classical ascetics, that this was an
impediment to prayer and religious meditation. About all
these things he had scruples, but there also his common
sense comes out. He did not condemn innocent pleasures as
evil, but, the *homme moyen sensuel,* he was inclined to indulge in them too much; they were God's creatures, but his
use of them was, as Ignatius Loyola would say inordinate.
Anyhow, he cut down the amount of indulgence he allowed
himself in "drinking tobacco," and in toasting other country
squires in the good Suffolk beer. The rough shooting he
gave up altogether after a good deal of soul-scrutiny, but his
motives were not wholly religious. It was "against the law,"
so perhaps a bit of poaching was on his awakened conscience; also it was over-strenuous and not without danger.
Lastly, he confesses, without conscious humour, that it was
a waste of time because he was a poor shot.

The second marriage was to Thomasine Clopton, the
daughter of a neighbouring landowner in Groton. The
young wife died a year later and was buried beneath the
chancel of the parish church. This loss affected Winthrop
more deeply than the death of the first wife, despite the
briefer period of the second marriage; perhaps this is at-
tributable to his greater maturity and the new-found Puritan piety. If his enumeration of Thomasine's virtues in his
journal is a frank appraisal and not just a good man's observance of *De mortuis* . . . , she was a truly admirable
wife and mother, and we can understand the devastation
her early death worked on his spirit. He writes touchingly
of her affectionate regard for the children of his first marriage and of her attitude towards himself, "so amiable and
observant as I am not able to express."

For nearly two years he remained very much shut up

within his own mind, low-spirited and hesitant where he had formerly been active and energetic. The cloud of depression and uncertainty was lifted in the spring of 1618, when he was betrothed to Margaret Tyndal, daughter of a well-to-do knight, Sir John Tyndal, with an estate at Great Maplestead, in the neighbouring county of Essex. The course of true love was not altogether smooth at first. The engagement was vehemently opposed by friends of the young woman's family, chiefly, it seems, because of inequality of fortune, John Winthrop being less wealthy than Margaret. That the marriage, which took place at the end of April, 1618, was a true love match is proved by the text of the two long letters written by John to Margaret in the weeks before the wedding. Winthrop, using his "scriblinge penne" as a poor substitute for endearments in the presence of his beloved, releases his feelings in a medley of religious sentiment and genuine erotic passion. When he wrote the still extant letter addressed to Mistress Margaret Tyndal three weeks before the wedding, wherein a quotation from the Song of Songs is immediately followed by a devout allusion to Holy Communion in the nuptial service, he was aware that his scribbling pen had indeed run away with him. Dating the letter (at the end) April 4, 1618, from "Groton where I wish thee," he remembers to send his parents' greetings to Margaret's parents and then adds to his postscript, "If I had thought my lettere would have runne to halfe this lengthe I would have mayde choyce of a larger paper."

Contemplating the extant portraits of John Winthrop we may wonder what in him called forth the deep affection of poor Thomasine during her brief married life and the passionate and lifelong devotion of the third spouse. We must recall, too, the trust given him by those who were his opponents in beliefs and principles—for instance, Roger Williams and Anne Hutchinson. Winthrop appears to exemplify Newman's motto *Cor ad cor loquitur* ("Heart speaks to heart"). Winthrop, despite his Calvinism, loved and trusted his fellow-men when he could. It is a fair guess that he owed little to his looks in winning love and friendship. The long nose and rather protuberant eyes do not repel, but they are without glamour. One is glad to see that he was not the crop-headed Puritan of caricature. He wore his hair long, had a neatly trimmed beard, and he is painted in a starched and ironed Jacobean ruff.

This third marriage (April 28, 1618) lasted for twenty-nine years, that is, to within two years of John Winthrop's own death. The betrothal and the wedding were decisive events in his life and it is clear that the character of Margaret Tyndal and her depth of affection brought out all that was best in him. It is to be noted that the correspondence of the two, mostly occasioned by Winthrop's absences for legal business in London in the earlier years and then, in America, when his official duty took him on slow and arduous journeys to outlying parts of Massachusetts, consists mostly of love letters. They were true love letters—written *after* marriage, the husband's in a difficult, cursive scrawl, the wife's in exquisite manuscript italics. While both man and wife were religious by nature and training, it is probable that Margaret's Anglican Puritanism had more of sweet reasonableness about it and that she unconsciously moderated her husband's tendency to scrupulosity and too much introspection.

It may have been under his third wife's influence and with the thought of new marital responsibilities that he finally gave up the idea of taking orders; the beginning of his married life with Margaret Tyndal saw him taking a more active part in local affairs. He worked at his job, an honorary one, as a justice of the peace and gave his personal

attention to the matters which came before him as lord of
the manor of Groton. That he gave some of his leisure time
to continuing his law studies is a reasonable surmise based
on his receiving an appointment in 1623 as one of the three
attorneys attached to the Court of Wards and Liveries under Sir Robert Naunton, another Cambridge University
graduate, later a Secretary of State, chronicler of Queen
Elizabeth's reign and, less admirably, a bitter persecutor of
the English Catholics. About five years later Winthrop was
made a member of the Inner Temple, a fact which suggests
that he looked forward to settling down for good as a practising lawyer in England.

His ethical standards led him to disillusion about the
Court of Wards and Liveries, which was honeycombed
with what we can only call legalized graft. His attendance
at its sessions, which might last for as long as six or seven
weeks four times a year, meant periodical trips to London
and long absences from his beloved Margaret and his Suffolk home. His letters from London to his "deare wife" or
"most sweet Spouse" in Groton while he was in the metropolis generally include a hint of his homesickness in the
medley of religious aphorisms, domestic trivia and thanks
for her "sweet Lettres." Sometimes he buys her a present
in town—in one letter a garment (unspecified) is mentioned—and, with a countryman's scorn for the townsmen's
drink, he praises the good Suffolk cider she had sent him:
"Thy Syder was so well liked that we must needs have more
as soone as thou canst." Her letters are equally affectionate
and informal, but less habitually pietistic. John Winthrop
had many admirable qualities, but a sense of humour was
not one of them. Margaret, who was a woman of character,
may, on the other hand, have had a touch of quiet irony
along with her capacity for enduring love. One of her letters,
for all its conventionally pious phrasing, suggests this.

"Those serious thoughts of your own which you sent me did make a very good supply in stead of a sarmon." She invariably directs her letters to "my very loveinge Husband, John Winthrop, Esquire," and they are full of the little details that give the correspondence a savour of continuing life. She is solicitous about his catching cold in a wet February, she asks him "to by a cake for the boyes" and a knife for one of her stepsons and promises to send to London for John's delectation "a turkey and some chese." On another occasion she includes a request from a neighbour: "Goodman Cole woulde intreat you to by him a pounde of such tobacko as you by for your selfe." Two "runlets of sider" are to be sent by the carrier, prepaid—"the carage is payed for."

The year of decision in John Winthrop's life was 1629. His appointment with the Court of Wards and Liveries came to an end. It is not clear whether he resigned from it in disgust or was eased out of it; he seems to have thought well of his chief, Sir Robert Naunton, but saw him as a man tied to a department irrevocably corrupt. The first vague hint of emigration as a thought in Winthrop's mind may be detected in a letter written to his wife in the spring of 1629, the year, moreover, when Charles I dissolved Parliament and made it clear he would be king in fact as well as in title. Winthrop, along with all the Puritans, saw England, more particularly the Church of England, as going from bad to worse and he became a prophet of woe as he unburdened himself to Margaret. "I am veryly persuaded, God will bringe some heavye Affliction upon this lande, and that speedylye," but he added, "If the Lord seeth it will be good for us, he will provide a shelter & a hidinge place for us and others."

Things moved quickly after that. From the time of his marriage to Margaret Tyndal there was none of the diffidence and self-distrust that followed the loss of Thomasine

Clopton. Winthrop made up his mind, impressed others with his ability and was readily accepted as leader and organizer. By midsummer he was at work on a statement of reasons for starting a new settlement (Plantation) in North America. The framework was ready at hand in the existence of a Massachusetts Bay Company, similar to that which had controlled the Virginia colony, that is, a council set up in London to manage the colony overseas.

The heads of the concern, Matthew Cradock, its governor, and Thomas Goffe, his deputy, had the happy thought of evading what had bedevilled Captain John Smith's efforts in Jamestown, namely, government by armchair "adventurers" three thousand miles away. This question was talked over in London and in the latter part of August a group of the men interested met in Cambridge. There, on the twenty-sixth of the month, twelve signatures, including Winthrop's, Thomas Dudley's and Sir Richard Saltonstall's, were put to a document, the *Cambridge Agreement,* stating the signers' design of "inhabiting" and "continuing" in New England, but with the significant proviso, "that the whole government, together with the patent for the plantation, be first by an order of court legally transferred and established, to remain with us and others which shall inhabit upon the said planatation." The original patent for the Company made no rule as to where it should have its headquarters and the twelve leaders shrewdly took advantage of this. Before the autumn was over they had legal authority for transfer to Massachusetts and on October 29 they met to choose, from four nominees, a governor for the "Plantation" in the first year of its existence. By "a generall vote and full consent they chose Winthrop, although it is interesting to hear that there were certain critics elsewhere who feared he might be too old for the job—at the age of forty-one. The whole responsibility for detailed plans now fell on the country

gentleman from Suffolk; he had to see to the choice of prospective colonists, getting supplies for the voyage and for the
first year on American soil, and the selection of ships and
their captains. Difficulties and hardship lay ahead, but at no
time did the enterprise come within sight of total failure, as
did the Jamestown settlement. Good organization, thanks to
John Winthrop and the transfer of actual government to the
colony itself, had much to do with this. John Smith's Virginia may be cited as an example of English "muddling
through" and coming out successfully at the end—but at
what a cost!

The great hegira began on March 22, 1630 (new style)
with the departure from Southampton of four ships, led by
the *Arbella* (or Arabella), originally the *Eagle* but renamed
for Lady Arbella Johnson, an aristocratic colonist, who afterwards died of sickness in the early Charlestown days before
the move to what is now Boston. A roster of the travellers'
names includes several, besides Winthrop's, that were to become famous in New England history—Saltonstall, Dudley,
Bradstreet, Coddington. Winthrop had two of his children
with him, but Margaret, now pregnant, was to follow him
the next year. Like the Virginian colonists before them,
Winthrop's voyagers were held up by contrary winds in the
English Channel, but with less harrowing effects. They
spent two weeks only within sight of England, off Cowes, in
the Isle of Wight. Winthrop at this time started the journal
which has served historians for so much of the early period
of North American colonization. Of more immediate importance was a document drawn up by the leaders of the expedition. It was to be read by their friends and fellow members of the Church of England at home. This "Humble
Request of his Majesty's Loyall Subjects, the Governor and
the Company, late gone for New England" had in view, it
tells us, to remove suspicions and misconstruction of the emi-

grants' motives. The gist of the letter was a protestation of loyalty to their "dear mother," the Church of England. It is probable Winthrop was the chief author of the document, for it states a position which he took at this time and held consistently for the rest of his life. He wanted religious reform *within* the framework of the established church; he regarded Archbishop Laud as a crypto-Popish wolf in sheep's clothing and he saw the English Church as encrusted with all manner of evils, but he wished to cleanse it, not destroy it or cut himself off from communion with it. We may compare him to a modern Low Churchman desiring to oust the "Anglo-Catholic" ritualists. The document is important in view of events in the new colony half a dozen years later.

The ships did not reach the Massachusetts coast until the early summer. On June 10 four hundred settlers, men, women and children, went ashore at the little shanty town that had been Naumkeag and now called itself Salem. Within a week Winthrop decided to move to the spot that is the Charlestown section of Boston and he at once set to work, as had Smith down in Virginia, buying corn from the Indians for the winter's food supply. The acting governor, John Endecott, a violent and impulsive man at times, was friendly and cooperative with Winthrop, willingly handing over authority to him. By the end of the summer the lack of a satisfactory water supply made a second, and final, move necessary, this time to the Shawmut peninsula, to be known henceforth as Boston, after the old Lincolnshire city. In the spring following this move a general court, which re-elected John Winthrop as governor, stipulated that no one should become a freeman of the colony who was not a church member. Almost at once Winthrop took the lead in planning the first church to be built in Boston, which, under the forceful cleric John Cotton a few years later, would become what someone has called the Vatican of New England.

In 1631 John Winthrop, Jr., a future governor of Connecticut, sailed from England and joined his father in Boston and soon showed himself as energetic and enterprising as his parent, less devout perhaps, but with an even keener eye for industrial progress. In the same year arrived a young clergyman destined to play a part in early colonial history as distinguished as Winthrop's. Roger Williams was a London tradesman's son who had the good fortune to attract the notice of Sir Edward Coke. The great legist arranged for the youth's education at the Charterhouse School and at Pembroke Hall, now Pembroke College, Cambridge. After his graduation he was chaplain in a noble household, fell in love with a girl so far above him socially that she refused him, and he then married one of the maids instead. By the time he sailed to America he was a Puritan of the left wing, as we should say, that is, he was a "separatist," one who saw the Church of England as wholly evil and who thought spiritual health could be regained only by breaking away from it. If we think of this young cleric as something of a fanatic, we must on the other hand recognize that he had traits of character which seemed to cast an aura of charm about him. The tough-minded parson John Cotton could indeed resist his charm, but Winthrop and others, who fought him and exiled him, found him very lovable.

Any percipient observer, perhaps Governor John Winthrop himself, might have seen trouble brewing as soon as young Williams and his wife had begun to feel at home in the new settlement. His academic record at Cambridge University, his chaplaincy in an armigerous household, above all, his own personality, marked him out for a career. This was in spite of his bourgeois marriage, for we must bear in mind that the Boston colony reproduced the class divisions and the class consciousness of England. Roger Williams was soon invited to become minister of Boston's new church, a flattering and a tempting offer.

He refused the offer. His motives should be understood, for in the pantheon of American heroes, where he rightly belongs, he has often been misrepresented. He was not a "liberal," like Jefferson or Franklin, willing to tolerate all creeds, however bizarre, so long as they were socially harmless, because indifferent to theological distinctions. He was an orthodox Calvinist, a sincere believer in certain basic doctrines which both Rome and Geneva held as essential to salvation. His concept of religious toleration, carried out to its logical end when he was in command of a new colony with a royal charter to back his authority, had its roots in a religious idealism, not in a deist's indifference to dogma, still less in political expediency. Christians, as Roger Williams saw them, were like the contemporary disciples of Dr. Buchman; they could not be satisfied with less than absolutes. The absolute purity of Christian faith, in which Roger Williams believed, could not be found in any "church," so long as it was part of, or attached to, the mother Church of England, herself hopelessly corrupt. A genuine Christian, therefore, must be a separatist. The innate depravity of fallen human nature tended to make all "churches" suspect, and the earnest "seeker" would soon find it well nigh impossible to know where pure religion could be found. Williams himself in later years felt he was in full communion spiritually only with his wife. All this ended logically in the complete religious toleration Williams advocated and practised, which has been so justly admired by later ages and so wholly misinterpreted at times.

For two years after he had refused the Boston offer, because Boston's church was still unseparated, he lived in Plymouth and did some preaching there. Then the Salem settlers invited him to their town and his preaching was well received there, the people resisting suggestions from Boston that he should be censured for denouncing the oath of civil obedience demanded by the colony's secular rulers. An oath, he said, was a religious act and the state had no lawful authority in matters of religion. Therein he comes closer to modern American concepts of the separation of church and state; we may feel even closer to him when he held that no royal charter gave anyone the right to dispose of land belonging to the Indians. So much at variance with official doctrine and practice of the Massachusetts Bay Company was all this that a decisive test of strength was inevitable. The governor and his assistants were fearful of trouble with Charles I's government. If a royal charter was invalid and if civil magistrates were stripped of the authority they held in church matters, England might intervene, revoke the charter and put an end to Massachusetts' virtual autonomy. Boston's leaders were now in the quandary that sooner or later troubles all revolutionaries. They had in practice broken away from the Anglican church establishment while stoutly protesting their loyalty to it and fighting separatism, but the separatists wished to push everything to its logical and usually unworkable extreme. Governor Winthrop, lawyer and statesman, saw the ever present need for compromise in human relations and knew that successful administrators must often be "trimmers," in the acceptable sense of the later stateman who invented the term. Mr. Williams over in Salem was the enthusiast and the firebrand. King Charles, well indoctrinated with divine right by his father, could view a man like Roger Williams only as subversive and seditious. Winthrop saw how things must appear to royal eyes at home, yet he loved Williams for his zeal, his kindliness, his sincerity, his unworldliness. The tone of affection and respect that pervades the controversial letters of the two men is a touching one.

Troubles descended on Winthrop's head in these years, apart from the administrative problems raised by the colony's rapid growth. By the spring of 1632, when he was re-elected governor, he had some two thousand British settlers looking to him for leadership. The difficulty of governing them was increased by the character of Winthrop's deputy, Thomas Dudley, a fiery, impulsive man with a tendency to quarrel with anyone, including his superior, with whom he had to work. In 1634 Dudley was elected governor, and Winthrop held the subordinate post. The new governor's zeal took diverse forms. He set up a free school for his citizens and bought Boston Common to provide them with a parade ground and a common pasture, as in English country townships, but he also introduced fantastic blue laws, as they were called, against such practices as wearing lace or smoking in public.

The annual election for the governorship put John Haynes in place of Dudley in 1635 and the controversy with Roger Williams now reached its crisis. In July Williams was called to Boston to appear before the general court on charges of teaching unsound doctrine. The accusation made much of his contention that civil magistrates had no authority to enforce by penalties the "first table" of the Decalogue, that is, the commandments relating exclusively to religious obligations as contrasted with civic or social duties.

Williams defended himself with ability and eloquence, yet with a courtesy and charity that won admiration from many of his bitterest opponents. The court decided against him; the governor and his assistants decreed his banishment, that is to say, they ordered him "to be enlarged out of Massachusetts"; perhaps the euphemism soothed some troubled minds. Winthrop, with what pain and searching of heart we do not know, supported Governor Haynes. The original verdict gave Williams six weeks' grace only, but this was extended to leave him in Salem until the next spring and an attempt was made to bribe him into submission by promises to cancel the sentence if he would pledge himself to silence. When he refused this, he was in danger of finding arrest and possible extradition substituted for banishment. He then fled to the wilderness, probably at a friendly hint which Winthrop contrived to give him. In the bitter New England winter he found refuge with his friends the Indians in their smoky wigwams in the wooded country that became Rhode Island.

The controversy with Roger Williams and the part which, as deputy to Governor Haynes, Winthrop had to play in supporting the sentence of exile was not the only mental and emotional crisis of his middle age. In the early sixteen-thirties a Calvinistic clergyman of the Church of England, the Reverend John Cotton, had caused something of a furore as preacher and spiritual mentor in the English Boston. He was vicar of St. Botolph's Church, whose tower, the famous "Boston Stump," dominates the level fields for miles around. Like all pulpit orators Dr. Cotton had a following of female admirers, some merely featherbrained, others serious and intelligent women. One of the latter was Mrs. Anne Hutchinson, herself the daughter of an able and courageous Anglican cleric, Francis Marbury, who had suffered persecution for his Puritan ideas. As Winthrop later described her, she was "a woman of a ready wit (i.e. intellect) and bold spirit." She was mated to a quiet and submissive husband, wise enough to accept his wife's domination and so ensure a peaceful married life. William Hutchinson, a Lincolnshire man, was, Winthrop tells us, "a man of a very mild temper and weak parts, and wholly guided by his wife." At this time the wave of Puritan emigration to New England was in full spate, with the old city of Boston very much in the movement. In 1633 the vicar of St. Botolph's, in trouble with the authorities of the English church, resigned his living and sailed for the spiritual Canaan of New England, as the Puritans regarded it, where "pure" English Christianity had made its home. On the same ship sailed Edward Hutchinson, Anne's eldest son. The following year another ship set sail for the North American Promised Land and among the two hundred passengers who went ashore on September 28 were Mr. and Mrs. Hutchinson. They settled down in the new Boston, where their friend the Reverend Mr. Cotton was already the accepted spiritual leader.

Anne Hutchinson was in her liftetime unjustly denigrated and since then she has been unofficially canonized by her admirers. She undoubtedly had delusions about herself as a mouthpiece of the Almighty, but she was well educated, had acquired a sound knowledge of theology and the Bible and, above all, was a woman of great fortitude and moral courage. For a time all went well with the Hutchinsons. Anne's admiration for Mr. Cotton's ministry was, if anything, greater than before and she made no bones about professing her belief that he was a chosen vessel of God, while the rest of the Massachusetts Bay clergy had all, like sheep, gone astray.

Mrs. Hutchinson soon became a New England *salonière,* or, as some American social historians like to see her, the first originator of American women's clubs. She held regular weekly meetings of earnest women, as many as a hundred at a time, in her house—one cannot think of it as William's house—for the study of theology and the Scriptures and for the recapitulation and discussion of Mr. Cotton's last sermon. Her religious ideas, tenaciously held because she was coming to believe herself directly inspired by the Holy

Spirit, began to take a heterodox turn. These ideas were not unlike those of Madam Guyon and the Quietists in France at the end of the same century. In the souls of the "elect" divine grace, freely given, and faith, the fruit thereof, were alone significant, good works meaningless. This must not be interpreted as a license for evil-doing, although it was inevitable that the enemies of these women as well as some of their less worthy followers should so distort it. The visionary's traits should not destroy our sense of Anne Hutchinson's genuine virtues—sincerity, moral and physical courage. She was, too, notably kind and charitable, her skill in nursing constantly exercised for the benefit of friends and strangers alike.

Her practical application of her doctrine to the religious life of Boston resolved itself into a distinction between a covenant of grace and a covenant of works, the former represented by John Cotton, the latter by the rest of the Boston clergy. This deviation from Bostonian orthodoxy gathered new strength in 1636, when a brother-in-law of Mrs. Hutchinson, the Reverend John Wheelwright, arrived from England and joined the Antinomians, as their opponents now called the Hutchinson coterie. It was a formidable movement, with some prominent citizens, lay and clerical, supporting it; Mr. Wheelwright, too, was tireless in work for his sister-in-law.

Anne's hero-worship of Mr. Cotton—she openly proclaimed Mr. Cotton and her brother-in-law the only sound clerics in New England—went too far for the ex-incumbent of St. Botolph's, Boston, Lincolnshire. He disavowed her claims and denounced her teachings on grace and works as bad theology. The Antinomian controversy rent the little settlement in two, interfering with such diverse matters as taxation and military defence against hostile Indians. In the late summer of 1637 came the crisis. Mrs. Hutchinson was cited to appear before a synod of the colony's clergy for an enquiry into her doctrine and its propagation. The clerics found her teaching unacceptable and enjoined silence. Strong in her sense of divine approval she disregarded the order and carried on her conferences and discussions. The rulers of the colony do not seem to have been very impatient, or they may have been awed by the moral authority she wielded. Not until November did they call her to account again. This time she was summoned before the general court to answer for flouting the veto on her propaganda. The trial lasted through two days, during which she defended herself with conspicuous ability. Her opponents were struck by her logic, her power of argumentation and her eloquence, but the court used its executive power, as in the case of Roger Williams, and imposed the penalty of banishment.

The onset of the New England winter moved her judges to the humane concession that she might spend the winter at Roxbury. Early the next year (1638) she left the Massachusetts Bay Colony and established herself with her family on Aquidneck—Rhode Island, as it was called later—under the aegis of Roger Williams. The rest of her story is tragic. Several years after the banishment she was left a widow and moved with her family into the Dutch territory that became New York State. A year later she and all but one of her children were murdered by Indians; the one survivor, a son, himself fell a victim to Indian savagery many years later.

The trial and banishment of Anne Hutchinson is of interest to us in studying John Winthrop's life and character. Anne's apostolate was viewed with a good deal of favour by Sir Henry Vane, governor of the colony, while Winthrop, then deputy, opposed it. When the trial took place Winthrop was governor again and found himself facing the same moral dilemma that had disturbed his conscience when Roger Williams was on trial. Here, again, was a person of lofty moral character, sincerity and the charm that goes with natural kindliness and altruism, suffering for the very thing that had estranged Winthrop and his colleagues from the authorities ruling their church at home, although not from the church itself. They had left England to live as Puritan Anglicans in America, since they could not so live in England. Mrs. Hutchinson and her followers now claimed the same freedom; they differed only in a more radical idea of what a Puritan Anglican could hold as his theology of divine grace. Governor Winthrop's quandary was worse than that of many revolutionaries, for he was a man of good will and Christian charity. Probably his distress was not so great as in Roger Williams' case, for he was aware of the taint of self-delusion in Anne Hutchinson's claims and, moreover, between himself and Roger Williams there had been a warm personal friendship. This friendship, indeed, survived all vicissitudes and it proved its strength when Williams' influence with the Indians enabled the exile to find allies for the Bay Colony in a time of peril from hostile tribes.

One feature of his work as governor was a source of quiet satisfaction to Winthrop, namely, the encouragement he was able to give to education in the colony. The early and vigorous growth of higher education in Massachusetts gives the lie to the popular travesty of the New England Puritans as a set of dreary fellows with close-cropped hair and steeple-crowned hats, ignorant of all literature but the Bible and with no gift to posterity but a rather repulsive cuisine and a more commendable taste in domestic architecture. The colony was still in swaddling clothes when it laid the foundations of a great university. In 1636 the sum of £400 was voted to set up a "school or college" at Newtown (or Newton) on the banks of the Charles River. Two years afterwards an English immigrant clergyman, one John Harvard, a graduate of Cambridge University, died in the Charlestown settlement and in his will bequeathed £750, together with his library, to the new college. Newtown had just been renamed Cambridge in honour of the *alma mater* of many of Massachusetts' citizens, and now the college was named Harvard in memory of its benefactor. Four years after John Harvard's death the college held its first commencement. Winthrop was again governor in that year and he now had a direct, personal interest in the college, for in that first graduating class was his nephew, young George Downing, later knighted and a diplomat in the English service. London's Downing Street was named after him.

From Newtown, shortly before it was re-christened Cambridge, we find Winthrop writing to his wife, who had remained at home in Boston. "Sweet Heart. I was unwillingly hindered from cominge to thee, nor am I like to see thee before the laste daye of this weeke . . . Have care of thy selfe this colde weather, and speak to the folks to keepe the goates well out of the Garden." Then follow instructions for Winthrop's brother on feeding the "sheep ramme" and Winthrop ends the letter with his usual affectionate valediction —". . . the Lorde blesse and keepe thee, my sweet wife, and all our familye, and send us comfortable meetinge, so I kisse thee and love thee ever and rest Thy faithfull husband."

John Winthrop's many years in high executive office, often alternating the governorship and the deputy's post, were disturbed at times by the friction between himself and Thomas Dudley who had sailed with him to America. The two men were alternately governor and deputy a number of times. Both were men of recognized ability, great energy and zeal for the colony's progress, but there was a temperamental disharmony between them. Dudley, like Winthrop, was a convert to the Puritan party in the Church of England, but, perhaps because of some innate trait of character, he did not, like his colleague, slough off the proverbial harshness of the new convert. Winthrop, we know, mellowed under the influence of the admirable Margaret Tyndal who was his third wife. Dudley was always an extremist Puritan, rigid in his Calvinism and a tireless heresy-hunter who tried to fasten suspicion even on that pillar of orthodoxy, John Cotton. Dudley's frequent disagreements with Winthrop, when the two men filled the two highest posts in the colony, may have owed some of their bitterness to rancour on Dudley's part. He lived in Newtown before it became Cambridge and he had taken an active part in the foundation of Harvard College there. He was very anxious that Newtown (or Newton) should become the settlement's capital; he resented Winthrop's decision that the town on the Shawmut peninsula—Boston—should be made the capital. The searching of heart which went with Winthrop's opposition to Roger Williams and Anne Hutchinson did not trouble Thomas Dudley. He was a Protestant Torquenada and the most damning epithet in his vocabulary was *toleration.*

Winthrop's talent for administration found scope for its exercise in 1643. He had already, with diplomatic skill, contrived to keep the colony's charter intact and in his possession when the colonial commissioners in London sought to withdraw it. The civil war in England probably found him with conflicting emotions, perhaps with a bias towards the Parliamentarian side, but resolved to maintain the virtual autonomy of Massachusetts. He persuaded the chief settlements of English north-eastern America, that is to say, Massachusetts, Plymouth, Connecticut (not the whole area as we know it), and New Haven, to unite in a federation, and he was elected as the first president of their representatives, who called themselves the Commissioners of the United Colonies of New England. The Massachusetts Bay Colony had grown rapidly in population during the years when Winthrop and Dudley shared its government and by the early forties of the century had some sixteen thousand inhabitants. Local government, destined to become a feature of New England life, was fostered by a division of the colony into shires or counties, four of them at first, Norfolk, Suffolk, Essex, Middlesex.

Winthrop's interest in the colony and his concern for its people's welfare did not slacken as he reached his middle years, the mature age when many a seventeenth century Englishman in his position would have reckoned himself an elder statesman, entitled to sit by his fireside with a tobacco pipe and a posset at hand. At forty-one or two Winthrop had been considered by some people too old for colonial pioneering, but more than eight years later, in one of his terms as governor, he was on a visit of state to Salem, by sea, to look into the progress of that "plantation." A brief letter addressed to "my deare Wife, Mrs. Winthrop" was sent back to Boston to reassure her of his safety. "My Deare. I prayse God we came safe to Salem, thoughe we had very strong windes. We found all well. I doubt I shall not returne before the 2: daye next weeke, & then my broth: P: will come with me. The Lo: blesse thee & all our familye, & send us a happy meetinge. I kisse thee and rest Thy faithfull husband J.W."

Not all Winthrop's zeal for the welfare of the colony and his spending much of his private fortune on it sufficed to protect him from bitter opposition at times and from what looks like sheer malice. Two years after he had organized the commission of "United Colonies" as a defence against both foreign aggression and arbitrary interference by king or Parliament—whichever came out on top—he was charged with dictatorial rule. One of the more active of his attackers on this occasion was a clergyman whose status gave his accusation undue weight in the minds of the hesitant. Winthrop was fully vindicated and one is glad to know that the clerical busybody was fined.

As mid-century drew near and the royal cause declined in the English civil war, Winthrop's sympathies veered away from the Parliamentarian side. Already an obscure Huntingdonshire country gentleman, Oliver Cromwell, was becoming the cynosure of all eyes in England. Thomas Dudley's narrow Puritan orthodoxy and his ruthless heresy-hunting were offensive to a man of Winthrop's magnanimous character, but he viewed with equal distaste the spawning of fantastic heterodoxies at home. The time had not yet come when Cromwell, the rebel in politics and religion, would become the essentially "bourgeois" leader; meanwhile freak religions and private revelations flourished unchecked. Sir Henry Vane, in his term as governor, had shown himself sympathetic to inspired religionists. Winthrop, however, always remained moderately conservative in such matters. We see him, in the latter years of his life, opposing the group of discontented citizens who wished to abolish the requirement of church membership for a full share in civic privileges. To us of modern secular states taking universal religious toleration for granted, even in countries like England with an established church, the position of the dissenting Massachusetts citizens appears axiomatic. To Winthrop and the conservative Puritans it was a proposal for a secularization of the colony's life that would destroy the religious significance of New England as a home of "purified" English Christianity. The leaders of the subversive movement, Robert Child and a small number of followers, threatened to appeal to the English Parliament. Governor Winthrop dealt with them as decisively as Cromwell himself might have done. He clapped all of the seven ringleaders into prison and imposed a heavy fine on them.

The summer of 1647 was the time of John Winthrop's greatest personal tragedy, the death of his beloved wife Margaret on June 14. For only a few months less than thirty years they had shared a married life almost startlingly idyllic in its setting of seventeenth century Puritanism, writing to each other during the absences caused by public duty with the exuberance of youthful sweethearts. In the early days when Margaret Tyndal of Great Maplestead, Essex, became the third Mrs. Winthrop, she had raised her husband from the gloom and melancholy that had overcome him on losing his second wife after a single year of married happiness with her. In later years Margaret's own affectionate nature combined with good sense and poise had a mellowing effect on the convert to the Puritan wing of the national church. Perhaps to Margaret Winthrop is due much of the credit for the liberal and humane spirit of her husband's administration as contrasted with the harshness of his associate and frequent opponent, Thomas Dudley. The personality of the governor's lady had made a deep impression on the austere and, usually, male-dominated society of early Massachusetts. Whatever the civic and theological storms raging in Boston, Margaret Winthrop was easily and always the best-loved woman in the colony.

When one has read the charming love letters which passed between husband and wife at intervals during nearly thirty years of marriage the fourth and final mating, in the last year but one of Winthrop's life, comes as an anti-climax. Probably the rational way to interpret an action which may offend sentimentalists is to bear in mind that the widower was an old man as age was reckoned then—seventy—and probably a lonely one, for his children were grown up and many of his contemporaries were dead. His nature, a singularly affectionate one, demanded companionship and a woman's love. Nor need this charitable way of regarding Governor Winthrop's marriage to the widow Martha Coytmore in 1648 blind us to the practical business sense of the first Bostonian. Winthrop was no longer a rich man; he had lost heavily through the knavery of a steward in charge of his property and he had spent much of his own fortune for the good of the infant colony. Mrs. Coytmore, a Rainsborough or Rainborow (English Puritan name) by birth, was well dowered when her first husband died.

We like to think that, apart from this material benefit, the last Mrs. Winthrop brought solace to the elderly and now ailing governor of the Massachusetts Bay Colony. His eldest son, the younger John Winthrop, a child of the first marriage, was undoubtedly a source of satisfaction to his father in these last years. The younger John Winthrop had been well educated, at Bury St. Edmund's Grammar School, in his native Suffolk, Trinity College, Dublin, and, for a time, as a law student in London. He had seen active service in the Duke of Buckingham's unsuccessful expedition to help the French Protestants in 1627, had travelled widely, for we hear of his visiting Constantinople, and then, still a young man, had joined his father in Massachusetts and was one of the governor's assistants at various times. He took a leading part in founding the Massachusetts settlement that became Ipswich, established a post on the Connecticut River that was the nucleus of a new state of which he became governor and, in his father's later years, started the "plantation" of Pequot, which became Connecticut's New London. Another son, the last by Winthrop's second wife, joined the Parliamentarian army in the civil war, rose to be a colonel and was well regarded by Oliver Cromwell.

The consolations of a new wife with a substantial dowry and of sons who had more than justified parental hopes have to be balanced against the annoyance caused by that Puritan gadfly Thomas Dudley. Winthrop, a genuinely religious man since his contact with the earnest evangelicalism of his youth, was a good friend to the New England clergy, almost, one may say, too good a friend, for they sometimes pushed him further in the direction of intolerance than his own liberal nature prompted. Dudley, the Puritan hammer of heretics, mindful of this, even when the governor was on a bed of sickness that was to be his death bed, pestered him for a decree of banishment against a citizen who had deviated from Calvinist orthodoxy. The governor refused his deputy's petition. Perhaps the dying man's memory conjured up a picture of the outspoken cleric, Roger Williams, whom he had loved as a friend and fellow-Christian, and the courageous woman Anne Hutchinson, whom he had sent into the wilderness. He had already, he told Dudley, done too many things of that kind.

The dreary end of the New England winter, the alternate frosts and thaws of late March, was the time of John Winthrop's death. He was buried in Boston on April 3, 1649, to the accompaniment of a military salute from the city's Honorable Artillery Company.

In an era and a region, seventeenth century Massachusetts, wherein history records so many things to dismay later ages—religious intolerance, the cruelties engendered by the witchcraft superstition, the flogging and the execution of Quakers, the violent rancour against Roman Catholics and, as the colony slipped away from its nominal adherence to the Church of England, the persecution of episcopalian Anglicans—the personality of John Winthrop stands out as, relatively to the spirit of his time, the exemplar of a liberal and humane spirit.

If we seek to ravel out the strands in his private and public character that have kept him a revered figure in history when so many reputations have been diminished, we shall not find great intellectual brilliance, deep erudition or the genius for statesmanship of a Burghley, a Richelieu or a Pitt. He had indeed excellent judgement of men and affairs, an ability to weigh causes without prejudice beforehand or vindictiveness afterwards, but perhaps it was above all as a supremely *good* man in public life that he won and held the affection of his fellow New Englanders, even his doctrinal opponents like Roger Williams, who loved him as a brother, the brave but self-deluded Anne Hutchinson and the harsh, intolerant Dudley. For most of our generation there are not many early Puritans whose lives smell sweet and blossom in their dust. Winthrop is one of the few.

4

★★★★★

William Penn

AND HIS HOLY EXPERIMENT

Those who admire the Society of Friends are inclined to dwell a good deal on Quaker simplicity. Surveying Quaker history from the days of George Fox to Quaker religion and philanthropy in the modern world, many people appear to see a kind of *Sancta simplicitas* as the outstanding Quaker trait. Is there possibly something fallacious about this idea? Perhaps friends of the Friends have been deceived by the simplicity of Quaker worship, its lack of ritual, its informality and its religious individualism, into viewing the Quaker mind as a kind of Protestant Franciscanism. Even if George Fox was something of a Puritan *Poverello*, it is clear that his followers soon learned to walk on the razor's edge between mysticism and the "world," between renunciation and acceptance of that world which, after all, they do not reject in Manichaean horror but hold to be the handiwork of a loving God. Something more subtle and complex than Franciscan simplicity is needed for a man to serve God and compete with Mammon's disciples, to win material success and yet pass through the needle's eye to the kingdom of heaven —something which by general consent the Quakers can claim to have done.

If along these lines we revise our estimate of a religious body that has fused worldly success with Christian mysticism, big business with perfect integrity, and that upholds a moderate Puritan practice without asceticism, we see the typical Quaker not as a holy simpleton but as a rather complex sort of Christian. We may then regard William Penn as the prototype of all good Friends in English and American history. Admitting George Fox to have been the true begetter of Quaker mystical religion, we must allow that he could not have founded what became the State of Pennsylvania nor devised the model of a Christian democracy in action. William Penn, by background, birth and education, was a gentleman in a rigidly stratified society; a gentleman he remained and was accepted as such despite his adherence to a newly born sect often persecuted and nearly always despised in its early days.

It is instructive to glance at the only portrait of Penn known to have any claim to authenticity. Readers of "improving" books foisted on the young a generation or two ago will recall, probably with disgust, the picture of a stout, rather stocky and presumably fussy old gentleman about to sign his famous treaty with the Red Indians: an unfortunate picture. At the time of the treaty Penn was only about thirty-eight years old; he was tall and had the bearing of a man trained to the management of a horse and a sword. The only picture done from the living model shows him, at the age of twenty-two, as a handsome young officer, complete with Cavalier locks falling to the shoulder, a fine cambric neckcloth spread out below his chin over the shining armour. The well-moulded features suggest a thoughtful nature, but nothing of fanaticism or perfervid zeal. The shapely mouth, with rather full lips, is not that of the ascetic or the world-hating Puritan. It is not hard to see in the young soldier of twenty-two the Quaker gentleman who, some six years later, would be the ardent wooer of the charming Gulielma Springett, herself as deeply religious as he and equally responsive to affection.

William Penn—the "Younger," to distinguish him from Admiral Sir William Penn, his father—was born on October 14, 1644, that is, towards the middle of the seventeenth century. This, perhaps, is not without significance. The brutalities practised in the name of religion were gradually fading, the end of the incredibly ruthless and destructive Thirty Years War was only four years away, and across the Straits of Dover Frenchmen of a new generation were being born, men who would teach and practise toleration and who would dream of Utopias where mankind recovered its pristine innocence. True, a war was in progress in England, with the battle of Marston Moor only four months past. The civil war between the royalists and the "Parliament men," however, though wasteful and destructive like all wars and fatal to much of England's heritage of beauty, was a relatively humane affair beside the "religious" wars on the European continent and such medieval atrocities as the Crusaders' rape of Constantinople.

There was little in William Penn's ancestry and inheritance to foreshadow the religious zeal of his work for the infant Society of Friends or the political idealism of his Pennsylvania foundation. His father and grandfather were seafaring men, the father, William, an authentic English captain of the old school, irascible but warm-hearted, always ready for a convivial evening, spasmodically religious and, it must be admitted, something of an opportunist. He had left the merchant marine for the king's navy and gone over to the Parliament side when he saw the way things were moving. Cromwell seems not to have trusted him overmuch, but found him too valuable to deny him promotion, and so for his "very noble and renowned" action in the naval war with the Dutch made him General of the Fleet and the recipient of a gold chain and a medal. History has preserved the valuation of these baubles—£300 and £100 respectively. All this, however, was some years after the birth of his eldest son. Mrs. Penn, Margaret Jasper before her first marriage, was the widow of a Dutchman, one Vanderschuren, with business in Ireland, before she met and married the young English sea captain. She seems to have been a lively, good-natured and very untidy little thing, the sort of woman whose slip is always showing and whose hair is never under full control. Before she became Lady Penn a kindly relative took her in hand and gave her a modicum of worldly polish. Samuel Pepys, who liked her but secretly disliked her husband, records certain evenings of high jinks when the Pepys and the Penn households, representing the Admiralty and the Fleet respectively, got together to "make merry."

At the time of his son William's birth, Captain Penn's family was in rather low water, living in a few rented rooms on Tower Hill. The naval officer's brother, George, lived with them. He was a broken man, impoverished, sick in body and soul after suffering at the hands of the Inquisition in Seville. Captain Penn had already made the changeover from royalist allegiance to the service of Parliament. Perhaps a hardworking and hard-fighting naval officer saw nothing very reprehensible in this. Blake had set the precedent. "It is not for us to mind state affairs," said the admiral, "but to keep foreigners from fooling us."

When his infant son was about four years old William Penn the father was in trouble with the government, and found himself in prison for a month. We do not know exactly what was held against him, for there seems to have been no trial, but it is probable that he was already putting out feelers for a second change of allegiance should the Puritan dictatorship come to an end. He was certainly on friendly terms with at least one royalist lord and may have made a tentative move towards the second transfer of allegiance which won him a knighthood twelve years later.

Baby William nearly died of smallpox in his infancy, but pulled through the illness with no greater loss than that of his hair. It never grew quite satisfactorily again and he wore a wig in adult life, a piece of worldly vanity in the eyes of more rigoristic Friends, but amiably condoned by George Fox.

When Vice-Admiral Penn had allayed the suspicions of his Parliamentarian masters and recovered his liberty the family fortunes improved. The Penns left their cramped and stuffy lodgings near the Tower and moved to a house in what was then thickly wooded country between Wanstead and Chigwell. Little William had the run of two noble forests, Hainault, now only a name and a memory, and Epping, still happily existent because in public ownership.

The prison shades of school closed early on little boys of the seventeenth century, but young Penn was not unhappy in the Chigwell Grammar School. It had been founded some twenty years earlier by the devout Archbishop Harsnett of York, a churchman in sound Anglican equipoise between Rome and Geneva who prescribed that the school's masters should be "neither Puritan nor Papist." There are anticipations of Arnold of Rugby and the stiff upper lip doctrine in the Spartan régime of the school and the archbishop's insistence on "character" rather than erudition. The curriculum, however, conformed to the pattern of the era, with Latin and Greek as the main subjects of study, but, perhaps because of its nearness to London and her counting houses, it also provided for penmanship: the boys were trained in "fair secretary and Roman hands." Young Penn took kindly to school, was neither a genius nor a dullard at his books, and was notably good at games. The archbishop had warned future headmasters of the school against "novelties and conceited modern writers," which may be the reason that the only English author ever mentioned in Penn's voluminous writings is Chaucer. The garrulous John Aubrey's description of the schoolboy Penn brings before the reader an attractive child, serious but not offensively so, "mighty lively, but with innocence, and extremely tender under rebuke; and very early delighted in retirement; much given to reading and meditation of the Scriptures, and at 14 had mastery over the Bible."

While the boy was busy with Latin and Greek, school games and the "fair secretary and Roman hands," his father's fortunes had steadily improved, but the glory and the material rewards of the Dutch war were soon followed by a set-back. An expedition against the Spanish in the West Indies was planned. Penn was to be in command of the fifty ships, while Venables was at the head of a land force of five hundred soldiers. Unfortunately the expedition failed to take its objective, the island of Hispaniola, which now embraces the territory of the two republics of Haiti and Santo Domingo. The commanders did, indeed, capture Jamaica, but that failed to assuage the Lord-Protector's anger. He put both the leaders in the Tower for over a month, but at the end of that time released them on their assurance that their return without hoisting their nation's flag over a captured Hispaniola was "not through refractoriness against superiors, but for advancement of the service." It is possible that John Thurloe, the shrewd little Essex lawyer in charge of an amazingly widespread and efficient secret service, had sown suspicion in his master's mind. Anyhow, Cromwell's navy did not call upon Penn's services for the remaining years of the Protectorate. The Penn family moved back to Tower Hill, but lodged more commodiously than before.

The infancy and early boyhood of the Quaker colonizer-to-be gave no sign of the precocious mystical awareness sometimes found in the lives of religious leaders. He was a normal healthy schoolboy, neither perverse nor strikingly the opposite. Then, when he was eleven years old, came a moment of religious enlightenment not unlike that revealed of his own boyhood days by Cardinal Newman. The young Penn, says an early nineteenth century editor of his memoirs, ". . . was suddenly surprised with inward comfort, and, as he thought, an external glory in the room, which gave rise to religious emotions, during which he had the strongest conviction of the being of a God, and that the soul of man was capable of enjoying communication with Him. He believed also that the seal of divinity had been put upon him at that moment; or that he had been awakened or called upon to a holy life." This illumination, however potent it may have seemed to the little boy, did not immediately result in the appearance of a religious infant prodigy. Perhaps this was as well, for precociously earnest children tend to be prigs; seldom was a notably good man less of a prig than William Penn. "His schoolmaster," John Aubrey tells us, "was not of his persuasion." This, too, may have been good for the youthful mystic.

A couple of years after this experience of the inner light, a basic concept in Quaker mystical theology, William was taken, along with his mother and his infant brother Richard, to Ireland. With the Penns on the ship from Bristol went a Negro servant and a parrot, the latter a gift from the older

Penn's comrade in arms of the unsuccessful Hispaniola expedition, General Venables. The Penn family had an estate at Macroom and the idea was to live economically, like other English expatriates, on land whose original owners had been expelled or exterminated.

In Ireland the Penns made their first contact with the new religionists whom the English nicknamed Quakers. Their founder, George Fox, a man barely literate but of magnetic personality and obviously sincere in his evangelism, won a kind of grudging admiration from those who loathed his ideas and his actions. Unfortunately the excesses of some of his disciples did much to stir up persecution. The Penns, cronies of the gossip-loving Pepys family, had heard of the fanatical Soloman Eccles or Eagle who, records the diarist, had gone "naked through Westminster Hall, only very civilly tied about his privities to avoid scandal, and with a chafing dish of fire and brimstone burning upon his head. . . . crying 'Repent! repent!'" The older Penn, an officer and a gentleman and an orthodox, if not habitually devout, Christian, must have taken a poor view of such antics; Pepys' unexpurgated report of them cannot have influenced him in their favour. Nevertheless, when he had heard that Thomas Loe, a Quaker of a very different type, intelligent, cultivated, eloquent, was preaching in Cork, he invited him out to Macroom to address a small private gathering. The effect of Mr. Loe's eloquence was astounding. The assembled English "settlers" were deeply moved, the Negro servant burst into uncontrollable sobs, and young Penn, then about thirteen years old, was amazed to see tears running down his father's cheeks. The question came into his mind, he recorded in a later account of his "convincement," "What if we should all be Quakers?" What indeed? Happily for his peace of mind he cannot have foreseen exactly what the near future held in store.

The education that had been begun in the Chigwell Grammar School was continued under a private tutor. The boy Penn was as active as ever, a good runner and all the time more and more proficient on horseback. The emotional effect of Thomas Loe's preaching had faded, along with the Negro's sobs and Admiral Penn's tears, but in the young schoolboy's mind a strange disquiet lingered. He was too immature to analyze or rationalize it and there was no one to whom he could turn. "I had no relations that inclined to so solitary and spiritual a way"; he says, "I was a child alone."

When the Lord-Protector Cromwell died, in disquiet of soul, on a night of equinoctial gales (September 3, 1658), William Penn the elder had already hedged his political bets wisely. He had discreetly made himself known to the still exiled king Charles II as a good crypto-royalist. The Protector's son Richard, Tumbledown Dick as the royalists scornfully named him, was, like his father, a country gentleman with the same rural tastes but, unlike Oliver, he was not the stuff of which dictators are made. England was saved from chaos and a new outbreak of civil strife by the hard common sense and effective action of General Monk. Less than two years after Oliver Cromwell's death things were ready for a most joyful Restoration. William Penn, again an admiral on the active list and recently elected to Parliament for Weymouth, sailed across to Holland in that happy May of 1660, was knighted by the king and made friends with the king's brother, James, Duke of York.

The Duke of York, who as King James II had become the whipping boy of Whig historians, was himself a fine sailor and, whatever his later mistakes on the throne of England, a man staunch in his friendships. Sir William Penn's tacit understanding with Charles during the years of the Puritan dictatorship was now paying dividends. He had indeed to give up his Irish estate at Macroom; it went back to its law-ful owner. The admiral was compensated with the gift of another Irish property, Shangarry, in County Cork. As it measured some four miles by two, the exchange cannot have been a cause for repining.

His rank restored, a knighthood, a seat in Parliament, a wife cheerful and lively and less slatternly than formerly and not unworthy the part of Lady Penn, a lively little daughter Peg, and young Richard, "a noble, stout, witty boy," above all, the elder son, sixteen now, ready for the university, handsome, athletic, intelligent—altogether the admiral's fortunes reflected the Restoration brightness which had, most people thought at the time, come to stay. Admiral Sir William, still under thirty-nine when so much good for-tune came his way, was an affectionate parent despite occa-sional rages, but not perhaps a very percipient one.

Son William's periods of wistful reverie and mental un-rest, alternating with zestful activity of mind and body, passed unnoticed. The earnest discourse of Thomas Loe, the Quaker preacher in Cork who, four years earlier, had moved the Negro servant to near-hysterics and drawn tears from the sea dog, had been forgotten by most of the auditors. But not by the schoolboy who had listened and watched, marvelling to see his father so affected by one of the despised Quakers.

For the moment all went well. The admiral, who now had the use of a fine official residence in the Navy Gardens in London, sent to Ireland for William so that he could start his higher education. Oxford was chosen; its ebullient royalism pleased Sir William and he was glad to see his son entered as a gentleman commoner of Christ Church. Young Penn enjoyed Oxford at first. His skill at games was combined with a lively wit; he was, we are told, "facetious in conversation." Withal he was not without intellectual interests. He composed a Latin poem on the death of the young Duke of Gloucester, possibly not in very flawless Latin, but still it was a proof of academic industry. He became interested in anatomy and while attending lectures on it may have met John Locke, then an older student acquiring the medical skill with which he served his friend and patron the first Earl of Shaftesbury.

Beneath the happy surface activity—games, studies, social intercourse—the preoccupation with religion made itself felt again. Young Penn now found a mentor whose teachings and personality impressed him deeply, not a Quaker this time, but a stalwart Cromwellian Independent, Dr. Owen, a former Dean of Christ Church and vice-chancellor of Oxford University. Dr. Owen, no time-server, would not pretend overnight conversion to royalism and orthodox Anglicanism when so many ex-Cromwellian clerics discovered that they had always loved Charles, who probably despised the lot of them, having no great affection for any faith except the Catholicism of his mother, Henrietta Maria. Dr. Owen was promptly thrown out of his deanery and his vice-chancellorship at the time of the Restoration, but at his home outside Oxford went on ministering privately to a number of devoted followers, one of them the admiral's son. Among the undergraduates, then and later, there was always a substratum of seriousness and readiness to be moved by anyone of patently genuine idealism. George Fox himself, visiting Oxford, had found that "the scholars were very rude, but the Lord's power came over them."

William soon got into trouble for absence from the services in the chapel of his college. He and other fervent young disciples of Dr. Owen were going on strike against the revival of the so-called Popish ritual of Stuart Anglicanism, the decorous practices of bowing to the cross, wearing surplices, kneeling for communion and so forth. In one respect Penn's contact with Dr. Owen seems to have some bearing on the future course of his life. The Puritan divine talked of a New England across the ocean where true believers, in this case the Puritan Independents, believed and worshipped in their own way, free of the restraints of the old country. Dr. Owen seems to have been unaware of the fact that New England had already set up a régime of intolerance beside which the Church of England was comparatively easygoing.

When Sir William heard of the trouble at Oxford he was understandably angry with his son and summoned him to London for a reprimand face to face, in the best quarter-deck style. The admiral's outbursts were generally violent but short-lived. Soon after the interview he took the youth to supper with Mr. Pepys and they all were very merry until supper time. A short time after this the undergraduate, home for Christmas, was allowed to take his schoolgirl sister Margaret, "Peg" in the family, to a dinner party at Mr. Pepys'. After dinner they went in a coach, the famous coach of the *Diary,* to the theatre to see Beaumont and Fletcher's *The Spanish Curate,* but not until they had fortified themselves with a barrel of oysters. After the play they all went back to the Pepys house to play cards. Altogether it is a picture of innocent merriment, less austere and brooding than any we have of the early days of the other great colonizer of North America, John Winthrop.

Sir William suddenly became dissatisfied with his son's being at Oxford, not on account of the university, but because of Dr. Owen's influence. The admiral turned in despair to his civilian colleague. Samuel Pepys remembered Magdalene College in the sister university and talked of it to the admiral, who was thinking of transferring his son to Cambridge. The question of leaving Oxford was settled without the father's intervention, for young Penn was "sent down" for some reason which history does not record. One unconfirmed story has it that Penn and other students, with evangelical zeal as excuse for a bit of riotous behavior, tore surplices from the shoulders of their High Church wearers. Penn himself later in life speaks of "writing a book"—a pamphlet or essay?—which the clerical dons disliked. Anyhow, he was expelled and sent home.

This time the father's patience, never his strong point, gave way altogether. He thrashed the youth and turned him out of the house. As usual Admiral Penn's rage soon spent itself; Lady Penn interceded and there was harmony once more in the house in Navy Gardens. Sir William, about to leave London for a visit to Ireland, had a brilliant idea—the Grand Tour. This was rapidly becoming the thing for young men of good family: the admiral saw a cure for his son's inner disquiet in a sojourn abroad, to say nothing of acquiring a good French accent and the easy bearing of a man of the world. Perhaps he would not have taken it amiss to see the young fellow kick over the traces a bit; a few wild oats might make him forget Dr. Owen.

In the summer of 1662 young Penn set out for the continent with some persons of rank, as he himself has related. One of them was Robert Spencer, the future Lord Sunderland, a brilliant and amoral worldling who yet remained a good friend when his travel companion had become an earnest Quaker.

Admiral Sir William Penn's recipe seemed to work at first. Young Penn took to French life with enthusiasm, went to the theatre, was dazzled by the court of Louis XIV, even came within an ace of fighting a duel; the last-named incident filled him with devout horror in retrospect. Then, still a serious student despite his taste for Parisian social life, he attended the theological lectures of Moïse Amyraut, a pillar

of French Protestantism, at the Huguenot college of Saumur. Amyraut's distinctive teaching was what we may call
a mellowed Calvinism, for it included freedom of the will
and departed from Calvin's ironbound predestination. Some
of the erudite French theologian's ideas which impressed
the young Englishman were akin to some he had heard of
as taught by the unlettered seer George Fox—his pacifism
and his belief in individual religious consciousness, the
"inner light" of the Quakers.

His grammar school in Essex, his sojourn in Oxford and
the studious period at Saumur had endowed Penn with
some valuable accomplishments. "He speaks well the Latin
and the French tongues, and his owne with great master-
ship," declares Aubrey in his *Brief Lives.*

Amyraut died in 1664 and Saumur without him had lost
its charm for Penn, so he set out for Italy in company with
young Robert Spencer. This phase of the Grand Tour was
ended abruptly at Turin by a summons from Sir William for
his son to hasten home before the expected second war with
the Dutch broke out. Until actual hostilities began an
English traveller could sojourn happily enough among
the Dutch. Penn was in Holland long enough to meet Algernon Sidney, the fiery, aristocratic republican, then living
in exile as a remittance man. Penn, more than twenty years
his junior, was much impressed. It is possible that some of
the principles—popular elections, religious toleration and
others—which went into the framework of Penn's constitution for his colony of Pennsylvania had their origin in con-
versations between the two men. Penn never accepted the
older man's out-and-out republicanism and it is sad to relate
that before Sidney was executed for a conspiracy of which
he was almost certainly innocent he and Penn had become
estranged on account of the Quaker's royalism. Sidney regarded him as tainted with the heresy of Divine Right.

Samuel Pepys, having met the younger Penn on his return to London, made one of his waspish entries in his diary about the admiral's son who had come home Frenchified, "most modish," and anxious to talk about his travels and experiences in France. Of these discourses there were "some good, some impertinent, but all ill-told." The fact is that Mrs. Pepys, a Frenchwoman, was entertained by the lively young Francophile fresh from his travels; her husband was secretly jealous. The relation between the two families was a strange one. Samuel Pepys disliked the admiral and was jealous of the son, but concealed his emotions. Sir William, an ingenuous and forthright sailor, liked Pepys and sought his advice. Mrs. Pepys and Lady Penn were good friends, both always active in the "making merry" which figures so often in the *Diary*. The women liked to tumble the admiralty official on to a bed and tickle him.

The admiral, who thought that his son was now cured of excessive religiosity, had him start law studies in Lincoln's Inn and then, when the second Dutch War broke out, he took him to sea and employed him as his courier to carry dispatches from the Duke of York, who was Lord High Admiral, to London. The young man was put ashore at Harwich, posted to London and, booted and spurred, reached Whitehall at daybreak. Charles II was still in bed, but, hearing there was news from his brother, rose quickly, "skipping out of bed" Penn wrote to his father, and in dressing gown and slippers conversed for half an hour with the messenger.

Young Penn was back at his law studies when the plague broke out in 1665 and he stayed in London all through that terrible year when the epidemic swept through the congested slums of Stuart London and the corpses were carted away in their scores and hundreds to be dumped into vast pits. At the end of the year the admiral retired from service at sea and with his family went to live at Wanstead again.

Early the following year he sent his son to Ireland to look after the family interests there. Dublin at that time, with the viceregal court as its centre and inspiration, was a brilliant little capital which charmed those who visited it then and in the next century.

The admiral's son, who had entered into Parisian life with gusto, showed at first the same enthusiasm for the social amenities of Dublin. "The glory of the world," as he called it, bade fair to seduce him, "I was even ready to give myself unto it," he said afterwards. Childhood memories of Thomas Loe's Quaker eloquence, undergraduate discipleship to the austere Dr. Owen, the pacifist teachings of Moïse Amyraut were now forgotten. Young Penn, well attired, skilled as fencer and horseman—the handsome young soldier of the only genuine portrait that survives—saw active service under the viceroy's son, Lord Arran, who had been sent to suppress a mutiny. The future Quaker leader showed himself possessed of the military virtues—physical courage, coolness in action. The viceroy heard good reports of him and suggested a military career. Admiral Penn held the nominal command of a garrison in Kinsale; why shouldn't he resign it in favour of his son? It seems a sensible idea, but the admiral took it ill, perhaps from jealousy, or, more worthily, because he thought his son could aim higher.

In the late winter of 1667 Penn went back to London, much of it still a desolate ash-strewn waste dotted with ramshackle dwellings of poor citizens made homeless by the Great Fire of 1666. His sister Margaret, rather plain but a precocious girl not above flirting with Mr. Pepys of the Navy Office, was being married at the age of fifteen. One gathers that brother William, even before his Quaker conversion, did not altogether approve of the frivolous Peg.

The religious crisis in Penn's life that deprived Charles II of a devoted courtier and a good soldier or diplomat gave the nascent Quaker movement its zealous propagandist and organizer. To the New World of North America it gave one of her great colonial founders. So far as we can tell, Penn had gone back to Ireland after his sister's marriage. There took place the series of events which completed the spiritual process of his "convincement." He was not a mystic in the sense that such men as Fox, Boehme and Swedenborg may be regarded as mystics. Temperate and chaste in his life, from childhood susceptible of religious emotion, he was yet neither ascetic nor visionary. His conversion was not so much the acceptance of new dogmas as the birth of a new attitude towards life.

Back in the region that held memories of childish stirrings of religious fervour he found himself one day a customer in a shop kept by a Quaker woman. To her he spoke of the preacher Thomas Loe, whose words so moved the Penn family and their Negro servant. Gladly, he said, would he travel miles to hear that Quaker saint again. Joyful surprise! Mr. Loe, said the Quaker shopkeeper, would speak at a Meeting of Friends in Cork the very next day. Penn was there in good time, a handsome young stranger, fashionably dressed, an object of surprise, perhaps of suspicion, to the gathering of humble, unobstrusive Friends. The Thomas Loe whom Penn saw that day had changed from the man, young and vigorous, he had listened to a dozen years earlier. Hard work, incessant travel, suffering and persecution had aged him, but when he spoke, the old magic was in his words and Penn's soul was filled with the mingled pain and sweetness known to all who undergo that kind of conversion—Saul on the Damascus road, Augustine in the African garden, Ignatius Loyola on his sick bed.

Penn turned his attention inward to "the thoughts and intents of his own heart." He was not pleased with what he found; he wept much, he tells us. After the Meeting he met

Loe, who was about to set out for another town. He had no horse and presumably would have to tramp wearily to the second Meeting. Penn impulsively offered his own horse; the offer was gently and courteously declined. Penn was grieved, for these devout men, bringing back, as he saw it, the brotherhood in piety of the early Christians, did not recognize him as one of themselves; he was no Quaker.

With a convert's zeal and the energy that was his distinctive trait Penn set to work to become a genuine Quaker. He attended Meeting regularly and began to speak in the gatherings of Friends. On one occasion he prepared to eject forcibly from a Meeting a soldier, possibly one who, in convivial Irish surroundings, "had drink taken" and was making himself a nuisance. The others present, less forgetful of their pacific tenets or fearful of stirring up trouble, persuaded the young convert not to throw the man out by the scruff of the neck. The intruder departed unharmed, but came back with a posse of constables. Several of the people present were arrested, Penn among them. His wish to be a veritable Quaker had now been fulfilled; he was a Quaker suffering for the cause.

The magistrate before whom he was taken was embarrassed and would have liked to discharge him forthwith. The young man, after all, was a gentleman and an admiral's son at that. Everyone knew, moreover, that Sir William Penn was on good terms with the king's brother, the Duke of York. Young Penn was adamant. He was a Quaker and if his friends went to prison he would go with them. So he did, but not for long. As soon as the jail door closed behind him he wrote to the nobleman who was governor of Munster and, incidentally a friend of Sir William, a shrewd letter—from one reasonable gentleman to another, as it were. The result was a speedy release for all who had been arrested. Penn had a strong sense of human dignity and the rights of a citizen and although he might welcome persecution as a test of his faith he was no pious masochist.

Sir William Penn, nursing his gout in London and restless now that quarterdeck authority had been replaced only by occasional advisory work at the Navy Office, knew at first nothing of his son's doings. Then news from Ireland reached him and he called the young man home. The letter was unanswered and was followed by another, rather more peremptory but still affectionate. One suspects that the young Quaker convert, fearless before mutineers, drunken soldiers and hectoring magistrates, hesitated to face his father's anger. The admiral was a warm-hearted man but, like many such, he had a quick temper and had not hesitated to take the stick to his son long after he had passed boyhood. Moreover, Penn the son always disliked "scenes" and throughout his life would do a good deal to avoid one.

For a time he toyed with the idea of disregarding the parental summons altogether, but an older Quaker companion, Josiah Coale, urged him to go home and face the music. Coale was a man of strong personality, good education, missionary zeal and a stern Puritan attitude to the world and its allurements. He had spent some time in America and had come back from the Delaware region with visions of a new nation wherein men of diverse faiths but common goodwill should live in peace together. Penn had heard something like that before and the name of America began to cast its spell over him as El Dorado had done to Ralegh and his contemporaries.

Meanwhile he had to muster up his courage for the meeting with his father. He made a bargain with the austere but kindly Josiah Coale. He would go obediently home if the other would accompany him. Although Coale was an active Quaker, he was, socially, a gentleman. Even the irascible admiral would have to exercise self-restraint in his company. He did so, controlling his impatience with the maddening Quaker quirks of keeping the head covered and using the second person singular.

When Coale had left, the admiral let himself go. He had seen all he wanted to see of Quakers in London, for the town was still agog with the doings of Solomon Eccles, the poor, crazed fanatic who had affronted the lawyers and the gentry with his calls to repentance as he ambled all but naked through Westminster Hall. After recalling this distressing incident and upbraiding his son for associating with fanatics, the admiral delivered his ultimatum. Young Penn could "thee" and "thou" those who liked it—that Sir William would concede—but there must be three exceptions: the king, the Duke of York and Sir William Penn. In the presence of these three, moreover, the head must be bared in token of respect. Even this not unreasonable demand was refused. The son was ordered off to bed and told to be ready to go out early with his father the next morning.

The next day started with a ride in the family coach in Hyde Park—a stratagem for a quiet talk away from prying domestics. The admiral argued with a good deal of patience and not without affection. No headway was made on either side and the father was the first to show signs of exhaustion. He made the coachman stop "at a tavern on the way, when Sir William ordered a glass of wine." Then he locked himself in the room with his son and announced that he would pray forthwith for the young man's renunciation of Quakerism. Thereupon young Penn opened the window and threatened to jump out of it. This, presumably, was bluff or it may be that the athletic younger Penn had looked out and seen that the jump was a safe one. That seems to have been the end of the incident.

Nothing much happened for a time. Pepys heard from an

acquaintance that the admiral's son "is a Quaker again, or some very melancholy thing." The strained relation between father and son was made worse by various minor affairs. Young Penn now changed his smart cavalier style of dress for the Quaker bourgeois fashion. Also he left off wearing his sword; it was as though a gentleman of our time were to go about in formal attire without collar or necktie. In the winter of 1668 he refused to attend the christening of his married sister's child because of his Quaker disbelief in sacraments.

The last straw, so far as the poor admiral was concerned, was a Quaker Meeting forcibly closed by order of a magistrate or justice, who wrote to Sir William complaining of his son's disturbing the peace. The angry father, feeling his family humiliated by the affair, swore that he would cut off his son without even the proverbial shilling, told him to collect his belongings and get out of the house. Young Penn kissed his mother and sister farewell and left the house, as he relates, with their distressful sobbing in his ears.

How he lived during this period of exile we do not know. The Friends, like the early Christians, have always been known for their charitable care for their brethren in trouble; they may have helped the young convert. Lady Penn, too, seems to have done something for her son, perhaps smuggled out part of the housekeeping money: her husband was unlikely to notice slight changes in the meals. The young man found abundant consolation for his troubles; he fell in love, deeply and, by prudent Quaker standards, rather romantically.

Wandering from Meeting to Meeting in the pleasant county of Buckinghamshire he had made friends with the Peningtons, who then lived at Amersham. They were pioneers of Quakerism, friends of its founder, George Fox, and fearless propagandists of its teaching. Isaac Penington had been a London alderman during the Cromwellian era, then Lord Mayor and Lieutenant of the Tower. He married Mary Springett, the young widow of a Parliamentarian knight who had fought in two battles of the Civil War, been wounded and died later. Along with a modest fortune Mary brought her second husband an infant stepdaughter, Gulielma Maria Posthuma Springett.

At the Restoration the Cromwellian Penington was jailed for a time and was impoverished by many fines and sequestrations of his property. The Springett inheritance enabled them to live very comfortably for a time and then that, too, was reduced by fines and sequestration. When Penn met them they were living frugally on the money from the sale of some land the wife had sold. With them lived Thomas Ellwood, the Quaker friend of John Milton who used to read aloud to the poet after blindness overtook him and whose suggestion for a sequel to *Paradise Lost* led Milton to write *Paradise Regained*. To avoid wounding his self-respect the Peningtons made him tutor to their children; he taught them Latin with the Italian pronunciation; it is amusing to reflect that Milton and other Puritans talked Latin as the Pope did. Ellwood is thought to have been in love with Gulielma, who is described as beautiful, gifted and a devout Quaker. She had many admirers and, until Penn came along, turned down numerous offers of marriage. John Aubrey records that she was much loved by the poor country people who lived near the Peningtons, "for the great cure she does, having great skill in physic and surgery, which she freely bestows."

By the time Penn was an accepted guest at the Penington home he had become a conspicuous figure among the Quakers. He spoke at Meetings very effectively, for he had a good voice and suited his language to his audience. He had been imprisoned in the Tower for "heresy," resisting not only the threats of the Bishop of London to keep him there until he recanted but also, what was more difficult, the genuine kindness of Dean Stillingfleet, a future bishop of Worcester. A subsequent trial at the Old Bailey, on the stock charge of disturbing the peace, was a nation-wide sensation. The defendants were Penn himself and a former Cromwellian, William Mead, and the trial became famous for the able defence put up by Penn and Mead themselves and still more for the heroic firmness of the jury that refused to be frightened, starved, browbeaten or fined into convicting the accused.

Penn came near to making a career of soldiering and then embraced a way of life essentially pacifist. The aggressive spirit that would have made him a good soldier found an outlet in religious controversy. Polemical writing was decidedly uninhibited in his time and he could always give as good as he received. In the defence of his fellow-believers he composed and wrote at lightning speed a host of books, letters and pamphlets and was always ready to meet all and sundry in public debate to justify his faith or combat attacks on it. The verbal duels, chiefly with Presbyterians or Independents, were definitely acrimonious at times, on both sides, for Penn seems to have inherited a touch of the admiral's testiness when provoked. History has preserved for our delight the piece of invective he hurled at the vice-chancellor of Oxford University for allowing the persecution of students who did not conform to Church of England ritual—"Better it were for thee thou hadst never been born! Poor mushroom, wilt thou war against the Lord?"

A complete reconciliation between father and son took place before Sir William's death. In the autumn of 1670 young Penn was in Newgate for a time after the battle for justice in which he was fighting alongside Bushel, the fore-man, and the stalwart eleven jurors who made their famous stand. There was an exchange of letters, deeply touching letters, between the admiral, now nearing death, and his son, who stayed in the fetid prison rather than pay a fine un-justly imposed. Sir William quietly settled the matter by sending money to pay the fines, for his son and the twelve courageous jurymen, and young William went home to com-fort his father in his last weeks on earth.

As death drew nearer, the admiral came to regard his son's Quakerism with tolerance, almost with sympathetic approval. In the most famous of his books, *No Cross, No Crown*, written in prison, Penn quotes what his father said shortly before his end: "Son William, if you and your friends keep to your plain way of preaching, and keep to your plain way of living, you will make an end of the priests to the end of the world. Bury me by my mother: live all in love: shun all manner of evil: and I pray God to bless you all: and He will bless you."

Long before his death Sir William had restored his son to his position as principal heir in his will: also he made him executor. The admiral was buried, with the ceremony due to his rank, beside his mother, as he had desired, in Bristol. Quaker unworldliness and Quaker pacifism notwith-standing, Penn prized as mementoes of his father the medal and the gold chain awarded in 1653 for prowess in action. After the funeral William wrote to the navy commissioners to ensure his receiving any small tokens—letters, scraps of writing and so forth—that had once been his father's. "I have yet superstition enough (as some are pleased to call it)," he wrote, "to value even the smallest relic that may be deemed a badge of his trade, which rendered him what he was, and us, his relations, what we are."

Soon after his father's death William was in trouble with

the law again, charged with violating the Five Mile Act by addressing a meeting in the streets of London. There was a good deal of recrimination between judges and defendant. Court procedure lacked the restraint of our days and Penn was not slow in repartee. When an irritated judge, who was also Lieutenant of the Tower, exclaimed, "I wish you wiser," the Quaker came back with, "And I wish thee better." A six months' sentence was imposed and the harassed judge ordered, "Send a corporal with a file of musqueteers along with him." "No, no; send thy lacquey;" promptly suggested Penn, "I know the way to Newgate." It was a busy six months in jail, filled with controversial writing.

When he came out of prison Penn visited his mother in the family home at Wanstead. Then he hurried away to Buckinghamshire for a brief stay with the family of his beloved Guli Springett. After that he crossed to the continent to spread the Quaker teachings in Holland and Germany. He encountered a good deal of opposition to his missionary efforts and it was with a good deal of relief that he found himself back in England the following year. He stayed with his mother at Wanstead and then with the Peningtons in Buckinghamshire. He was now formally engaged, with the full approval of the Quakers in Meeting assembled, to Penington's beautiful stepdaughter Guli.

For a couple of years before his marriage Penn was very busy, an apostle of Quakerism, with missionary journeys and with writing. Early in 1672 he was back in Buckinghamshire for his marriage to Guli. His bride had a sizable dowry as well as much charm and a lovable nature and was no less zealous than her husband in the Quaker cause. He was very much in love and the first few months of their married life made up an interlude of idyllic content in the pleasant countryside. Perhaps Penn felt the temptation to settle down to a placid life as a country gentleman. His vast reserve of energy would not have let him remain a country squire for long and, anyhow, it is probable that his wife's interest in spreading the Quaker doctrine was as urgent as his own.

The year after their marriage they met George Fox at Bristol, the port at which he landed on his return from a visit to America. What he had to tell them recalled to Penn many things he had heard vaguely already—of a new, vast country where Englishmen might plough, sow and reap on a virgin soil and where they might hope for the freedom of worship they were denied at home. Maryland, under Lord Baltimore, had set a new pattern. In that colony, named in honour of Charles I's Catholic queen, a Catholic lord-proprietor had established freedom of worship for all who accepted the basic Christian belief in Jesus Christ. Penn had, it is true, written a controversial *Caveat against Popery* and one of his friends, Perrot, a spiritual stormy petrel who was eventually ejected from the Quaker body, had years ago made a toilsome journey to Rome to convert the Pope to primitive Christianity. In spite of all this, Penn had a soft spot in his heart for Catholics, sympathizing with them in their sufferings under the penal laws. He discussed religion with the Duke of York after the latter's conversion and is reported to have told his royal friend that there was little difference between Quakerism and Catholicism except the trimmings.

Gulielma, in her zeal for Quaker missionary effort, shared many of her husband's journeys as he went about England preaching, writing and arguing with opponents. Perhaps she endured too much for her own welfare. Several of their children died before she gave birth to one who survived infancy. This was the boy Springett, but he was always delicate and did not grow to manhood.

In the controversies of his early years with Guli all manner of opponents were tackled, either in public debate or in a paper war of pamphlets. Penn crossed swords with the learned Protestant divine Richard Baxter. There was a certain amount of heat generated on both sides, but both men were too magnanimous for a long feud and, anyhow, Penn's own genial nature invariably won over all but the most dour of his critics. At times it seems as though Penn's ardour in the defence of the faith that was in him quite obscured his sense of humour. How otherwise could he have engaged in a war of words with Lodowick Muggleton, the most grotesque of all the religious "enthusiasts" thrown up in the ferment of the Puritan dictatorship and the years just after it? Muggleton, a tailor by trade and a visionary by avocation, with a Messianic destiny, was not impressed by Penn's family background, education, breeding or his obvious sincerity. Having told the Quaker that he, Lodowick Muggleton, inspired of God, "did not care a turd" for Penn and all the other Quakers, he concluded the interview by assuring Penn that he was damned—by a special decree known to Muggleton.

The spate of books, pamphlets and letters continued and, as though all that and the cares of married life were not enough, Penn set out on another missionary journey on the continent. This time he set off in company with George Fox and Robert Barclay. They form an interesting triumvirate of Quakerism—Fox, the leader and founder, the mystic and "enthusiast," almost uneducated, a man of one book, the Bible, yet of a magnetic personality; William Penn, the energetic organizer, adding all the graces and accomplishments of a man of the world to his religious zeal: Robert Barclay, less ebullient than either of his friends, erudite, a good Latinist, a keen intellect, the Thomas Aquinas of Quakerism.

The national hysteria which was aroused by Titus Oates'

bogus Popish Plot seems to have left Penn unmoved. He was a staunch Protestant, but, with friendly feelings for the Duke of York and with an unwavering loyalty to the House of Stuart he could have no sympathy with the party of anti-Catholic politicians who were seeking to use popular bigotry as a weapon against the heir to the throne. It is unlikely that, other things being equal, Penn would have welcomed a Catholic monarch in preference to a Protestant one, but he was in line with the spirit of the times in England, where legitimacy outweighed all other claims.

Eight years had passed since his marriage before Penn's attention was seriously drawn to America, if we except the talks with George Fox and the latter's report of religious toleration in Maryland. Pennsylvania may be said to owe its birth to an accident, although devout believers may see the finger of God in it. The accident was the need of an arbitrator in a business dispute between two Quakers. The Friends, understandably, look askance at litigation among their members and until modern times they were debarred from effective action in the courts by their refusal to take oaths. In this case Penn was the arbitrator and so was brought directly in contact with American affairs.

The dispute had arisen over some land in the partially settled territories of the East and West New Jerseys. A Quaker, John Fenwick, was acting as trustee for a fellow-Quaker, Edward Byllinge, who had bought out the holdings of Lord Berkeley. Then came the disagreement about the outcome of the deal. Fenwick was a litigious fellow, but both men agreed to accept the decision of the respected young Quaker, Mr. Penn. When, however, Penn gave his verdict in favour of Byllinge, his opponent refused compliance and Penn had to trounce him rather severely by letter into a sullen acceptance of the judgement given. Byllinge was none too good at business and when he found himself in difficulties of his own making he called on Penn to help him. The outcome was the division of the territory so that one part, already colonized by British and other European settlers, was held by Sir George Carteret, of a Jersey family, hence the name of New Jersey, while the western part, with Indians as almost the sole inhabitants, was to belong to a group of "adventurers," that is, investors. They were controlled by trustees, one of whom was Penn.

Thus at the age of thirty-six he found himself in the responsible position of lawmaker and administrator for an important piece of England's expanding colonial empire. The troublesome Fenwick's claims had been met with a grant of about one tenth of the land held by Penn's "adventurers," while the rest, bought from the Indians, was mostly resold to Quaker immigrants. Already, in the rules which Penn drew up for the colony he foreshadowed what, a few years later, he would carry out when he established Pennsylvania.

The settlers were to elect their own rulers. Freedom of belief and worship was to be absolute and no man was to be convicted except by the verdict of a jury. All went well until 1680. Then trouble started with a claim from the neighboring province of New York, the domain assigned to the king's brother when it had been taken from the Dutch. New York sought to put a tariff on all merchandise entering or leaving the country by way of the Delaware estuary. This threatened the economic future of the new settlement, wholly dependent at that time on Delaware Bay for its overseas trade. Penn's friendship with the Duke of York, his father's fellow-seaman, saved the day for the Quakers of New Jersey. To Penn's appeal the duke replied generously by accepting the decision of the colonial commissioners against him; the New York tax was withdrawn.

This success whetted Penn's appetite for colonization.

When Sir George Carteret died, East New Jersey was up for sale; seventeenth century Europeans saw no incongruity in putting a whole province, with its inhabitants white or red, on the real estate market. Penn saw his opportunity and seized it. Drawing on his own considerable means and inviting investors, eleven at first and then an additional dozen, he bought the whole territory and issued a prospectus to attract would-be colonists. It was the first large scale business venture almost entirely in Quaker hands. We are not unrealistic in seeing it as the birth of the Quaker reputation for sound business instincts wedded to business integrity.

Perhaps Penn was at first appalled by the magnitude of what he had undertaken. Knowing his vast energy and gift for enthusiasm in whatever he undertook, we may surmise that, good Latinist as he was, he said with the Roman poet," . . . *majus opus moveo.*" ("I now tackle a bigger job.") He aspired to have a colony of his own, where the Quaker ideals of social life on a Christian basis could be put into practice. Early as well as later ages would call it a crusade. He called it an experiment; "the Holy Experiment" was the phrase he used in a letter to a fellow-Quaker.

A colony based on Christian ideals is rather anomalous if its territory has been won by conquest or piracy. Penn was resolved that land held by the Indians should be bought, not just seized. If the purchase prices are somewhat comical beside later land values, that can hardly be held against him; anyhow, he never drove as hard a bargain as the Dutch when they acquired Manhattan. He had plenty of money, but he knew he would need plenty before his Christian commonwealth could become self-supporting, so he thought out a means to get his land advantageously. As heir to his father's estate he had taken the late admiral's place as a creditor—with the King of England in debt to him. At one time Sir William Penn had made a loan of some

£10,000 to Charles II and by the time William Penn the second was thinking of his Holy Experiment the principal and accrued interest came to £16,000. A proprietary province in North America—there was a heaven-sent way for Charles to pay his debt and for Penn to get the land for his Holy Experiment. Late in 1680 he petitioned the king for the grant of territory.

Some of the royal officials looked askance at a scheme that would put a sizable portion of England's empire under the control of a Quaker. A religious, or more properly an ecclesiastical bias still entered into English poltical thinking. Further, Lord Baltimore, to whose family Maryland had been granted, raised objections to what he thought was an encroachment on his own province. These difficulties were smoothed out—on paper; only the sketchiest of geographical data were to be had, and there was trouble in the future.

Charles was glad of this easy way to pay a big debt; a lover of ships and the sea, like his brother, he had a warm feeling for the dead admiral's family. Early in March, 1681, (New Style), the king signed the royal patent in Penn's presence. One version of a pleasing story—whether true or merely *ben trovato* we cannot tell—attaches to this interview the account of Penn's keeping his head covered, Quaker style, in the royal presence and the king's uncovering his own head. This drew from Penn the question, surely with good-natured malice, "Friend Charles, why dost thou uncover?" The king is said to have replied, "Because it is the custom here for only one man to wear his hat." True or not, the story mirrors Charles II's satirical good nature. The traditional account of the origin of Pennsylvania as the name of Penn's American domain is authentic, preserved for us in a letter written by him the day after the meeting with Charles.

Penn had made up his mind to call the colony New

Wales, basing his choice on a report of the land as "a pretty, hilly country," but to this name objection was raised by a secretary, a Welshman, who thought it derogatory to his country to bestow its name on a raw colony. Penn, drawing on his Latinity, then offered Sylvania. This satisfied Charles II, but he insisted on prefixing Penn to the name, in honour of the admiral. Penn, proud of his father, could appreciate that, but feared people would see it as vanity in himself. The king refused to have it changed, saying he would be responsible. Penn was still uneasy and tells us ingenuously, ". . . nor could twenty guineas move the under-secretary to vary the name."

Penn left the royal presence with joy in his heart. Throughout his life he threw himself into all his enterprises with an almost boyish enthusiasm. He concludes the letter in which he tells how Pennsylvania got its name: "It is a clear and just thing, and my God that has given it me through many difficulties, will, I believe, bless and make it the seed of a nation. I shall have a tender care to the government, that it be well laid at first." This tender care he did indeed exercise until he was no longer able to do so.

At the home he had made for his family in Sussex he set to work on a constitution for his province, which was about the size of England and was sparsely populated by Indians and scattered groups of European colonists. The document containing the royal patent spoke of Penn's "commendable desire to enlarge the English empire, and to promote such useful commodities as may be a benefit to the king and his dominions." Rather materialistic, some may think, for a Holy Experiment, but a loftier note was struck when it was stated that the proprietor of Pennsylvania wished to "reduce the savage nations, by just and gentle manners, to the love of civil society and the Christian religion." For officials this may have been a stock formula, but not to William Penn. The union of practical business aspiration and religious idealism was characteristic of him. Perhaps it is not inaccurate to say that in this respect Penn rather than George Fox is the typical Quaker.

A month after he had received his patent Penn wrote a letter to his subjects in Pennsylvania, a Quaker encyclical. He wished to reassure them that their welfare rather than his own pecuniary gain was uppermost in his mind. As a lord-proprietor under a royal patent he had almost feudal powers over his people. He was resolved that they should be given freedom in governing themselves, but he had no objection in starting off as a benevolent autocrat. Perhaps his political ideas were rather lacking in clearness; he believed in a democratic form of government, but saw it as resting on the prince's free gift, not on an implied contract. Therein he differed from his one-time friend Algernon Sidney, an authentic republican. It seems fair to say that his practice was better than his theory and he annoyed Sidney by introducing mystical concepts into a philosophy of civil government. In practice he saw the need to allow growth through experience and a process of trial and error. Governments, he said, depend on men, not men on governments.

His rules for the administration of Pennsylvania were set out in detail in the *Frame of Government*. He had consulted Sidney while at work on it, but the final product so displeased the fiery and uncompromising republican that it led to a breach between the two men which was never healed. Sidney was especially critical of what he called Penn's hydra-headed executive, a Council of seventy-two members, as legislature, and an Assembly of some two hundred. The latter body had no powers beyond approving or vetoing the legislation of the upper house. As, moreover, the same electors chose members of both chambers from the same section of the population, it would seem that there is reason for Sidney's criticism.

The letter to the settlers was sent across the Atlantic

in the care of Captain, afterwards Colonel, Markham, a cousin of Penn. Markham was to deputize for Penn until his own arrival in America. Penn, always a quick and facile writer—too facile at times—next produced a brochure for stirring up interest in the colony and followed it with another giving advice to prospective emigrants. It was full of practical details—the amount of money needed for a start in the new world, the cost of various things required, even such matters as the kind of nails to be taken over for shingling roofs.

In the enthusiasm of starting his Holy Experiment the benevolent lord-proprietor conjures up for his citizens-to-be a picture of pastoral simplicity that anticipates the Utopias of eighteenth century social philosophers. In his *Information and Direction to Such Persons as are Inclined to America, more especially Those related to the Province of Pennsylvania* the author writes, "If Jacob dwelt in tents, and herds and flocks were his revenue, a life like his should be no stop with those that love his plainness and integrity." Nor were the aboriginal Indians overlooked. Penn instructed his deputies "be tender of offending Indians" and he wrote a letter which was to be translated and passed on to his redskin subjects. About this time a mercantile concern offered him a tempting bribe—£6,000 and 2½% of their profits for the monopoly of trading with the Indians of Pennsylvania. We must multiply the sum by something between six and ten to appreciate what acceptance could have meant in easing the financial burden of starting to colonize. Penn turned down the offer. He knew what it would have meant in exploitation of a race ignorant of money and commerce and ready victims to a demoralizing liquor traffic.

There was a gratifying response to the call for emigrants. The modest sums asked for grants of land, reports of the fertility of the soil and of the natural wealth of the province, and, for harassed non-conformists in religion, the prospect of toleration, attracted large numbers of intending settlers. Quakers were in the majority at first, although the government at home insisted on the appointment of an Anglican minister as soon as the number of Anglicans justified it. Penn, despite his disbelief in sacraments and, copying George Fox, his use of the term "steeple houses" for the English churches, readily acceded to this. Later he was equally tolerant of Catholic worship; it is significant that the Mass was openly celebrated in Philadelphia long before it was legally tolerated in England.

Two shiploads of colonists set out from the river Thames aboard the *Amity* and the *John Sarah* and a third ship, the *Bristol Factor,* carried passengers from the west country by way of the River Avon. Cousin Markham was hard at work in Pennsylvania. One of his tasks was to supervise the clearing of land for Pennsbury Manor, the future home of the lord-proprietor. An enterprising printer, William Bradford, was induced to take his press across the ocean and set up in business in the new province.

As the autumn of 1682 drew near, Penn completed his arrangements for his own migration. He sailed from the Kentish port of Deal aboard the *Welcome,* a little, overcrowded 300-ton ship, on September 1. Guli and the three Penn children were left at home in Sussex until Penn had a home ready for them to go to in America. He addressed a touchingly affectionate farewell letter to them, for a journey across the Atlantic in the days when a quarter of the people aboard ship might never disembark was a gamble with life and death. While the ship lay at anchor in the Downs he sent another good-bye letter—to all "faithful Friends," as well as a personal one to his great friend Stephen Crisp.

When all seemed to be ready, the sailing was postponed because of an outbreak of smallpox on the crowded and insanitary little ship. Careless of the danger to himself, Penn nursed the sick, consoled the dying and kept up the spirits of the rest. There were thirty-nine deaths before the *Welcome* could start on her long and tedious voyage. It took nearly two months, for it was almost the end of October before the travellers went ashore at New Castle, the present-day Newcastle, Delaware, at that time a port of entry doubtfully belonging to the proprietor of Pennsylvania.

Until the disability of his closing years overtook him Penn always had immense physical and mental vigour and remarkable resilience. He displayed it now after the hardships, discomforts and perils of that Atlantic crossing. The day after landing he assembled the citizens of New Castle and formally took possession of his territory; on the next day he sailed to Upland, the later Chester, and thence set out to choose the site for his capital and to make plans for its lay-out. It was to be at Coquannock, a tiny settlement occupied by a few Swedes, who readily agreed to move away to generous grants of land elsewhere. The settlement Penn renamed Philadelphia. He saw it in his vivid imagination as truly a City of Brotherly Love, where men of various faiths—all "Christians" in his tolerant vocabulary, even if they were Unitarian in creed or Red Indian worshippers of a Great Spirit—would live together in amity and bring his Holy Experiment to fruition. That his picture was unduly optimistic may be admitted; he shared with his contemporary John Locke the not unworthy delusion that men, being rational animals, would choose the best and the most reasonable way of living when it was shown to them.

His Philadelphia was the offspring of a creative imagination. His vision was not shared by his assistants and advisers. He saw in the future a garden city arising on the site of the miserable little settlement, a metropolis of broad avenues and tree-lined streets, of well-built houses, each in its own grounds, a noble city hall as civic centre, and a spacious and well-planned waterfront. He proposed to mark out ten thousand acres for the Philadelphia of the future. His subordinates were aghast. Whether from sheer good nature or because the surveyors were "experts," he let himself be talked into reducing the area to twelve hundred acres.

Of all Penn's early work as a colonizer the thing that has most impressed the mind of posterity is his treatment of the Indians, perhaps because it was in such marked contrast to what was done by other settlers in the western world. His attitude was simple and undeniably logical. The Indians, by inherent right, the *jus gentium,* were the owners of the land where they dwelt; to take it away from them forcibly or to refuse payment was as much robbery as to do the same to a fellow-European. Penn was alert to detect and forestall any sharp practice on the part of the settlers. The result was the high prestige he always enjoyed in Indian eyes and, it may be added, the peaceful state of the country so long as his influence was paramount.

Even before his arrival in the province his letter to the Indian inhabitants had made a good impression and they soon learned to trust and, later, to love this white man who was an honest broker when they wished to trade and whose word was never broken. It was, therefore, in an atmosphere of good will that they agreed to send delegates to confer with him and to decide on a treaty between the two races. The meeting was at Shackanaxon, the modern Kensington, in the early days of November. There was much speechmaking, exchange of compliments and giving of presents and then the red men gave a display of bodily skill and agility.

They were delighted when the English chief joined in with them, hopping and jumping as in the old days at the Chigwell Grammar School.

This first meeting was followed by a second, more formal one for the actual treaty-signing. At the end of November the Indian chiefs and their attendants appeared, all in full war array—feathered headdresses, faces painted with the juice of the wild bloodroot. Penn, who was accompanied by his cousin Markham, advanced unarmed to meet them. They were deeply impressed by this token of confidence. Painters and writers have tried to reproduce this scene for us, not always with the happiest results, portraying a stout, elderly gentleman dwarfed by the towering braves. Actually, Penn had just passed his thirty-eighth birthday and had not yet acquired the portliness of his middle life. He was tall, dignified, athletic, described by one who saw him as "the handsomest, best-looking, liveliest gentleman."

With an old English captain beside him to act as interpreter, Penn addressed the Indian delegates from a manuscript text of the treaty of amity he had drawn up. It set a precedent for the relations between Indians and the newcomers which was, unhappily, only too seldom followed in later years. Of it Voltaire remarked that it was the only treaty made between such tribes and Christians that was not sworn to with oaths and that was not broken by the signatories. Penn somewhat shocked his more rigoristic followers by referring to his Indian friends as Christians because of their belief in a supreme Great Spirit. There were critics in England who did not hesitate to declare him a deist; that was loose thinking, but it must be admitted that a certain vagueness sometimes appears in his excursions into theology.

Penn, who became known as *Onas,* the Indian word for a pen or quill, held a unique position in the minds and hearts of his barbaric neighbours. Benjamin Franklin, speaking of Penn's dealings with the Indians, says that he "united the subtlety of the serpent with the innocence of the dove." It is probable that the subtlety was unconscious in this case and anyhow what the Indians saw and respected was the innocence. Had the innocence been continued by Penn's countrymen, before and after the War of Independence, the white settlers in North America would have been spared many massacres.

The effect made on the Indian mind by Penn's moral stature was enhanced by a sobriety of manner which appears to have been a distinctive trait of the early Friends. He himself was aware of the value of this and in giving advice to his subordinates on dealing with the tribesmen warns them, "Be grave; they love not to be smiled on."

Friendship was established with the Indians on a basis of fair dealing and, it is worth noting, of equality with whites before the law. Penn's early law-making had provided for the trial of Indian law-breakers by mixed juries—six of the Indian's countrymen, six white men. Philadelphia had already arisen in its founder's imagination above the few score of wooden shanties that stood on its site. He bubbled over with enthusiasm for his undertaking and in a letter to his old friend of Grand Tour days, the Earl of Sunderland, he says, "I will show a province in seven years equal to her neighbours of forty years planting." While the spell of North America was still on him Penn wrote of Virginia, where his friend Lord Culpepper was one of the proprietors, "I am mightily taken with this part of the world; I like it so well that my family being fixed with me and if no other thing occur, I am like to be an adopted American."

Unhappily the course of true love as between Penn and America did not run altogether smoothly for very long. There were difficulties over boundaries and territorial claims with the neighbouring province of Maryland, held by the

Calverts, who had become ennobled as the Lords Baltimore. The lord-proprietor of Maryland at the time was the second Lord Baltimore, a man somewhat high-handed, it seems, and at times rather disingenuous. In justice to him we must bear in mind that the disputes were complicated by hazy geography at home and the allocation in different patents of overlapping boundaries. To sum up in a few words a tedious controversy that dragged on for several years, we may say that legally Lord Baltimore was in the right, but that Penn, with his huge territory needing an outlet to the ocean in order to survive and prosper, had a moral claim to some concession from the Maryland proprietor.

There were meetings between the Catholic nobleman and the Quaker gentleman, marked by mutual compliments and the exchange of hospitality, but the dispute was not brought to an end. There was even a show of violence when one of Baltimore's subordinates, a colonel, entered what Penn regarded as his territory and set up a garrison there. Penn saw that if he hoped to have the matter settled in his favour he must go to London and work for it. Lord Baltimore had already gone to England, "that, making an interest before I arrived, he might block up my way, and carry the point," says Penn, writing to his friend the Duke of York. He was anxious to visit England, also, because he had news that his wife was ill.

He wrote parting letters to some of his friends, for he did not know how long he would be away from them. To his fellow-Quakers of Pennsylvania he sent a valedictory letter which rises to eloquence as he bids farewell to the city which was, he hoped, to be the focus of what we may call Quaker humanism: "And thou, Philadelphia, named before thou wast born, what love, what care, what service, and what travail, has been to bring thee forth and preserve thee from such as would abuse and defile thee."

In mid-August, 1654, he sailed in the *Endeavour*, leaving behind him a flourishing province, with a new charter whereby, not too willingly, he had given up a good deal of his authority to his Council and Assembly. Immigrants were arriving in considerable numbers, new towns being built, and the friendship made with the Indians was still unruffled. The Holy Experiment seemed to be in a fair way to success.

Penn was still in his prime, not quite fifty, when he sailed for England. Although he did not know it then, his best work was already done, his happiest associations with America at an end. It would be many years before his return to Pennsylvania and then he would be an elderly man as age was reckoned in his time, harassed in many ways and feeling that his Holy Experiment was, after all, but one more colonial venture, tainted by men's unreasonableness and ingratitude.

Apart from finding that his wife and children were, after all, in good health, there was little to cheer Penn on his arrival in England. The Whigs had fallen from power after the execution of Lord Russell and Algernon Sidney and the flight and death of the Earl of Shaftesbury. A strong Tory resurgence had brought with it a revival of religious tests and persecution of non-conforming bodies. The Quakers were doubly victims of the state of things, in ill odour with the authorities of the established Church because of suspected heterodoxy and hounded by the judiciary because of the refusal to testify on oath in court. Penn heard of a thousand or more of his co-religionists confined, often under horrible conditions, in the Marshalsea, Newgate and the Gatehouse. He journeyed to Newmarket to see the king and his brother, the Duke of York. He was graciously received, but could achieve nothing. Charles II was a tolerant man by nature, but he had his finger on the pulse of his turbulent, bigoted, unbiddable people and knew the limits

of his power. He had known poverty and exile and was resolved, he said, not to go on his travels again.

After doing what he could for a number of individuals
among the worst victims of persecution, Penn composed a
long letter for the king to read, a mixture of pleading, ex-
hortation and advice. Probably Charles would, with cynical
good nature, have taken it all with a smile, but it is more
probable that he did not see the letter. He was taken ill that
winter, 1685, and died on February 1, received into the
Catholic Church on his deathbed by the Benedictine Father
Huddleston who had helped his escape after the Battle of
Worcester three and a half decades earlier and, recipient
of a king's gratitude, had been protected during the hysteria
of Titus Oates' so-called Popish Plot.

The respect for legitimacy in monarchical England was
stronger than the dislike for the religion of Rome. Only a
small minority, worked upon by the Whig party that was
Shaftesbury's legacy to Stuart England, would have preferred to see Charles' bastard son the Duke of Monmouth
on the throne instead of James, Duke of York, the king's
brother. James had made his peace with Rome and, more
the zealot and less the politician than his brother, made no
secret of it. Nevertheless his accession took place peacefully
with the usual junketings. There was a short-lived rising afterwards, a tragic fiasco which led to the execution of the
hapless young Monmouth and the hanging of a number of
poor, misled peasants in the west of England.

To William Penn, now settled with his family in Sussex
and working to help Quakers in distress, the accession of
James II brought new hope. The king, when he was Duke
of York and Lord High Admiral, had been very friendly towards Sir William Penn and had given his word that he
would do what he could for his friend's son.

That James truly believed in the desirability of general

religious toleration for its own sake and not merely as a way to free Catholics from their disabilities, seems more than probable, Whig history to the contrary notwithstanding. His concept of English kingship, however, was that of medieval times and his hope of restoring it to its old status was a will o' the wisp which led to his downfall. Perhaps Penn shared the king's ideas, for his attitude to the people of Pennsylvania was very much that of a king, a loving father who would give his children what they wished—even self-government.

The prospects of the English Quakers at the beginning of James II's reign took on a rosy look. William Penn, the Friends' spokesman and champion, had access all the time to the royal presence and it was known that he and the king saw eye to eye on religious toleration. To a petition setting forth the plight of fifteen to sixteen hundred Quakers in prison the king responded with a proclamation, in the spring of 1685, suspending all prosecutions of them and immediately releasing those who were in jail merely for the refusal to take oaths. There was also an interim settlement of the boundary dispute with the Maryland proprietor. The eastern portion of the Delaware territories was awarded to Lord Baltimore, while the western area was to be under crown control until a new title to it could be set up for Penn. He was now living in London with his wife and children. He was a frequent visitor at Court, always, of course, wearing his hat, a breach of courtly etiquette which King James, though lacking his brother's satirical sense of humour, seems to have accepted good-naturedly.

Until the blow fell in 1688 Penn does not appear to have guessed how precarious was his position in England. The tide was running against James II because of the widespread hostility to his religion and his own maladroit actions which aggravated that hostility. Penn himself, illogical as it sounds, came in for a measure of anti-Catholic suspicion because of his friendship with the king. He was accused of being a crypto-Catholic and even a Jesuit; the latter charge was based on the fact that he had sometimes been seen in the company of Father Petre, James' Jesuit adviser. Even so intelligent a churchman as John Tillotson, the future archbishop of Canterbury, suspected that Penn was secretly a Catholic, but had the generosity to disavow these suspicions on Penn's assurance that they were groundless. Penn, unlike some of the early Quakers, was invariably on good terms with the Anglican clergy and he disapproved of the brawling in churches some of the brethren regarded as a laudable way of bearing witness against the "superstitions" of Anglican worship.

As the founder of Pennsylvania and the compiler of its *Frame of Government* Penn may be regarded as possessed of qualities of statesmanship, but he lacked the qualities of a politician. It is proof of this and perhaps of his own straightforwardness that he let himself become involved in James II's quarrel with the fellows of Oxford's Magdalen College when the king sought to impose his nominee, a Catholic, upon the voting dons. In the spring of 1688, when James had played into the hands of his enemies by the imprisonment of the seven bishops for their refusal to order the reading of the Declaration of Indulgence from their pulpits, Penn awakened to the danger—to his royal friend and to his fellow-Quakers. It was too late. By the end of the year William, Prince of Orange, and his wife Mary, James' elder daughter by his first marriage, were king and queen of England. James, with his wife and his infant son, were exiles, with their Court of St. Germain under the protection of Louis XIV.

Penn now found himself suspect in the eyes of the triumphant Whigs. William and his wife were too intelligent to believe the crypto-Catholic and Jesuit canards, but they were hostile to Penn. He was, after all, an out-and-out Jacobite, loyal to the House of Stuart; he had been something of a royal favourite and the fate of royal favourites when their patrons are deposed is proverbial. Almost overnight he had fallen from his privileged position and was officially a criminal suspect on bail, for he had been haled before the Lords of the Council, questioned closely and released under a £6,000 surety. He left London for his place in Sussex to await events. A long interview with King William III seems to have convinced that dour Dutchman that Penn was innocent of any intention to partake in attempts to subvert the new order. It also gave William a chance to see something of what moral courage was, for Penn assured him that while he would avoid the guilt of conspiracy, he would not be mealy-mouthed about an old friendship. "Since he had loved King James in his prosperity, he should not hate him in his adversity." It was a very different state of mind from that of William's Whig supporters. Penn was kept in mild imprisonment for a time, but was set free before Christmas.

There was more trouble for him in 1690. While the king was in Ireland, Queen Mary included Penn's name in a proclamation denouncing suspected "traitors." Some of the men listed were put in the Tower, but Penn was allowed bail on the score of ill-health. Finally, he was freed altogether; there had been no specific charge against him. It is not surprising that he began to think of an early voyage to his beloved Pennsylvania. He saw George Fox, then a dying man, about this time. The Quaker founder's last plea to his friend and disciple was to remember the Friends across the Atlantic.

The next few years were full of vicissitudes. Informers bore false witness against Penn and he was compelled to live for a time in hiding, a pariah in his own country. Then

came bad news, of political and religious quarrels, schisms
and moral deterioration in his American province. The Holy
Experiment of a Quaker Utopia had failed. Pennsylvania
had joined with New York, the East and West New Jerseys,
Connecticut and Delaware to take up arms and oppose by
force the French and their Indian allies. Harassed and depressed, Penn sought consolation in spiritual reveries and
the stimulus of writing. The *Fruits of Solitude,* one of the
anthologies of religious and prudential maxims in the fashion of the times, was the outcome of this enforced retirement
from more active life.

Then, late in 1693, came the first piece of good news in a
long time. Some of his friends—Tillotson, the archbishop-
to-be, now that his suspicions were removed, a loyal de-
fender, John Locke the philosopher, Somers, a bright young
Whig lawyer of liberal ideas, Lord Rochester and several
other peers—petitioned the king in Penn's favour. William
III, an unpredictable man, generally cold and aloof, was in
a melting mood that day. He spoke in a kindly manner of
the Quaker Jacobite and said he was free to do as he would.
Henry Sidney carried a written confirmation of this to Penn,
who was afraid at first that it was a pardon rather than a
recognition of his integrity. Like Fox in jail in Worcester
many years before and Locke as an exile in Holland, he
said, "Pardon? For what? I have done no wrong." The king
allowed a friendly peer to reassure Penn; he was free without conditions or qualifications. He might return to his
American province if he wished.

Six years passed by before Penn crossed the Atlantic
again. The year after the restoration to royal favour his wife
Gulielma died (February 23, 1694). He had loved her
dearly, as "one in a thousand," and for a time he was borne
down by his grief. Pastoral journeys and talks at Quaker
Meetings were the anodyne for his sorrow. These talks or

addresses—for to call them sermons savoured of ritual and a professional ministry—were much appreciated in his day. The secret of his popularity as a religious teacher is lost to us. Probably it was chiefly due to his kind and generous nature, to a good, resonant voice and to his hearers' knowledge of what he had done and suffered in the cause. His devotional writing is prolix, often turgid and tending to platitude and when he descends to whimsy, as he sometimes does in his letters, it is heavy-handed.

The summer of 1694 brought him the satisfaction of being once again put in full authority over his American province. The governor of New York, called upon to care for the two provinces, had not been a success. A military man, he had a soldier's outlook on life, but the Pennsylvanians of the Council and the Assembly were not given to being ordered about brusquely as though on a parade ground. Moreover, they disliked their acting governor's morals; he was reputedly overfond of wine and women. William III's government was now willing to authorize Penn's immediate return to the colony, but he could not yet bring himself to accept the terms on which he might go, namely, the raising of a militia for possible warfare with the French. That, he felt, would destroy the last vestiges of his Holy Experiment. Meanwhile he was hard put to it to raise enough money to keep up his house in Sussex and to educate his children. We read of his selling the timber on his estate to meet these expenses.

There was something of a sensation among the Quakers in 1696. Their leader and benefactor, a staid householder and father of a family, had fallen in love at the age of fifty-two and was about to marry again. He had met his beloved in the course of his missionary journeys in the west of England. She was a Miss Hannah Callowhill, the daughter of a well-to-do merchant in Bristol. She was a level-headed woman with a gift for business and we are told that she had no striking attributes of physical beauty. Penn, however, in middle age was still capable of youthful ardour, whether in religion or love. It is pleasing to find him, fifty-two and inclining to portliness, writing thus to the merchant's daughter: "I cannot forbear to write where I cannot forbear to love as I love my dearest Hannah, and if that be a fault, till she ceases to be lovely I need no apology for it." The monthly Meeting near Penn's home in Sussex duly approved the espousal after the members had looked into the matter; the couple were married in February.

A few weeks later happiness was turned to sorrow by the death of Penn's elder son Springett. He had from birth been a sickly child, and with poor health and the inability to live and grow as other children he had developed a precocious piety. Penn wrote an extended obituary, *Sorrow and Joy,* in the loss and end of Springett Penn. To his father the poor youth was indeed a paragon, an exemplar of Christian piety and all the virtues. Reading of him we sadly conclude that he must have been a singularly priggish youngster. A younger son, William, gave no promise of juvenile piety. By Quaker standards he turned out badly, nor did the daughter Letitia make up for him; she was always tepid towards the Friends' devotional life and in adult years broke away from the movement.

At length, in the autumn of 1699 Penn set out for America again, sailing in the *Canterbury* with his wife, Hannah, and Letitia, a daughter of the first marriage. William, the younger son, did not go; he preferred the amenities of English life. To us, who know the sequel to this journey, there is pathos in the second departure for the Quaker Promised Land, the Holy Experiment that had already failed. Although Penn knew part of the depressing reality he did not know it all. When he was once again in the midst of his people, he may have thought, surely they would rally round him, forget their schisms and squabbles and help to build the New Jerusalem among the wooded hills of Pennsylvania.

Of one factor making for humiliation and much distress in the future he was happily unaware as he sailed across the Atlantic. Penn had the defects of his qualities, we may say of his very virtues. He was a philanthropist in the strict derivative meaning of the word, optimistic about human nature, without the Calvinistic rigour of other seventeenth century creeds, but he was no judge of men or, anyhow, singularly inept at spotting a bad man. He had put his financial affairs in the hands of a very bad man. This was Philip Ford of Bristol, to whom he had given virtual power of attorney. Ford bore the name of Quaker, but he was a sad departure from Quaker standards of integrity. Penn, calumniated by his enemies, worn down by bereavements and beset by rapidly mounting debts, borrowed money from Ford, allowing him to hold the American estate as collateral security. In plain terms, he had taken out a mortgage on Pennsylvania as the price of a "friendly" loan. Even that was not the whole of the affair, as Penn was to discover before very long.

At the end of November the travellers disembarked at Chester and went on by boat to Philadelphia. In February Hannah Penn gave birth to her first child, John, in the house her husband had rented for the winter. It was a severe winter, with great ice floes on the Delaware River and there were ice storms, freezing rain, that coated the forest trees, "as if candied" Penn reported. In spite of his fifty-five years, his tendency to stoutness, the bitter weather, his wife's confinement, he still spent himself in work for the Quaker cause. From Meeting to Meeting he travelled, preaching, praying, giving his approval to Quaker marriages, organizing a Quaker youth movement.

For a brief time he was able to forget the nagging cares of

government and the burden of indebtedness. Almost imperceptibly he had come to accept the idea of a secular government operating alongside a religious movement, but not fused with it or even much affected by it. He had reached this point when he wrote his *Essay on the Peace of Europe,* an anticipation of the ideals which prompted the setting up of the League of Nations and our United Nations. Penn's scheme, like its more grandiose successors, failed to find a way of making sure that aggressors would be controlled. By the time he took up residence in Pennsylvania the second time, he had made a frank declaration of his concept of government. "Government is not a means, but an end," he says, and states that he was "grieved" to hear people make it "a matter of religion." The Holy Experiment had been replaced by something akin to the nineteenth century "Free church in a free state" of the Abbé de Lamennais.

The happiness of the early months in Pennsylvania this time was short-lived. By 1699 the Assembly, designed as an advisory body only, with veto powers over the Council's lawmaking, had become a legislature. Penn now found it quarrelsome, obstructionist, a hodge-podge of cliques, secular and religious. Almost at once it ran foul of the founder's humanitarian ideals. Two bills, which he had very much at heart, were before the Assembly for ratification. One was to forbid the sale of rum to the Indians, the other to regularize the marriages of Negro slaves.

The question of slavery, so courageously tackled by the Quaker saint John Woolman in the next century, was beginning to disturb the Quaker conscience. Penn himself was an owner of slaves, although their position at Pennsbury was to prove happier than that of most indentured servants and their freedom after a number of years service was provided for. Penn's moral sense was affronted by the attitude of a large number of the wealthier colonists. They saw slaves only as negotiable chattels, valuable stock whose fertility was an asset. They saw no reason for lessening their wealth by any scruples about monogamy and Christian marriage in the slaves' quarters on their estates. The Assembly threw out both the bills.

Bitterly disappointed at seeing Christian morality as well as his own wishes thus flouted, Penn betook himself to his country manor as summer drew near. His vexations could be put aside for a while when he set to work landscaping his gardens—with exotic trees and shrubs to delight his Scots gardener—and helping the efficient housewife Hannah Penn to furnish the house. There is a gratifyingly un-Puritan touch about his care for good food and drink in the house. He instructs his agent to buy specified delicacies—chocolate, a flitch of bacon, Madeira wine and coffee; he is insistent on the coffee, expensive as it was, thus setting the precedent for a coffee-drinking North America. Moreover, he liked to feel that others were sharing these pleasures. He was careful to tell his secretary to see to the entertainment of the sea captains who arrived at Philadelphia. They were to be given "a small collation with a bottle of wine." For the workmen engaged on the Pennsbury estate he ordered a fresh supply of rum; the stocks were running low and he did not wish to seem niggardly towards these honest fellows.

Among the Indians of the province there was no lessening of the respect and affection towards the man who had met them unarmed and had said he regarded them as equals and fellow-Christians. *Onas* was always welcome in their settlements and as time went on and his difficulties with his white citizens multiplied, he found his chief solace, next to his domestic life, in the company of the red men. He was more than loved by them; he was idolized.

The first blow in a series of misfortunes fell on Penn in

the summer of 1700. An order from England, which in the original patent retained authority over the laws of Pennsylvania, told him to provide a contribution of * £350 to New York for aid in defending her frontier. The Assembly members whined about their poverty when the order was put before them and did not hesitate to make it clear the lord-proprietor ought to foot the bill for defence himself. That was not the worst of it. Penn was a zealous Quaker, committed to George Fox's belief in non-violence, yet he could not shut his eyes to the reasonableness of the royal demand. It was a question of conscience and he saw no easy answer to it—even if he forgot for the moment that he had promised King William III to carry out loyally all orders from the crown as to the running of his colony.

The Assembly was not only unco-operative about the money for defence; they would not vote a sum adequate to the day-by-day administration of Pennsylvania. Penn himself was deep in debt, as he pointed out to these callous politicians, for expenses he had incurred on their account in the long dispute over the Maryland claims. So charged with bitterness and opposition was the atmosphere that he was convinced he could do no good by staying in Pennsylvania at that time. He prepared to sail back to England. We know that he intended to go back to America, for he sought to persuade his wife Hannah and Tishe (Letitia), his daughter, to stay at Pennsbury and await his return. They would not be persuaded; colonial life had lost its charm for Hannah; it never had any for Tishe.

The rest of Penn's story is a sad anti-climax. His financial affairs were going from bad to worse. His dream of going back to America and living the quiet, retired life of a colo-

---

* Sums quoted in sterling in Penn's time should be multiplied by at least 6 or 7 to give an adequate idea of their value in terms of English money at the present time.

nial gentleman in the bosom of his family never became a reality. He remained in England, more or less suspect in the eyes of his suspicious king, William III, and worried by reports of quarrels and confusion in Pennsylvania. At one time he had hoped to be asked back as governor, at a salary of £600 a year, leaving to the elected bodies all legislative power. They refused to raise the £600.

When William III died in 1702 after injuries caused when his horse stumbled on a mole hill, Penn the Jacobite can hardly have felt much sorrow, although Penn the Quaker may have drawn the line at joining the other Jacobites in drinking the health of the little gentleman in black velvet. Something of the glory of the good old days when he was befriended by the Papist King James II was revived for him once the period of court mourning was over. He was again in favour with royalty and found a good friend in the thoroughly Protestant Queen Anne. She, the younger daughter of his old friend James and now ruler of the kingdom which had rejected her father, liked Penn's Jacobite sympathies and respected his decorous Quaker piety. The queen and the elderly Quaker hobnobbed over their dishes of tea in Kensington Palace.

This seeming dawn of happier days as the eighteenth century opened was, alas!, a false dawn. To monetary worries parental ones were now added. After the depressingly pious Springett had died, Penn fastened his affection and his hopes on the younger son, William, a lively and high-spirited youth, quite unlike his devout brother. William nearly broke his father's heart. He trod the primrose path, showed an un-Quakerish contempt for thrift and industry and, although still nominally a Friend, made no pretence of living like a Friend. His father did what was often done with troublesome sons, then and later—sent him overseas. He was to be cured of his wild oat sowing by the simplicity of life in Pennsylvania, visits to Penn's Indian friends and the company of God-fearing Philadelphia Quakers. The father drew up a list of the last-named for his son's guidance. William must have found these good citizens almost comically uncongenial.

Penn's failure to detect the flaws in men's characters led him further astray in dealing with his problem child. The governor of Pennsylvania had died recently and it was for Penn, as proprietor, to appoint a successor. He chose a certain Colonel Evans, not for his military experience, for he seems to have had none, but because he appeared to be a young man who would have a good influence on William. Colonel Evans was, unfortunately, very much a man who shared the tastes of William Penn, Jr. They drank, gamed and whored together and Evans helped young Penn to dispose of his patrimony. William crowned his misdeeds in Philadelphia by being arrested for the offence, fashionable among well-born young hooligans, of assaulting the watch. Governor Evans pulled wires for his release, but could not prevent a grand jury from bringing up the offender in the mayoral court. The young man, indignant, angry and humiliated, cursed all American Quakers and boarded the next ship for England.

His father travelled from Sussex and met him near London for a serious talk and a discussion of his future. Of the interview we know chiefly of Penn's indignation against the unenlightened Philadelphia Quakers and their maladroit handling of his child. They had, he said, "stumbled him from the blessed truth."

Letitia—Tishe in the family—was not much consolation for the misdeeds of her brother. She broke away from Quaker piety and submission to Quaker control and married one William Aubrey. Penn, with his habitual good nature, welcomed the son-in-law with open arms, but soon found him a new source of worry. Mr. Aubrey was of the opinion that a lord-proprietor, with all the wealth of a North American province at his disposal, could easily finance his daughter's husband whenever he needed money. When Penn was unable to meet his excessive demands, he became abusive. Writing to his faithful secretary Logan in Philadelphia and urging him to raise what money he could, the harassed father-in-law complains of his "son Aubrey," of whom he would gladly be rid. "He has a bitter tongue, and I wish I had nothing to do with him in money matters."

While Penn was thus scraping the bottom of the barrel and trying to cope with his difficult offspring, the worst blow of all fell on him. The full extent of Ford's villainy came to light. The first Philip Ford had died in 1702, but he left a widow and a son, also Philip, both as crooked as himself. Two years after her husband's death Mrs. Ford and the younger Philip set to work. They presented a bill for about £14,000; the alternative to payment was the foreclosing of a mortgage on Penn's patent, that is, on the whole of Pennsylvania.

In desperation Penn did what he should long since have done—checked the accounts. He had indeed borrowed some £16,000 altogether, but he had repaid nearly £18,000. What, then, could be owing except a small amount of interest? Ford had charged up interest semi-annually to swell the account, but even so Penn could not see that he owed more than £4,000 and he offered that sum in settlement. The Fords still held out and then the too-trusting Penn, who had not thought to look into papers he signed for the good Friend Philip, discovered that what he had thought was a mortgage was in fact a bill of sale—for the territory of Pennsylvania! Widow Ford and her son had the effrontery to take the case to court and, amazing as it sounds to us, in 1707 judgment was given against Penn. Early in the new year, as he was leaving a Meeting in London one Sunday morning, a writ was served on him. Two Quaker friends came to his rescue, offered to stand surety and obtained a writ of *Habeas corpus*. This saved him from the final humiliation of being arrested and haled off to prison, but he had to accept voluntary detention by taking rooms in the Fleet.

Mrs. Ford and her son naturally had great confidence in their lucky star after this. They claimed to have become the lawful proprietors of Pennsylvania and sought to have a new charter drawn up in their own names. At last they had overreached themselves. The Lord-Chancellor decided against their claim and ruled that on repayment of the original loan Penn would recover all his rights in Pennsylvania. Philip Ford now proposed a compromise—the withdrawal of all further claims if Penn would settle for £6,800. Although Penn sold his Sussex house and collected such small sums as he could, he would still have been unable to make the settlement had not his father-in-law, the Bristol merchant, and a few other generous Friends come to his rescue. His hopes of going back to America rose again and he was full of optimism on getting a report of a silver mine that was to restore his fortunes. Again he had to face a disappointment; the mine was valueless. It is not surprising that after all these vicissitudes he was anxious to sell his patent back to the crown. The negotiations hung fire for the rest of his life because of his unwillingness to surrender full authority and all revenue in the colony.

In spite of everything life was still not without its consolations. Although Quakers remained a "peculiar people" in the eyes of most of their countrymen, the days of violent persecution were over. Penn, known to be on good terms with the queen, was generally treated with respect. He had become a Quaker elder statesman, the accepted head of deputations to royalty or persons in high station. Dean

Swift, in his *Journal to Stella,* records such an occasion, the visit of a Quaker delegation to the Duke of Ormonde. "My friend Penn came there, Will Penn the Quaker, at the head of his brethren, to thank the Duke for his kindness to their people in Ireland. To see a dozen scoundrels with their hats on, and the Duke complimenting with his off, was a good sight enough."

As the years went by and old acerbities were forgotten, the hearts of the Philadelphia legislators softened towards their aging lord-proprietor. For a time he still clung to hopes that before he reached the Biblical threescore years and ten he would cross the Atlantic and address the American Friends in fervent Meetings or sit in grave converse with the Indians who loved him.

It was too late for these happy dreams to come true. One day in 1712, as he was writing at his desk, he felt a sudden twinge of pain in his hand and found he was unable to hold and guide the quill. He diagnosed the trouble as incipient gout, but actually it was the first warning of a stroke that he suffered shortly after. His wife took him to their country home in Berkshire and for a time he appeared to be doing well, but a second stroke followed, affecting his speech and his mind.

The clouding over of that active brain took a merciful form, for he lost all memory of his sorrows and disappointments and settled into a state of childlike unconcern, glad to wander about the house and garden. He would gaze for a while at the flowers and shrubs he had always loved and from time to time come out of his absorption with them to play with his grandchildren as though himself their contemporary. His friend Queen Anne died and was succeeded by the Hanoverian prince who became George I, but Penn was unaware that the Stuarts, the family to which he had been loyal, no longer ruled England. His own end came peacefully and rather unexpectedly at the end of July, 1768, when he was in his seventy-fourth year. Within the week his body was taken to the Friends' burial ground at Chalfont St. Giles, in Buckinghamshire. There his remains lie with those of Gulielma, his first wife, and Springett, his son, in the cemetery of Jordans. It is a place of pilgrimage for Friends and, as he would have wished, for many who are not Friends but who honour his memory as that of a man whose outstanding trait was, simply, human goodness.

Amid the disillusionments of his later years while his mind was still active, Penn may have thought of his Holy Experiment as a total failure. Could he, however, have been granted prophetic foresight of the course of history, he would have been consoled for the earlier slings and arrows. As one who had written, as far back as 1696, a pamphlet to advocate a federation of the various English colonies in North America, he would have rejoiced to hear of the *United* States of America. With his strong royalist loyalty, though, he would have needed much prescience to see in the War of Independence and the building of the Republic a more fertile experiment than his own. He would, of course, have been happy to know that the State of Pennsylvania would be whole-hearted in its rejection of slavery and of secession. And one can imagine his pleased surprise to see his much abused *Frame of Government* seriously studied and pondered by the constitution-makers who assembled in his Philadelphia to put together their frame of government for a mighty nation.

5

★ ★ ★ ★ ★

James Oglethorpe,
SOLDIER-PHILANTHROPIST
IN GEORGIA

By a happy paradox soldiers, whose trade of necessity calls
on them to kill some of their fellow men, have often been
associated with efforts to serve their fellows, spending themselves in adding to the welfare of mankind. We think of
Robert E. Lee's years of devotion to the young men of the
post-bellum Southern States when he was president of
Washington College, later the Washington and Lee University, or of Baden-Powell's gift to the boys of all nations
when he started the Boy Scout movement. General Oglethorpe, whose long life began in the last years of the seventeenth century and spanned most of the eighteenth, stands
worthily with these later exemplars of the humanity which
is, perhaps, stimulated by the sight of war with its squalor
and its suffering. Hogarth and Rowlandson have accus-
tomed us to think too much of the brutality and viciousness

of eighteenth century life. We should bear in mind that the era of Gin Alley and the Harlot's Progress was also the time when European man began to develop a sensitive social conscience and to concern himself with the hard fate of orphans, prisoners, ruined debtors, Negro slaves. The word *philanthropist* too often evokes a picture of an incredibly rich man writing large cheques for good causes, administered by a battalion of "executives." The Greek etymology of the word is worth remembering—one who loves his fellow men and, like anyone who loves anyone else, seeks to serve the beloved. Such was James Edward Oglethorpe.

The family name of Oglethorpe lives in English history as that of the bishop who officiated at the coronation of Queen Elizabeth I in 1559. The young queen had made it clear she was going to walk in the Anglican footsteps of her father, Henry VIII, not in the Roman ones of her half-sister, Mary I. All the Marian bishops refused to have any part in the coronation service, all but Owen Oglethorpe, bishop of Carlisle. The queen and he came to terms; she would allow the Catholic ritual; he would place the crown on her head. This act of compliance did him little good. Queen and bishop fell out over the elevation of the Host and she soon put him out of his diocese and threw him into prison, and he died in 1560. His family was a Yorkshire one, his father a George Oglethorpe who was thought by the later Oglethorpes to have been responsible for a bar sinister in the episcopal coat of arms. Bishop Owen, said the general's brother, "was an Oglethorpe, but of a spurious race." George Oglethorpe and his bride were, indeed, espoused but not yet married when the future bishop was born.

The more distant ancestors of the founder of Georgia need not concern us except in so far as three distinguishing traits run through their history and are all three prominent in the general's life. The first is their loyalty to the crown; they fought as royalists in the Civil War and were ardent Jacobites after the revolution of 1688. General Oglethorpe's transfer of loyalty to the Hanoverian line may be seen as a defection or as common sense realism according to one's prejudices. In the second place, the Oglethorpes were a soldierly clan, and, thirdly, they held a family tradition of serving the nation by membership in Parliament.

The future general's father, Theophilus, born in the middle of the seventeenth century, was very much a soldier. He had his training under the great Turenne and for a time served in the army of Louis XIV. Then, when he was a major of dragoons, at the age of thirty, serving Charles II in England, he fell in love with Ellen, or Eleanor, Wall, an attractive and spirited young Irishwoman. She was of good family, but in reduced circumstances—as were most of the Irish after Cromwell had been in their country. At the time Major Oglethorpe wooed and married her, she was working as head laundress and sempstress to the king. She had entered his service through Louise de Quéroualle, his French mistress who became Duchess of Portsmouth. The supervision of Charles II's laundry was a better job than it sounds, as it carried a salary of two thousand pounds a year. Theophilus continued serving in the royal forces under James II and took part in the suppression of the Duke of Monmouth's rebellion in 1685. Soon he was knighted and took his seat in Parliament and we hear of his supporting Pepys in his advocacy of systematic naval training. The son who was to become the colonizer of Georgia was born in London in 1696* and was baptized in the church of St. Martin's-in-the-Fields by the Archbishop of Canterbury, Dr. Tenison.

---

* Not 1688, a year erroneously quoted by certain biographers who were misled by the record of an earlier child called James who died in infancy in 1690.

The time of James' birth and infancy was an anxious one for the Oglethorpes. Known as ardent Jacobites after the deposition of James II, they were suspect when William and Mary ruled. Sir Theophilus Oglethorpe was denounced, as was William Penn, in the proclamation which Queen Mary issued while her husband, William III, was in Ireland. Nothing seems to have been done against these hypothetical "traitors" by the usurping Dutchman and it is pretty certain that a few years later both the dashing army baronet and the zealous Quaker managed to send assurances of their loyalty to the exiled king in France. In the year of our James' birth, however, the Oglethorpes found it convenient to take the oath of loyalty to William III. This did not prevent Lady Oglethorpe, "so cunning a devil," as Swift called her, from devoting herself to a succession of Jacobite activities. Her husband died, when only fifty-one, in 1702, leaving her with seven children to care for. Another grievous blow fell on her two years later; her eldest son, Lewis, died of wounds while serving as A.D.C. to the Duke of Marlborough. The duke appears to have had no prejudice against so intransigent a Jacobite as Eleanor Oglethorpe, who appealed to him on behalf of her male children. The girls she fended for very successfully, establishing two of them in the Jacobite court in exile at Saint Germain and marrying off another to a French nobleman—thirty years the girl's senior, a hunchback disfigured by smallpox. One son, another Theophilus, was manoeuvred into a job in India, started well and then was sent home in disgrace, after piling up debts. Later, however, he got into Parliament.

It was now time to do something for the younger son, James Edward, and again the irrepressible Eleanor Oglethorpe appealed to the great Marlborough. He was no longer in favour with Queen Anne, but somehow or other Lady Oglethorpe pulled wires successfully and we hear of

James with a lieutenant's commission in Her Majesty's First
Regiment of Foot Guards when he was about seventeen. We
know nothing of his boyhood. It must have been a wholesome one, for he was always, into extreme old age, healthy,
vigorous and active. His early education must have given
him a sound enough foundation for his sojourn at Eton and
at Oxford and for his later Parliamentary work. From his
letters, however, it is evident that he was allowed a good
deal of freedom in spelling, even for those days.

Young James Oglethorpe's receiving an army commission
did not, as we might have expected, lead directly to military
service; it led to boarding school! Whether his mother was
dissatisfied with his early education or she wished him to
have the social cachet of attending a good school and a
university we do not know. Anyhow, this seventeen-year-
old, with his army commission just signed by good Queen
Anne, was packed off to Eton College. He was there only a
short time, which suggests that social rather than academic
distinction was in Lady Oglethorpe's mind. In 1714, the
year Queen Anne died, he went to the university—Oxford,
predominantly Tory and Jacobite in sentiment, and to the
most strongly Jacobite of its colleges, Corpus Christi. A non-
juring bishop, one of Lady Oglethorpe's Jacobite friends,
recommended James to the president of the college as "a
very ingenious, understanding and well-bred youth." Of
what he did at Oxford and what his academic interests
were, we are as ignorant as we are about his life at Eton. It
is interesting to know that one of his associates may well
have been Theophilus Leigh, a grand-uncle of Jane Austen.

Fresh from the Jacobite family circle and influenced by
his mother's fervent loyalty to the Stuarts, young Oglethorpe
was in his element at Oxford. When Queen Anne died, the
scholars cut down to a minimum the celebrations for her
successor, the Hanoverian George I, and when, next year,

the observance of the king's birthday was ordered, the Jacobite Oxonians by a gala celebration the next day—com-
memorated Charles II's birthday. That year, moreover, was
1715, marked by the unsuccessful attempt of James II's son,
James III to good Jacobites, the Old Pretender to the Whigs,
to regain the throne of England. There were riotous clashes
in Oxford between "town," the Hanoverian bourgeoisie, and
"gown," the Jacobite students.

Oglethorpe stayed in Oxford University somewhat longer
than in Eton College. He was still in residence in 1716, had
his name on his college register in 1719 and kept it there
until 1727. We do not know if he lived or studied there
after 1716. Despite his family's Jacobite sympathies, his
army commission was renewed by George I, but James resigned it before leaving the university, not from any aversion to soldiering, but because of his desire to travel abroad.

For many years the Oglethorpes, despite their very English roots in Yorkshire's West Riding, had much contact with
France. The attractive young superintendent of royal laun-
dering, Eleanor, or Ellen, Wall from Tipperary, was originally in the service of Charles II's mistress, Louise de Quéroualle, the "French whore," as Nell Gwynn, with national-
ity rather than morals in mind, called her. When James II
had been forced into exile and set up his court at Saint
Germain under the protection of Louis XIV, the Oglethropes
were constantly back and forth across the English Channel.
Theophilus, an older brother of James, lived permanently
on the continent, and three of his sisters, one of them married to a French marquis, made their homes in France. It
was natural for James to seek a fuller and more exciting life
overseas. In 1716 he left Oxford and went to Paris to study
military science in its Academy, where James Keith, a future
field marshal, was a fellow-student. There was fighting in
central and eastern Europe, where Prince Eugene of Savoy

was campaigning against the Turks. To keep the students in Paris at their books and lectures and possibly to avoid international squabbles, the French government forbade the young men to engage in foreign army service. James Oglethorpe managed to get round this, made his escape and offered himself to Prince Eugene, who at once took him on as his aide-de-camp.

Boswell, who as a young man was a friend and admirer of General Oglethorpe in the latter's old age, has preserved an anecdote recording James' spirited treatment of an aristocratic snob. At a military dinner party a prince of Württemberg set to work arrogantly to humiliate the junior English volunteer officer by flipping some wine from his glass into the aide-de-camp's face. James took the affront with imperturbable good humour, smiled across the table at the princely lout and with the remark, "That's a good joke, but we do it much better in England," contrived to shoot the contents of a full wineglass into the other's face. One is gratified to read that this riposte drew forth the admiration and laughter of the whole company.

Although he was a staff officer in personal attendance on a prince, James was no drawing room warrior. He took part in the fierce struggle at the siege of Belgrade in the summer of 1717, when a faithful batman was killed fighting at his side. In a letter to one of his sisters James describes the engagement as "very bloody and sharp."

When the Turkish campaign was over in the autumn of 1717 James took leave of his chief and set out on his travels again. He wished to visit his sisters in Paris, but planned to go by way of Turin so as to see his elder brother Theophilus. The Oglethorpes were an affectionate family and, scattered geographically, were united by family feeling and by their Jacobitism. Theophilus' Stuart loyalty had been rewarded by a Jacobite title of nobility: he was Baron Oglethorpe of

Oglethorpe, Yorkshire, with reversion to his brother James should there be no male heir. Theophilus felt that Jacobite sentiments had taken firm root in Jamie's soul, for he wrote to the Duke of Mar, "I am very well satisfied with him and love him the more, because I see he is entirely affectionate to the king (i.e. James III) and that the Germans have not in the least prevailed on him." Some time after this, "Jamie" went to Urbino to kiss the royal hands and he made an excellent impression on the royal mind. When Oglethorpe was making ready to go back to England and look after the family seat near Godalming, his sister Fanny wrote to a Jacobite friend, "Jimmy is here and going home, very sensible of the goodness *the King* had for him, which he'll never forget." In the light of after events one may question whether James Oglethorpe's undoubted affection for the Stuarts was quite as intense as his brother's and his sisters'. Theophilus, indeed, was criticized by one of the leaders for his "imprudent zeal."

In 1719 James was settled on the family's Surrey estate, Westbrook, near Godalming, deputizing for brother Theophilus, now a permanent expatriate. The older brother had not been a great success as squire. He was too much the *enthusiast*—the word had a perjorative meaning in the eighteenth century—and got into squabbles with the local parsons, doubtless Whigs who, outwardly at least, were pro-Hanoverian. James' Jacobitism seems to have had no impact on the Surrey gentry, while his interest in local affairs made him popular. He made a good impression by a subscription for repairs to the market building, just as, twenty years later, when he was a general, he again won local approval by another gift of money for repairs to the town fire engines and for buying leather buckets.

Until he was twenty-five he lived tranquilly as a country squire, well regarded by those of his own class and pretty certainly loved by what were known as the lower orders. Although he could be irascible on occasion, he was of a kind and generous nature. The rigid social divisions of eighteenth century England were taken for granted as part of the natural order of things, but in James Oglethorpe the awareness of them was, at most, subconscious. When his sense of justice or his innate benevolence was aroused, then and later, he seems to have been unconscious of social status, colour or religious differences.

Some two to three years of idyllic life in rural Surrey were enough for James; his energy and his interest in the world around him called for a wider field than a country seat and the affairs of a little country town. At the age of twenty-five he determined to stand* for Parliament. In the early spring of 1722 he and another Tory, Peter Burrell, were candidates to represent the town of Haslemere. They won the election in the face of strenuous opposition from the wealthy Whigs, who sought to have the election results declared invalid. They failed in this and had to content themselves with the scurrilous paper attacks that flourished in the days before modern libel laws.

Whig journalists, or any others for that matter, were little troubled by factual accuracy when a point had to be won, so in one of the London newspapers they made much of a little unpleasantness between rival politicos on the streets of Haslemere. Evidently an insult of some kind gave offence to the newly elected M.P., for, says the newspaper, "Mr. Oglethorpe drew his Sword there on Mr. Sharp (Secretary to the present Bishop of London) and wounded him in the Belly." The news item continued with a statement that "Mr. Oglethorpe was disarmed by Mr. Sharp's companion, a

---

* It may be noted that Americans *run* for public office, Britons *stand* for it. Perhaps the terminology is symptomatic of a difference of temperament on opposite sides of the Atlantic.

Captain Onslow, and his life spared through the magnanimity of the gallant captain." This garbled account, as he claimed it to be, roused Oglethorpe's indignation and, like all Englishmen with a grievance, he wrote to the newspaper. He admitted that "in the Scuffle Mr. Oglethorpe wounded Mr. Sharp in the Belly," but branded the rest of the account as untrue and gave his own version of the affair.

The young M.P.'s quick temper landed him in worse trouble less than a month later. He had, perhaps, been celebrating his Parliamentary victory with some cronies in London. The *Daily Journal*, the London paper which had angered him with its account of the Haslemere fracas, now came out with a more sensational item about James Oglethorpe, Esq., lately chosen at Haslemere in Surrey "a Representative for the new Parliament." Surely there was malice in the formal "Esq." as contrasted with the plain "Mr. Oglethorpe" of the previous article. At six in the morning James, "being overcome with Wine," entered some kind of proletarian dive—"a Night-House of evil Repute" says the paper—and mixed "with a promiscuous Company of Hackney-Coachmen, Shoe-Blackers, and Linkmen." This democratic freedom had an unhappy sequel. Oglethorpe had his pocket picked or, possibly, confused after a night's drinking, imagined he had lost the "piece of Gold." He accused a linkman of the theft, "high Words arose," violence followed and again that too-ready sword was drawn. The linkman was mortally wounded; James was taken before a justice, who committed him to the Gatehouse jail. Beyond the fact that the linkman died, we do not know the outcome. Probably Oglethorpe pleaded self-defence and was bound over. Anyhow, he was at liberty by the autumn, for when Parliament reopened (October, 1722), he took his seat as member for Haslemere.

The street brawl in Haslemere and the deplorable incident in London made an unpromising start for a young Parliamentarian's career. Happily the record of what followed forms a very different picture. The greatness of Oglethorpe's achievement in Georgia has diverted attention from the fruitful decade of Parliamentary work that preceded it. He was a hard-working member, active on innumerable committees dealing with a great variety of problems, always ready to speak and act for humanitarian measures or against injustice. During this period he threw himself ardently into the fight to improve the well-nigh hopeless lot of imprisoned debtors. It was his work for these unfortunates that inspired the first idea of what became his great colonizing scheme in Georgia.

His position in politics was an anomalous one: he was a Tory in a predominantly Whig Parliament, but, more than that, he was a known Jacobite. A law-abiding and constitutional Jacobite was a novelty not yet thoroughly assimilated by his contemporaries. To the Whigs, of course, it was something unsound, and that was to be expected, but it was more trying to know that your own family and friends, paying court to the exiled King James III over the water, also viewed you with suspicion.

The new member delivered his maiden speech in the spring of 1723. We may take it as symbolic that it set the pattern for the speaker's lifelong crusade for the victims of injustice, harshness or just sheer bad luck.

When, in 1720, James III, the Old Pretender, was blessed with a son, the future Bonnie Prince Charlie, there was a revival of Jacobite enthusiasm and activity. Various plots, real or imagined, titillated the public mind and when several years had gone by without anything being done the Prime Minister, Sir Robert Walpole, felt the time had come for a victim. He found one ready to hand, an aged Anglican cleric, Francis Atterbury, bishop of Rochester. Atterbury was a perfervid Jacobite, outspoken and unafraid, but innocent of everything except his scorn for the Whigs and the Hanoverian dynasty. Parliament was now considering a bill to punish this Jacobite prelate by a sentence of exile. Oglethorpe opposed the measure, shrewdly basing his argument on expediency. If the old prelate, admittedly "a man of great parts," were exiled he would join the real plotters overseas and give them the benefit of his knowledge and ability. Left in England he would remain "under the watchful eye of those in power." Oglethorpe moreover discounted the Whigs' fear of the Old Pretender, who, said the speaker, "had none but a company of silly fellows about him." Mr. Oglethorpe, M.P., Tory and Jacobite, had come a long way from the true-blue Jacobitism of his mother, his expatriate brother Theophilus and his sisters at the Stuart court of Saint Germain. The appeal for clemency, based on expediency, was unsuccessful; the bill was passed and the bishop was banished.

For half a dozen years following the Atterbury affair Oglethorpe was not in the public eye, although he did a great deal of committee work in such varied matters as the naturalization of foreigners—to help persecuted Jews—road works, fisheries, poor relief, the aftermath of the South Sea Bubble, and funds to rebuild the church of his own baptism, St. Martin's-in-the-Fields. His most important humanitarian work in these years was done on a committee for the relief of insolvent debtors, often the innocent victims of misfortune. They were the true forgotten men of the period, thrust into disease-ridden jails to repay debts which their imprisonment made it impossible to repay.

The six years of unspectacular committee work were followed by two achievements which gave Oglethorpe a worthy position among eighteenth century humanitarians. He had learned a great deal about the living conditions of sailors in the Royal Navy—bad food, cramped and insanitary quarters, ferocious punishments, sick and disabled sailors thrown on the parish or left to starve. One of the worst abuses was the cruel and arbitrary method of recruitment by the press gang when volunteers did not appear in sufficient numbers. In 1727 the methods of the press gang had been so callous that even the tough minds of eighteenth century Englishmen were shocked. Next year there was published a pamphlet entitled *The Sailor's Advocate,* which appeared anonymously, being described as "composed by most respectable members of the Opposition." This ascription was a cloak for the authorship of the member for Haslemere. He gave a forceful exposition of the evils of the press gang system, but without hysteria and with a logical attack on what he saw as a violation of English liberties implicit in *Magna Carta* and explicit in the Petition of Right. Unhappily the pamphlet had no effect on legislation. Although Britannia ruled the waves, it was a long time before she did anything much for her sailors.

The year following his attempt to help one of the most cruelly exploited bodies of his countrymen Oglethorpe threw himself with characteristic energy and tenacity into the other campaign which ranks with his Georgia scheme as a great philanthropic work of his era. Experienced in Parliamentary committee work and interested in social problems of the day, he was ready for the assignment that came his way in February, 1729. He undertook the chairmanship of a committee appointed, at his own insistent plea, to enquire into the state of the British jails. Lecky's history of eighteenth century England and the novels of Charles Dickens may give their readers some idea of the sad plight of debtors until comparatively modern times, but they fail to depict the full measure of the insolvent debtor's mental and physical misery, the hopelessness of his condition and the squalor of his surroundings. The whole thing was brought home to James Oglethorpe by a tragedy that touched him very closely.

One of his more intimate friends was Robert Castell, an architect. It was this man's misfortune to find himself at the mercy of his creditors, who were entitled by the law as it stood then and for a long time afterwards to seize—literally —the body of the debtor. That was bad enough, but it *was* the law. Alongside the operation of this harsh enactment had grown up a gross abuse, under a cover of legality, by which the jailers in the various debtors' prisons were in charge of the lodging and feeding of the inmates. This, of course, invited exploitation by grasping and brutal petty officials; one hears little of humane jailers. The prisoner who had hidden assets or well-to-do friends might buy a measure of comfort, at an exorbitant charge. The lot of the truly impoverished debtor without such advantages was intolerable. Oglethorpe's friend Castell had come to the end of such resources as he had when he was thrown into jail. Unable any longer to pay his jailer's crushing fees for his keep, he was put into overcrowded quarters where there was an epidemic of smallpox. He caught the infection and, left without medical care, nursing or proper food, died of the disease.

As he grew towards middle age the M.P. who in a street brawl had wounded a political rival "in the Belly" and in a low-class dive had killed a linkman in a scuffle gained control over his quick temper. We see him grow in moral stature as well as personal dignity as he gave himself to the service of his fellow men.

He pushed forward the enquiry into prison conditions with great assiduity, examining witnesses—some of them afterwards victimized by chains and solitary confinement—compiling minutes of meetings, exposing abuses and, finally, presenting to the Commons a set of three reports on the appalling evils that came to his committee's notice. The worst scoundrel in a whole rogues' gallery of prison officials was Thomas Bambridge, warden of the Fleet Prison. Near to him in infamy was William Acton of the Marshalsea Prison. Oglethorpe and his colleagues gave chapter and verse for a multitude of cases of torture, starvation and insanitary conditions. All that, however, was in the lower strata of officialdom. He struck higher at bribery and tampering with witnesses in Newgate, the apparent culprits being the Lord Chief Justice and a member of the Privy Council! "If this be law," Oglethorpe concluded, in putting the case before the House of Commons, "all England may be made one extended prison."

By the spring of 1730 he had gained a body of support in the House. Men of good will, Whigs and Tories, applauded his work as a reformer. The romantic Jacobitism of his mother and sisters had been replaced in his mind by a more farseeing crusade. His sound work on the committee and his speeches in Parliament met with a gratifying response. The Commons voted unanimously for measures of reform and for the criminal prosecution of the worst offenders, especially the brutal and corrupt Bambridge. Able lawyers among Oglethorpe's backers undertook the prosecution. It speaks ill for the judiciary that all the accused men were acquitted.

While he was attacking cruelty and extortion in England's jails Oglethorpe tackled another curse of the period, the excessive drinking of spirits. He was no Puritan and he did not make the Prohibitionist's error of regarding abstinence, especially when compulsory, as temperance. He sought to discourage the vicious gin-drinking recorded in Hogarth's pictures by raising the duty on imported spirits and at the same time encouraging "the drinking of malt liquors."

The work of Oglethorpe and his fellow committee members in the prison enquiry had given back their liberty to a number of unfortunates, but for many of them their freedom was a doubtful blessing. "The miserable wretches let out of Gaol are starving about the town for want of employment," Oglethorpe wrote to his friend Sir John Percival, later the Earl of Egmont, who had served with him on the committee. Oglethorpe's contemplation of the sad case of many of the released debtors was the first stage in his foundation of Georgia. As a beginning he proposed sending a hundred or so of the ex-prisoners to America; a small group of men who shared his ideas began to collect money for the undertaking.

With all his philanthropy and his zeal for social reform Oglethorpe was not just a starry-eyed dreamer of Utopias. An English government, especially one in an age of imperial expansion, would not vote material aid to idealists for Utopias. Oglethorpe had studied his map of North America and saw the need for a buffer state between the jealous and aggressive Spaniards in Florida and the English settlements to the north of them. Nor was there any insincerity in putting before the government a plan for a new colony south of Carolina as a means to imperial safety. Oglethorpe *was* an imperialist, in the sense that he wished to see England's dominions extended and her wealth increased. He would, too, have maintained stoutly that a British empire was a better thing for the world and posterity than a Spanish one—and who shall say he was wrong?

The idea of the settlement that became Georgia was not wholly new. A dozen years before Oglethorpe set to work on prison abuses, an enthusiastic but not very competent would-be colonizer had brought forth a scheme for a Margravate of Azilia to be set up in what is now part of the State of Georgia. A pamphlet, to attract settlers and capital, was published as *A Discourse concerning the designed establishment of a New Colony to the South of Carolina, the most delightful country in the Universe.* Nothing further happened and by 1730, when the original Carolina province was divided into North and South Carolina, England's colonial governors on the North American seaboard were uneasy not only about the Spaniards south of them, but also the French north and west of them and what we should nowadays call infiltration among the Indians.

One day in the early spring of 1730 Oglethorpe called on his friend Percival and, with a gift for passing his enthusiasm on to others, kept him entranced for three hours as he developed his plan to send a "colony of poor and honest industrious debtors to the West Indies" (i.e. North America). There were various obstacles to be overcome before the scheme got under way—the extreme caution of Sir Robert Walpole, the Whig premier, which to men of Oglethorpe's and Percival's ardent nature, looked like pusillanimity, and, in Oglethorpe's case, the question of retaining one's seat in Parliament while taking on the rule of a colony. There was also the usual time lag between the government's promises to supply funds and its payment of them.

By the early months of 1732 the difficulties had been smoothed out and the king signed the charter for the new colony on April 21. Oglethorpe and nineteen others were appointed "Trustees for establishing the colony of Georgia in America." James Oglethorpe, the former intransigent Jacobite, was now to become a hard-working servant of the Whig oligarchy, helping to rule in the name of the Hanoverian king George II a vast North American territory. It was indeed vast; on the north and south it was shut in between South Carolina and the disputed boundary of Spanish Florida, but westward it extended to the Pacific Ocean.

Money for the project had come in from various sources —gifts of individual donors and of corporate bodies, chari-

table legacies and some of the £20,000 originally voted for
Bishop Berkeley's plan for a Christian college in Bermuda.
The usual delay between promise and payment had oc-
curred, the scheme had come to seem impracticable and
Oglethorpe had written to the philosopher-bishop, then in
Rhode Island, asking him to help the Georgia project.
Berkeley returned to England and helped the Georgia Trus-
tees in a petition that some of the money might be diverted
to their scheme. Parliament agreed to a grant of £10,000.
Oglethorpe, with the destitute men from the debtors' prisons
still in mind, was delighted, but did not yet think of himself
as more than one member of a philanthropic committee.
Filial piety kept him close to his ageing mother in London.
Lady Oglethorpe was in her seventieth year; she had been
widowed thirty years earlier and, as time went on, looked
for affection and companionship to her youngest, and probably her favourite, son James.

The year 1732 was a decisive one in James Oglethorpe's
life. The Georgia Committee was set up in May. A few weeks
later, on June 19, Lady Oglethorpe, a venerable figure now,
whose ardent Jacobitism was regarded without bitterness in
Whig society, died in her house in Westminster. She was
buried beside her husband and her eldest son in St. James'
Church, Piccadilly. Even the Whig newspapers were re-
spectful and sympathetic. Then James Oglethorpe made
his great decision. By July the Trustees had chosen suitable
emigrants for the new colony from among deserving ex-
prisoners, Swiss volunteers and Salzburg Protestants seeking
religious freedom. Oglethorpe had no domestic ties now. He
offered himself as leader of the emigrant party. His colleagues on the committee, including his friend Percival,
showered congratulations on him, while the Reverend Samuel Wesley, father of the famous brothers John and Charles,
wrote a special ode on the subject. There was one hitch; the

committee urged delay, on the score of unpreparedness. Even the enthusiastic Percival was with them in this, although he made a speech to express his satisfaction with Oglethorpe's offer. "My great pain," he said, "was that although we were ever so well prepared, it would be difficult to find a proper Governor, which post he has accepted."

Oglethorpe overrode his colleagues' too hesitant prudence, which would have imposed a delay in starting; he insisted on an early beginning of the enterprise. Before October was over he had worn down all opposition. Stores were collected, the Admiralty helped by offering ships, and the governors of the American colonies were instructed to welcome the pioneers. Appointments were made for the party's spiritual and bodily comfort—a chaplain, a surgeon, an apothecary and an engineer.

By mid-November Oglethorpe judged that all was ready for the departure. On the 18th he left London and drove to Gravesend. Two days later he sailed, with a hundred and sixteen people in his party, on the little frigate *Ann*. The authoritative *Gentleman's Magazine* adds the pleasing item that the cargo included ten tons of Alderman Parson's best beer, "for the service of the colony."

Oglethorpe and his colonists travelled in the middle of the winter, for it was January 13 before they reached South Carolina and disembarked at Charles Town (the modern Charleston). As voyages were reckoned then, it was a good one, for the total casualties on the way were two infants. The South Carolinians were very hospitable to the newcomers, for they felt grateful to the intrepid soldier and his pioneers who would serve as an outpost against Spanish aggression and Indian raids. The Assembly not only supplied boats for the further trip to the wilderness, but also voted a gift of "105 head of cattle, 25 hoggs, and a quantity of rice for provisions." In February, when winter is already ending in those southern latitudes, the party set out for its new home, shepherded by a guard of twenty rangers under their colonel.

Ten miles up the Savannah River from the ocean lay the tract of land which, by agreement with the Indians, was to be the site of a new city. Oglethorpe had brought the plans with him. If the sight of them as he spread the papers out in his tent thrilled him with the anticipation of a great undertaking, there was an undertone of sadness. These designs for a spacious and noble city were based on drawings in a book by Robert Castell, the architect friend who had died of smallpox in a debtors' jail, victim of a petty official's criminal spite. In time the new city, rising in a wilderness of palmettos and trees draped in Spanish moss, was to have a full-fledged municipal government. So the Trustees in London had ordained, but there was no hurry about it, "because till we come to that," said Percival, "the laws of England take place." Oglethorpe was glad enough to deputize for the city government-to-be as well as for the English crown. He had been a soldier before he became a Parliamentarian and was not averse to independent command.

Like any conscientious officer he had reconnoitred the ground ahead of his people. He let them rest at Beaufort, South Carolina, while he went on to view the country and decide on the exact spot for his new city. He wrote to the Trustees telling them that he had fixed on a healthy situation where the river banks were about forty feet high, "and on the Top a Flat, which they call a* Bluff."

Oglethorpe was not insensible to the natural beauty of the south, for he remarks, "The Landskip is very agreeable,

---

* A term in use among the English colonists in America, but not yet domiciled in the mother country. Long after Oglethorpe's time, we find English writers putting the word in quotes, as though to mark a certain distaste for a crude Americanism.

the Stream being wide, and bordered with high Woods on both Sides." He speaks also of the "vast Woods of Pine trees" and conjures up the picture of a Georgia that may still be seen where Industrialism has not taken over. He remarks, as though with approval, the absence of Spanish moss in a particular spot. "There is no Morse on the trees, though in most parts of Carolina they are covered with it, and it hangs down Two or Three Feet from them." He deduces the healthfulness of the site of Savannah from the fact the Indians had chosen to live there.

With these same Indians, the Yamacraws, belonging to the Creek tribe, Oglethorpe quickly established good relations. He had the initial good luck to make friends with Mary Musgrove, the half-Indian wife of a British trader and she, acting as intermediary and interpreter, paved his way to an understanding with the tribes. If the first satisfactory contact was made through her influence, it was owing to the Englishman's own character that the thing developed into a lasting friendship and that the local chieftain Tomochichi became a loyal and even an affectionate ally. It is the story of the Quaker William Penn and his redskin friends over again. The pacifist Quaker and the army officer who had fought under Prince Eugene had certain traits in common, especially a sense of the dignity of man and an entire freedom from the racialism that tainted later colonial ventures. Both men saw the Indians simply as fellow humans and treated them as equals, without self-consciousness or patronage. Oglethorpe, like Penn, mixed freely with the Indians and learned something of their language. "They know Mr. Oglethorpe as their Father," said a German pastor working in the colony, "and ask his Advice in all their circumstances."

By the end of the year since the landing at Charles Town, when Oglethorpe decided that his affairs called him back to

England for a time, good progress had been made in the new town on the bluff above the river. Oglethorpe, however, still slept under canvas and fared frugally, as though on campaign. We note the contrast with Penn. The Quaker was something of a gourmet and a connoisseur of wines, insistent, too, on his chocolate and coffee, rare luxuries in early Pennsylvania. The soldier-aristocrat, who had been the staff officer to a prince, lived like an ascetic. He did not ask his Georgian colonists to embrace his own Spartan mode of life, anyhow no further than they had to. By the end of the first year forty houses had been built, there was a good stock of provisions and a supply of pure water. Nearly a dozen other settlements had been made in addition to Savannah, described rather grandiosely by the Trustees' secretary as "the metropolis of a country."

When, in March, 1734, Oglethorpe started north for Charles Town, bidding farewell to a crowd of his friends, English and Indian, he may well have felt a glow of satisfaction to think of all that had been done. The former inmates of English debtors' prisons and the Lutheran and Anabaptist refugees from central Europe had experienced nothing to compare with the vicissitudes of the first New England settlers and the Virginia colonists in Jamestown. There had been no awesome record of disease and death. A London paper of the time says that, "when he (Oglethorpe) came away, the people were healthy and orderly."

The only cloud on the Georgia Trustees' horizon was Oglethorpe's casual manner of doing business with them. When he was short of money for colonial activities and had spent all of his own that was handy, he would draw on the accounts of the Trustees in London without troubling to warn them beforehand; they had to honour the notes to avoid a scandal that would have harmed their colony. Even his good friend Percival, now the Earl of Egmont, was annoyed by this.

The eastward voyage across the Atlantic was made in a warship, the *Aldborough,* which had been assigned for Oglethorpe's use. He had made up his mind to impress the people at home. He took with him his devoted friend Tomochichi, the Indian chief, a lively and active redskin of ninety, full of the enthusiasm of youth. With him went his wife, his grand-nephew and five warriors. The formal excuse for taking them all to England was that they might learn the English language and the Christian religion—in that order—but Oglethorpe was not without a sense of their value as publicity for Georgia. Their presence in London helped to win appropriations from Parliament and when the Trustees had a group portrait painted, a phalanx of Oglethorpe's dark-skinned friends was a conspicuous part of the picture.

The *Aldborough* arrived off the Isle of Wight in mid-June. Oglethorpe rushed up to Surrey for a brief visit to his home near Godalming and he was in London within the week for a "grand entertainment" planned by the Trustees, who had apparently forgiven him for the excessive number of drafts on their bankers. The Indians were a great success, definitely the high spot of the evening, which ended, the contemporary newspapers tell us, with bell-ringing, a bonfire and "other Demonstrations of Joy and Gratitude." During the ensuing weeks the Indians met the king, the Archbishop of Canterbury and the famous physician and scientist Sir Hans Sloane. All were impressed by the red men's dignity, as well as by their obvious affection for Oglethorpe. Tomochichi, that lively nonagenarian, took it all in his stride, until he lost his nerve in the presence of "the Magick Lanthorn." Then tragedy overtook the party. One of the Indians fell ill and died of smallpox, despite Oglethorpe's solicitude and Sir

Hans Sloane's medical care. At the end of October the Indians sailed from Gravesend, having been accompanied to the ship by Oglethorpe, from whom they would not part until the last farewell was uttered.

Oglethorpe himself, as founder of Georgia, had a share in all this enthusiasm. Two poets, Pope and Thomson, sang his praises in verse; the newspapers in lush prose lauded him as "a Roman hero" and, less imaginatively, as a gentleman whose services as the colonizer of Georgia would "render him ever famous in English History." In the riverside village of Rotherhithe, once famous for cherry gardens and sailors' doxies, the shipwrights built a 250-ton vessel launched as the *Oglethorpe*. The city fathers of Inverness made him an honorary burgess of their council without even requiring him to make the journey to Scotland.

Sometime before he bade farewell to his Indian friends at Gravesend he had said goodbye to another friend of alien race who had been the object of his fight for justice and humane dealing. At one time Oglethorpe had held stock in the Royal African Company, but he sold it and retired from a position on the board, probably because of his dislike of slavery. Some time afterwards an educated West African Negro, a Moslem, whom the records call Job ben Solomon and Job Jolla, was kidnapped by slave-dealers and put up for sale. He was taken to Maryland, escaped and was recaptured, but sent a letter in Arabic, telling of his woes, to his father in Gambia. The letter, by way of the Royal African Company's officials, came into Oglethorpe's hands and he sent it to a pundit at Oxford University to be translated, after which he paid, out of his own pocket, for poor Job's manumission and his journey to England. There, by his zeal and his usefulness, he won the esteem both of his benefactor and of his benefactor's friend, Sir Hans Sloane. In July, 1734, Job, a free man bearing gifts from his English friends, sailed at last for his home in Africa. The proneness of human beings to forget their benefactors being what it is, one is glad to record that this admirable Negro in after years sent letters to express his gratitude to the two Englishmen who had done so much for him.

The year after his return to England Oglethorpe persuaded the Trustees to pass three laws for the good of the new colony. The first of these forbade the sale of rum in Georgia. Ale and beer, wine if they could come by it, would do the colonists no harm, but rum-drinking, especially in the summer climate of Georgia, was a peril for both white men and Indians. The second law, which Oglethorpe had very much at heart, showed him—and the Georgia of the early years—as ahead of their century. Negro slavery was forbidden in the colony. Oglethorpe's insistence on this does credit to his head as well as his heart. His sentiments about slavery were those of Wilberforce and of Abraham Lincoln. Moreover, apart from his ethical stand on the subject, he saw slavery as inimical to his people should they become slave-owners, blunting their sense of justice and removing the incentive to personal exertion.

The third piece of legislation, whose object was described as "maintaining Peace with the Indians in the Province of Georgia," set up a plan of licenses for traders among the Indians. The idea behind this was strategic rather than humanitarian or even commercial. The people of South Carolina had for a long time been suspicious of the Spaniards to the south of them, but by the time Oglethorpe settled Georgia they had become more apprehensive of French influence to the south-west—in the settlement of Moville (the modern Mobile, Alabama). The French were working on the Indian population in the area so as to win customers in time of peace and allies in war.

The new scheme gave the control of such licenses as were

to be issued to Oglethorpe. It is an irony of colonial history that the South Carolinians welcomed with enthusiasm the establishment of Georgia as a military outpost and a buffer state and promptly became embittered when Georgian competed with Carolinian traders in commerce among the tribes. They resented, too, a plan which seemed to place them under the authority of someone outside their colony. The news of this tension between the two colonies and of grievances of his people against some of their own officials disturbed Oglethorpe and made him hasten preparations to return to America.

By the latter part of September, 1735, he was ready. He gave a farewell dinner to the agents of the various North American colonies, entertaining them "splendidly at Pontiack's" reports a London newspaper of the time. He then went down to the Isle of Wight and boarded his ship, the *Simmonds,* at Cowes in the middle of October, but the ship was held up by unfavourable winds until November had passed. The delay was not only annoying; it was expensive. The passenger list was the biggest so far, 257 persons who had to be fed and cared for all this time. Oglethorpe himself had been ill with a fever, but early in December he wrote that he would rather run the danger of an earlier start "than have risqued the losing of the season in Georgia." His impatience to sail could not overcome the captain's refusal to leave his anchorage until he had the wind in his favour. The voyage did not start until nearly the middle of the month. Oglethorpe sent a farewell message ashore as the Needles fell astern. "God be praised," he wrote, "we at last have got an Easterly Wind in the morning."

Oglethorpe was a religious man in the mode of the eighteenth century, that is to say, he believed in God, in the brotherhood of man and in the widest toleration of other faiths than that of his Anglican baptism. He had, for example, welcomed two parties of Jewish settlers to Georgia in the face of opposition from some of the Trustees. There was one exception to toleration in Georgia—that of "Papists." This apparent residue of bigotry, from which Quaker Pennsylvania was free, was more a matter of geography than of dogma. It is doubtful if the Earl of Egmont and the other Trustees troubled themselves very much about Catholic dogma. The point with them was that Catholics in the colony might be too closely drawn in sympathy towards their fellow-believers in the Spanish and French settlements. The Trustees as a whole were more strictly orthodox than Oglethorpe himself, who had no thought of doctrinal tests for his colonists. His friend the Earl of Egmont, on the other hand, records in his diary that on a Sunday in July, 1732, when the Georgia venture was in its infancy, he received communion and took "a certificate thereof, it being necessary upon the passing our charter of Georgia."

As a matter of course the Church of England was given first place among the varieties of Protestant Christianity in Georgia, but the church had not been fortunate in its ministers. The first one appointed had fallen ill after a short time in the colony and had died at sea on the way home. The next choice of the Trustees was an unstable cleric who had tried being an Independent or Congregationalist and a Presbyterian before he turned Anglican. He was not the stuff of which pioneer missionaries are made. He grumbled about conditions and the state of his health and, altogether, was a disappointment to the Society for the Propagation of the Gospel, which had sponsored him.

Oglethorpe resolved that his colonists, most of them Anglicans, should not be left without zealous ministers and so it came about that among the passengers who sailed in the *Simmonds* were the Wesley brothers, John and Charles, and their friend Benjamin Ingham. These three young men came fresh from the fervent prayer meetings and conferences of the religious brotherhood that had received the nickname "Methodists" at Oxford. When they joined Oglethorpe they were still earnest Anglicans; eighteenth century dislike of "enthusiasts" had not yet driven the "Methodists" out of the church they regarded as their spiritual home.

On what turned out to be a tempestuous and uncomfortable journey Oglethorpe's character displayed its most admirable traits. He spent himself in care for the sick and those who were too poor to buy small comforts or extra services for themselves. When a woman emigrant about to bear a child was in danger of death, Oglethorpe gave up his own cabin to her. Others insisted she was as good as dead anyhow, so why trouble about her? He refused to despair of her recovery and saw to it that she should have proper attention. She survived to bless her benefactor. His care for all the emigrants was unending and it paid dividends. The voyage was completed without a single death, no small achievement in those days. Oglethorpe would not allow the sailors, in their crude fashion, to make fun of the poor seasick and homesick travellers. "We can't be sufficiently thankful to God for Mr. Oglethorpe's presence with us," wrote John Wesley in one of his letters.

Wesley's admiration for Oglethorpe's truly Christian charity and his abstemious way of life did not prevent him from trying to achieve something akin to his own effusive piety in his patron. Wesley had a Buchmanite's fondness for "sharing" and for a certain amount of spiritual exhibitionism. Not so James Oglethorpe. He did not "open his heart" as Wesley would have liked him to; his Anglicanism was moderate and decorous, more a matter of ethics, probably, than of eschatology. However, he won the general goodwill of all the sects by his respect for their clergy. Oglethorpe and John

Wesley worked together wholeheartedly to nurse the sick and cheer the downhearted as the ship was tossed about on the wintry Atlantic.

Christmas was celebrated at sea, a bitter January went by and it was not until February 6, 1736, that the ship arrived at Savannah. The colonists welcomed their founder with enthusiasm; their South Carolina neighbours sent delegates to offer the governor's greetings and those of the Council and Assembly. There was much to please Oglethorpe in Savannah; new buildings had gone up since his departure and the land was being brought under cultivation. There were also problems calling for his attention—dissatisfaction with Causton, the colony's storekeeper, accused of harshness and corruption, the lack of Anglican clergy, and a growing extravagance among the settlers of independent means. The last-named abuse sounds strange as told of a colony so recently established in the wilderness. Yet we have Oglethorpe's word for it. Within a week of his arrival he wrote to the Trustees, "The People who come at their own charge live in a manner too expensive which will make sumptuary laws necessary for the Province."

Despite all these calls upon his consideration he did not stay long in Savannah. During the previous autumn it had been determined that he should establish a settlement in the southern part of the territory to serve as defensive outpost for his people and for the South Carolinians. He journeyed southwards in the middle of February to the mouth of the Altamaha River and marked out the site of his new town on St. Simon's Island. He called it Frederica, in honour of Prince Frederick. The one-time ardent Jacobite was thus doing homage to the Hanoverian royal family and he seemed quite happy to have his beloved colony named after the king whom his mother had regarded as spurious.

At this time began Oglethorpe's closer association with

the Wesley brothers. There arose a series of incidents much to be regretted, because good men were at logger-heads. The story is not without its comic aspects. Charles Wesley had joined the colony with the impressive title of Secretary of Indian Affairs, but when he reached Georgia he found that his title might as well be just "secretary." Ogle-thorpe at Frederica was so overwhelmed with business that a secretary was indispensable. The founder, left to himself, was inclined to be remiss about reports, minutes of meetings and paper work generally. Early in March young Charles Wesley joined his patron at Frederica and noted in his diary, "Mr. Oglethorpe received me very kindly."

Unhappily Oglethorpe's kindness did not reconcile Charles to the arduous and humdrum task assigned him. "I was wholly spent in writing letters for Mr. Oglethorpe. I would not spend six days more in the same manner for all Geor-gia." A week later he wrote in his journal that he saw Ogle-thorpe as the chief of all his enemies, although he records that he prayed earnestly for him. It all sounds rather hys-terical. The pioneer American life, the climate or the young man's emotional fervour led him astray. He squabbled with his benefactor over Sunday church services, objected to his going to hunt buffalo on Sunday and, finally, listened to some irresponsible gossip which credited Oglethorpe with keeping *two* mistresses, former converts to John Wesley's missionary zeal on shipboard.

Things went from bad to worse after that. Oglethorpe, perhaps without knowing of all the prurient gossip to which the gullible young man had listened, was angry and im-patient with his secretary's moods and quirks and so a kind of sniping warfare went on between the two men for weeks at a time. The colonists nearly all took Oglethorpe's side in the quarrel. Poor Charles, who had started with dreams of a great apostolate among white men and red, found his congregation reduced to "two Presbyterians and a Papist."

John Wesley went to the aid of his younger brother at Frederica and made things worse by his tactless interference. Charles gave up all attempts to better the situation, wrote in his diary, "I resigned," went back to Savannah, made his way to Charles Town and sailed for England in August. Whatever the faults on both sides—Charles Wesley's credulity and morbid soul-searching, his benefactor's impatience and peppery temper—there was no vindictiveness in either of them. They met in England years later and were the best of friends. Oglethorpe even invited the cleric to return to Georgia and take over a parish there. He declined; perhaps it was as well for the ecclesiastical peace of the colony that he did so.

John Wesley's ministry in Georgia began more auspiciously than his brother's secretaryship. He had impressed Oglethorpe favourably, although he had not been able to effect an emotional "conversion" in the soldier's soul. Not all the Georgians took to the Reverend John Wesley as kindly as their founder, for he managed to estrange many of them by too much zeal. He had followed Oglethorpe to Frederica, but decided he could achieve nothing there and went back to Savannah. Again there was a promising start and he wrote enthusiastically to the Trustees, "the Good I have found here has indeed been beyond my expectations." Between the ardent young churchman still in his early thirties and the mature soldier and colonizer entering on middle age there was a bond of affection and mutual respect. Perhaps Wesley lost a needed moderating influence when Oglethorpe returned to England in the latter part of 1736. Anyhow, during his patron's absence he entangled himself in a skein of emotions, partly erotic, partly religious, which made him a sore trial to the devout and a figure of fun to the ungodly. It all started, harmlessly, over a young woman of eighteen. Troubled by the attentions of a young man of loose morals, she turned to the Reverend Mr. Wesley for advice. Shielding her from the young rake's evil desires, Wesley found himself falling in love with her and began to dream of marriage.

All might have been well, for at the start of the business Oglethorpe was in favour of the young clergyman's marriage. The girl seems to have had second thoughts about it, or perhaps she was just a coquette. Wesley was full of scruples and hesitations. His love for Sophia ran counter to an earlier resolve of lifelong celibacy, made when he was the leader of the "Holy Club" in Oxford. He had a shock when the girl's aunt called on him to announce the banns of marriage for her niece and a young colonist who was a relative and a subordinate of the unpopular official, Causton. Wesley had, it seemed, overcome his yearning for the girl and had embraced once more his celibate ideal. Then the layman, fearful, one supposes, of a change of mind in the cleric, rushed the girl up to South Carolina and married her there.

This was too much for John Wesley. He brooded morbidly and lost his peace of mind. When the bride and bridegroom had come back to Savannah, he publicly refused to let the young wife receive communion, alleging some fault or other in religious practice. The angry husband charged the clergyman with defaming his wife's character and had a warrant made out for Wesley's arrest. Perhaps this was merely a gesture, but Wesley did not wait to see. He went to Charles Town and just before Christmas, 1737, boarded a ship about to sail to England.

The young woman's husband had to content himself with a letter of complaint to the Trustees. John, like his younger brother Charles and like Oglethorpe himself, was a man of generous nature. In the midst of the emotional turmoil that led to his departure, John Wesley wrote to Oglethorpe, "I bless God that ever you was born . . . I am indebted to you for a 1,000 favours here. Though all men should revile you, yet will I not." As the years went by, he and his brother kept alive their interest in the religious welfare of the Georgia settlers.

The defection of Charles Wesley and the folly of his brother were a trial to Oglethorpe, who had a genuine fondness for the young men and had chosen them to minister to his people in Georgia. A third member of the "Holy Club" in Oxford, Benjamin Ingham, had sailed with Oglethorpe in 1735. He had learning, ability and good looks. He antagonized the Wesleys by deserting their "Methodist" Anglicanism to join the Moravians and disappointed Oglethorpe by giving up his missionary work to marry a lady of title.

All these events were but ecclesiastical storms in a teacup. Oglethorpe was a soldier with a strategic task laid upon him by his government, frontier defence as England's empire began to spread southward along the Atlantic coast. Until the beginning of the Georgia settlement there was a debatable area between Anglo-Saxon, Protestant Carolina, whose hub was Charles Town, and the Spanish colony of Florida, with its Latin and Catholic civilization centered in St. Augustine. There were conflicting claims on the intervening region, but a wilderness of palmettos and moss-draped trees, with a population of Indians and alligators, was not prize enough to provoke more than a cold war of diplomatic exchanges.

When Oglethorpe settled in Georgia, the case was altered. Here was a soldier, with an active commission and a record of service in the field, sent to establish new, aggressive frontiers for an England impinging on part of Spain's colonial empire. The Spaniards knew, of course, that the Georgian males of military age were exercised in the manual of arms; moreover in the Scots Highlanders at New Inverness (now Darien), on the Altamaha River, the colony had a nucleus of tough fighting material. The Highlanders were largely survivors of the Jacobite rising of 1715 and were very much an élite corps whose plaid the founder often wore in compliment to them. England's enemies have always feared the Highlanders who fight under her colours; the Spaniards were no exception.

In theory Spain claimed most of what had become Georgia. Either her forces had conquered it or her missionaries had evangelized it. The English settlers, on the other hand, had been pushing their boundary steadily southward and now, by setting up the fortified town of Frederica on the Altamaha River, Oglethorpe had planted the English flag at a spot only about thirty miles from St. Augustine. There was a constant exchange of diplomatic protests between Savannah and St. Augustine, with an occasional diversion to Cuba. While in London a tenacious Spanish ambassador besieged the Duke of Newcastle, in charge of colonial affairs, with complaints about the doings of Oglethorpe. The duke was at length badgered into sending an agent, one Captain Dempsey, to look into matters on the spot.

This official undertook so many journeys between Savannah and St. Augustine that Oglethorpe began to suspect a policy of appeasement, and, disregarding Captain Dempsey's enquiries, wrote directly to the Duke of Newcastle, "I cannot deliver up a foot of ground belonging to his Majesty, to a foreign Power without the breach of my allegiance to his Majesty. I will alive or dead keep possession of it till I have his Majesty's orders."

Meanwhile he had stationed soldiers in a fort set up at the mouth of the St. John's River, undeniably in Florida, which he claimed as rightfully British in virtue of a tradition—

unfounded—of its conquest by Sir Francis Drake in the time of Queen Elizabeth I. His soldierly declaration to the Duke of Newcastle notwithstanding, Oglethorpe received with due ceremony the delegate whom the Spaniards sent to Frederica for discussions during the summer of 1736.

Spain now demanded the withdrawal of the English from all territory below Port Royal, within the borders of South Carolina. This may have been bluff, but Oglethorpe would not risk unpreparedness. He wrote to the lieutenant-governor of New York and was assured of help should the Spaniards attack. Virginia kept her troops ready for anything that might threaten the security of the colonies south of her borders.

At length, in the autumn of 1736, Oglethorpe made a treaty with the Spanish governor, Don Francisco del Moral Sanchez. He was a reasonable man and the terms he offered were satisfactory to the Englishman. Both parties would keep their Indian auxiliaries in check and would refrain from any aggression, awaiting settlement of the boundary dispute by Madrid and London. Oglethorpe made the concession of withdrawing his troops from the fort on the St. John's River. South Carolina was pleased that diplomacy had staved off the threat of war and in London both Oglethorpe's firmness in opposing outrageous claims and his compliance with reasonable ones met with approval. Less happy was the lot of Don Francisco. After a time he was recalled to Spain and put to death by hanging.

If there was for the time being peace on Georgia's borders, there was no peace of mind for her founder. The friendliness of many of the South Carolinians changed to hostility when laws made for the good of Georgia affected South Carolina's economy adversely. The prohibition of the sale of rum in the new colony deprived South Carolina of a market for one of her products. It also led to the first appearance in American history of bootlegging; plenty of rum was smuggled into Georgia to compete with the ale which Oglethorpe considered strong enough for his settlers. The South Carolina merchants felt that insult had been added to injury when they had to get their trading licenses from the man whose opposition to rum had cut down their profits. Further, his friendliness with the Indians was viewed with suspicion, despite the fact that it strengthened both colonies in the face of French propaganda amongst the tribes.

Meanwhile in London the Spanish ambassador was striving with all his might to exploit Walpole's leaning towards appeasement and a policy of peace at any price, or, anyhow, at the price of Oglethorpe's security in Georgia. The founder, unfortunately, had not improved his position with the Trustees by his casual habit of dipping into their funds in London for the needs of the colony but without authorization on their part or prior warning on his. They complained also of being kept in the dark about colonial affairs because of the "short, unsatisfactory accounts" he sent them. Towards the end of 1736 it was clear to him that the time had come for a visit to England.

About the end of November he sailed in the *Two Brothers*. He had a fearsome voyage, thanks to bad weather and a poor-spirited crew. In a moment of peril the sailors decided that things were hopeless and sat down to wait for the ship to break up, as it would have done had not Oglethorpe and Mr. Tanner, one of his constituents from Haslemere, jumped out of bed "In their shirts to pull the ropes." Finally, five weeks after the start of the voyage, the ship, having been "drove" into the Bristol Channel, made port safely at Ilfracombe. The stormy weather on the Atlantic had made people on both sides of the ocean despair of the safety of Oglethorpe and his fellow travellers. When the good news of their safe arrival in England reached Georgia, it was celebrated "round a bonfire" by the citizens of Savannah, records Thomas Causton, in charge of the commissariat, and he adds, "I have given them a Barrell of Beer."

At home, as the new year began, Oglethorpe saw his colony in danger from the machinations of a tirelessly persistent Spanish ambassador and the attitude of the Prime Minister, ready to throw Georgia away for a peace without honour. At the end of January, 1737, Oglethorpe asked Parliament for £30,000 for Georgia's defence; he hoped to get £20,000. Walpole had indeed asked his advice about defence, but found it unpalatable when it was given, nor was he mollified by the soldier's frankness. . . . He was "not used to have such things said to him." Mr. Oglethorpe replied, "Yes, he was when he was plain Mr. Walpole; but now he was Sir Robert, and Chief Minister, he was surrounded by sycophants and flatterers who will not tell him the truth." If Walpole starved Georgia of defence, Oglethorpe threatened, Spain would immediately seize the colony and then the way would be open for France to take the Carolinas and Virginia.

At length Oglethorpe got what he wanted, or the chief part of it, anyhow. Parliament granted him £20,000, and Walpole agreed that he should command the joint forces of South Carolina and Georgia, but it was the middle of March before he had got that far. South Carolina, afraid of the French down in Moville, forgot her grievances against Georgia and hailed Oglethorpe as friend and saviour.

The Spanish ambassador now intrigued to prevent Oglethorpe's return to America. He could not manage this, but he did persuade Walpole to ask for the disbanding of Oglethorpe's infantry regiment. This was going too far. Oglethorpe was indignant, asked the Prime Minister what sort of man he took James Oglethorpe to be and demanded a straightforward *Yes* or *No* to the question whether Georgia was to be left in the lurch. More usefully, perhaps, Oglethorpe went hunting with the king and before August was over he had his commission as colonel of "the regiment of Foot for the Defence of His Majesty's Plantations in America." Walpole, the adroit politician, was badly beaten in this contest with the forthright soldier who dealt in simple Yea and Nay.

He went ahead with recruiting for his regiment during the following months, while an angry Spanish ambassador, vainly protesting against this threat to his country's colonial interests, was shuttled back and forth between the evasive Walpole and the suavely procrastinating Duke of Newcastle. Military business was not enough for Oglethorpe's great fund of energy. He took an active interest in the Westminster Infirmary, of which he had become one of the governors, spoke in Parliament for Georgia's needs, met Charles Wesley again, and helped a struggling, poverty-stricken author, still unknown to the world, by putting down his name for a subscription to a poem ready for publication. The poem was Samuel Johnson's *London*. The two men, more than a dozen years later, were to begin a close friendship which would last until Johnson's death.

Meanwhile Oglethorpe had his hands full as the Spaniards pressed their charges against him. Undoubtedly they were correct in regarding his establishment of Fort St. George on the St. John's River as a violation of their territorial rights. The Duke of Newcastle questioned him on the subject and for once the plain soldier showed himself as competent at double-talk as any of the politicians. He deftly confused Fort *Saint* George, on the St. John's River, the subject of Spanish complaints, with Fort *King* George, on the Altamaha River, indubitably a British fort on Georgian territory.

By the spring of 1738 he was ready to sail to Georgia. He

had won royal support over the head of the Prime Minister, got his regiment assembled, and overcome the apathy of the Trustees, who had been uneasy about friction with Spain. These Trustees were a great disappointment. Oglethorpe had trained his soldiers, prepared an impressive review, to be followed by a dinner, and invited the whole body of the Trustees to attend. Only four of them, including the colonel's friend, the Earl of Egmont, turned up. Oglethorpe was proud of his regiment, which the newspapers of the time described as making a good show, being "finely armed" and "well cloathed" and made up of "strong, middle-sized young men." In mid-May they assembled at Southampton and were inspected by their commander, who then made his way to Portsmouth, whence he was to sail. In a parting interview the king had impressed on him the need to keep up "the strictest friendship" with the Spaniards in Florida. To George II and Sir Robert Walpole, the arch-opportunist, Georgia was only a pawn in the game of European politics. To James Oglethorpe it was an ideal, compounded of warm-hearted philanthropy, soldierly sense of duty and an enthusiastic imperialism in the mood of Sir Walter Ralegh, who had dreamed of an "English empire" spanning the North American continent.

The weather seemed always to bear a grudge against Oglethorpe when he set out on a journey. This time he lost over a month waiting for favourable winds, from mid-May to the end of June. On June 26 his ship, the *Blandford*, left Portsmouth and then, accompanied by transports and a warship, made her way to the open sea early in July. The voyage ended in mid-September with only two deaths on the way, again a good record for the times. The soldiers disembarked and were marched to Frederica. The execution of the hapless Spanish governor for signing a peace pact had made it clear that war was not far distant.

Oglethorpe had founded his colony as a philanthropist, had been its lawyer and administrator and worked for its spiritual and material welfare; now he would have to serve it as a soldier. In his own chosen profession, strangely enough, he was least successful, so far as Georgia was concerned.

The urgency of military problems tended to sink the administrator in the soldier and before long the Trustees set up a new civil government for half the colony. Gradually Oglethorpe was more or less stripped of his civil administrative authority, the Trustees saying that they did not desire his "interfering in their civil concerns while he is employed in his military ones which are distinct services." He had to sacrifice the old paternal intimacy with his English settlers, but he made up for the loss by more contact with the Indians. Like Penn he drew closer in friendship to them as his own people repulsed him or grew indifferent to his ideals. Long ago he had said to his friend the Indian chief Tomochichi, "I am a red man, an Indian, in my heart; that is why I love them."

A great conference of Indians and English took place in the summer of 1739 to strengthen the bond between the two races. Oglethorpe made a long and trying journey inland to Coweta for this ten-day meeting with his aged Indian friend and the other Creek chieftains. Before the autumn was over, old Tomochichi died and Oglethorpe mourned for him as men mourn only for a very dear friend. There was policy as well as personal affection in his dealings with the Indians, for they were allies against both the French and the Spaniards, but the affection came first and long survived the fears of aggression.

Oglethorpe's philanthropy suffered no diminution during the years when he was aware that sooner or later war would come, and that the very existence of Georgia as an English colony might be at stake. His zeal for the religious welfare of his colonists had met a setback in the affairs of the two Wesleys, but with another clergyman from England he had greater success. George Whitefield, one of the group of earnest young Anglicans at Oxford derisively called Methodists, joined Oglethorpe in the early years of the colony and thereafter made a number of missionary journeys to America, eventually dying in New England. Both in England and Georgia his preaching, emotional and fervent, deeply impressed his congregations, but his greatest colonial achievement was the Bethesda Orphanage in Georgia. With Oglethorpe's support he founded it to improve education among the colonists as well as to exercise Christian charity among the unfortunate. Benjamin Franklin, no friend to religious "enthusiasts," sought to have the work of the orphanage transferred to Philadelphia—Franklin had a poor opinion of the people of Georgia—but Whitefield would not agree and thereby lost Franklin as a subscriber to the charity.

When war came it brought Oglethorpe misfortune and disappointment at first. He retrieved an initial failure by a subsequent victory, although malicious tongues sought to belittle his success. For a long time he saw his colony treated as a mere bargaining item in the cold war between England and Spain. His friend Egmont and a few other far-sighted Parliamentarians kept up the contest with the appeasers, but for a time the fate of Georgia hung in the balance. William Penn, several decades earlier, had written to a friend, "We see so little of an American understanding among those whose business it is to superintend the American empire." So it was now. Much of the greatness of Britain's immediate future lay in her expansion on the North American continent, yet Whig statesmen would have sacrificed Georgia to placate a power whose star had been sinking since 1588.

When war broke out, it was not merely a war between Spaniards and English for the disputed region between English South Carolina and Spanish Florida. That, Oglethorpe's war, was only one facet of the War of Jenkins' Ear, a struggle for mercantile supremacy in the Caribbean and along the American Atlantic coast. The English sea captain's ear allegedly slashed from his head by a Spanish official in a quarrel about West Indian trading provided the useful lever for propaganda that brought English sentiment into line with government policy and assured it of popular support. England declared war, from London, that is, on October 23. Oglethorpe, now a brigadier-general, issued Georgia's declaration of war on October 3. He had known for some time that the outbreak was on the way and he hoped to take the Spaniards at a disadvantage. His action was justified in London by the fact that months before the two countries were officially at war an English naval unit in the West Indies had been ordered to attack Spanish vessels whenever they were encountered.

A letter from the general to his Trustees shows that he, like the naval commanders, had orders to anticipate the formal declaration of war. "I have received the King's Commands to anoy the Spaniards and am going to execute them" he writes. He planned an attack on St. Augustine by his own regiment and a detachment from South Carolina, both under his command. An English naval unit was to blockade the town from the harbour. All went well at first. Georgians and Carolinians advanced side by side into Florida and early in the new year (1740) the San Juan or St. John's River was under the general's control. He was within a couple of dozen miles of St. Augustine, the enemy's capital and the nerve centre of Spanish operations. The Spaniards were pessimistic; even if it took Oglethorpe a year to do it, he would capture their town, said one of them. He was correspondingly optimistic. "God has been pleased to Bless us with a great Success," he reported to his South Carolina opposite number.

Then things went wrong. The British blockade failed and the Spaniards were able to take help to their hard-pressed townsmen, who had endured a thirty-day battering by Oglethorpe's artillery. By the late summer the position was one of stalemate. The English forces had started their retreat northwards, pessimistic now and fearing the loss of Georgia to Spanish arms, but the Spaniards, although joyful at the raising of the siege, were too weak to follow the besiegers and seek a decisive victory in battle. Worst of all for English colonial unity, the former cooperation between Carolinians and Georgians had given way to bickering and recrimination, while irresponsible critics in Charles Town accused the general of all manner of evil. One poison-pen agitator even wrote to the Duke of Newcastle to "reveal" a plot of Oglethorpe to massacre the English settlers for the benefit of the Spaniards and their Indian allies. It is not surprising that Oglethorpe's health broke down for a time and that he was, as one of his friends noted, "reduced to an extraordinary Weakness by a continual Fever."

Fortunately his constitution and his spirits were equally resilient. By early winter he was himself again, writing reports to London, arguing for more support in men and money, and getting ready for a new attack on the Spaniards. All through 1741 his appeals for support were disregarded, a state of things the more galling to him that he saw more clearly than his masters at home that Spain's empire was crumbling. She was, however, still able to muster considerable forces, by sea and land, and in the early summer of 1742 they were moving northwards from their base at St. Augustine.

Oglethorpe's situation at this time was gloomy in the extreme. The statesmen at home, taken up with the European struggle and intent on British supremacy on the high seas, gave neither encouragement nor material aid to Georgia. The South Carolinians, embittered by the squabbles after the failure at St. Augustine, and now frightened by the French bogey once more, paid no attention to appeals for help from their southern neighbours. Almost in despair, Oglethorpe wrote early in June to the Duke of Newcastle, that it was too late for forces from England to do any good. He ended his letter, ". . . before they can arrive the matter will be over. I hope I shall behave as well as one with so few men and so little Artillery can." To the South Carolinians three weeks later he said, "If we should be defeated and they (the Spaniards) take Fort William and Frederica, I know nothing can stop them on this side Virginia." This, at least, took effect; South Carolina appealed to Virginia and both colonies came to the aid of General Oglethorpe.

The Spaniards, with the help of a renegade pilot from South Carolina, advanced northwards by sea and took St. Simon's Island as soon as Oglethorpe left his position there and retired inland. They followed him, struggling through the swampy wilderness until they were within a mile of Frederica, where Oglethorpe had decided to make a stand. In the stifling July heat a battle was fought at Bloody Marsh, where a successful ambush by the English accounted for some two hundred Spanish deaths. The Spanish forces retreated and so Carolina and Georgia certainly, Virginia and the more northerly colonies probably, were saved. This was the high point of Oglethorpe's military career in North America. The rest of the story from his day of thanksgiving, July 25, 1742, to his return to England a year later, is one of anticlimax.

The Whig government was still in power, but the leadership had passed to the Pelhams, the Duke of Newcastle and his brother. Oglethorpe might well have hoped for more attention and help from the new rulers of the oligarchy. The victory at Bloody Marsh had been a setback for Spanish power in Florida, but not the destruction of it. Oglethorpe was very conscious of this fact and sought to awaken the Whig politicians to the danger of leaving England's southern colonies in North America without adequate defence. His warnings were not heeded and, acting on the old military axiom that the best defence is a vigorous offensive, he organized another attack on St. Augustine in the early spring of 1743. It was a failure, for he found the town too strongly defended for the forces he had available and was compelled to retire to Georgia.

To add to his troubles, there was a fresh outburst of recrimination from critics in South Carolina. About the same time a disgruntled subordinate commander, allowed to go to England for convalescence, charged his general with corrupt handling of army finance, specifically of "defrauding his regiment by making them pay for the provisions the Government sent them over gratis." The War Office, even in the eighteenth century, could not disregard this, and it was unfortunate for the general that at the same time the Treasury was annoyed by complaints of his irresponsible drawing of bills of exchange. That he spent much of his own money to fill up gaps in the military budget for Georgia seems to have been overlooked. Anyhow, the War Office wanted his answer to the charges made against him in London and before the summer was over he had made his way to Charles Town and embarked on a ship for England.

Whether, in his disappointment he still hoped to return to Georgia we do not know. He was still, in his forty-sixth year, only on the threshold of middle age and could reasonably look forward to many years of active work. As things fell out, he had reached the high-water mark of achievement when, on a basis of warm-hearted philanthropy, he founded Georgia to rebuild broken lives and give hope to a section of his countrymen who until then had despair for their portion.

He landed in London in September and met a mixed reception—the friendliness and goodwill of many who valued the work he had done in Georgia, the hostility and backbiting of a South Carolina faction that had listened to the malicious gossip about peculation in army supplies. By the spring of 1744 the War Office had got around to convening the Board of General Officers that would enquire into the charges made against the general. The outcome of the enquiry was a forcibly expressed vindication of his character, a stern rebuttal of all the accusations against him and a recommendation that the officer who had made the charges should be dismissed from the army.

General Oglethorpe had come through his ordeal with flying colours and thereafter could look back on his North American achievement more happily. As the years passed, however, there were developments that undid some of the things he had worked for. Shortly after the army enquiry in London the prohibition of the rum trade in Georgia was repealed and, later on, the anti-slavery law was annulled. Oglethorpe's colony, which he had planned as a community of free men, white, black or red, became a slave-owning territory and so remained until the freeing of the slaves by Lincoln.

That Oglethorpe was looking forward to an early return to Georgia seems likely from a note in a London newspaper contributed by its Charles Town correspondent to say that the colonists hoped to see him again soon. A month later, however, the announcement of his forthcoming marriage was in the London journals. So far as the evidence goes, we may not picture the forty-eight-year-old soldier bowled over by a romantic passion. The baronet's daughter whom he married by special license of the Archbishop of Canterbury in Westminster Abbey the year after his return to England is discreetly specified in the document as "Elizabeth Wright, of Cranham, Essex, spinster, above 25." She had a yearly income in her own name of £1,500. The general, who had been spending money freely for the good of his colony, was hard up.

A marriage of convenience it may have been, but it proved a happy one and those who knew the couple in later years describe a pleasing Darby-and-Joan domesticity. Even if Oglethorpe was, as the record suggests, a bit garrulous and something of a showman at times, he was a warm-hearted man, full of kindness, tolerant and always faithful to the woman he had married. The spinster above 25 had made a good choice. The honeymoon was spent at Westbrook, the family seat in Surrey. The couple went to London and then as Christmas drew near returned to Westbrook, taking with them as guest an Indian chief who had accompanied the general from Georgia.

The year 1745, that of the last serious attempt of the Stuarts to regain the English throne—in the person of Prince Charles Edward, the "Young Pretender"—was a time of vicissitude for General Oglethorpe. Despite his Jacobite background and connections, including a nephew serving in the Stuart forces, he was appointed to an active command in the army that was to repel the invaders. He was praised for allowing the diversion to government use of a ship about to carry soldiers and supplies to Georgia. In Yorkshire, his ancestral county, he organized a body of fox-hunting country gentlemen in a cavalry unit that became the Royal Regiment of Hunters. With these volunteer patriots and a detachment of his Georgia Rangers he made, says a London paper, "a grand Shew."

Towards the close of that eventful year, as several times before in his career, something went wrong. Under orders from General Wade and the supreme commander, the Duke of Cumberland, he was sent to the north when the tide had turned against the invading Jacobites to harry their retreating forces, cut off isolated detachments and, generally, help to turn a defeat into a rout. The weather was bad, the country under snow and ice, communications disrupted and Oglethorpe apparently halted by orders from his superiors. The Jacobites escaped until their defeat at Culloden and Oglethorpe had missed a chance of capturing Prince Charles himself. The general found himself under suspicion. Was he merely unfortunate, the victim of mistaken orders and a scapegoat for them or was he, as some people suggested, reverting to the Jacobitism of his youth and giving the Stuart prince a break?

Again he had to face an investigation, a full-dress court-martial this time. Again he came out victorious. He was acquitted "most honourably," although it was known that the Duke of Cumberland heartily disliked him. Many people felt that, the acquittal notwithstanding, Oglethorpe would still be under a cloud, but in 1747 the army bigwigs seem to have wished to compensate him for what he had gone through and he was made a lieutenant-general. There was no more active service, although in 1755, when the Seven Years War broke out, he tried, although nearly sixty, to get himself sent to North America again. We know that he did not think much of Amherst and Wolfe as commanders in the field.

During these years he was active in Parliament on behalf of the army, characteristically in efforts to better the lot of the common soldier. One of the bitterest disappointments of his long life came in 1768, when he lost the Parliamentary seat for Haslemere, which he had held through so many years of hard work in committee and on the floor of the House of Commons, invariably for some cause with a humanitarian feature in it. England had all but forgotten him in the excitement stirred up by John Wilkes and the affair of No. 45 of the *North Briton.*

The septuagenarian soldier, who had been given the full rank of general in 1765, retired to his country home in rural Surrey. Apart from the companionship of his wife and the normal duties and recreations of a country squire, life seemed to hold little in store for him henceforth. Fate was kinder to him than he may have thought at the time. When he was seventy-two he entered on what turned out to be the happiest and was certainly the most peaceful portion of a life full of activity, trials, physical hardship and not a few disappointments.

For nearly two decades more the general lived on, healthy in body and young in spirit, enjoying the friendship and respect of the various gifted men who formed a group around Dr. Johnson. Thirty years earlier Oglethorpe, to encourage budding talent, had helped an impecunious young author by subscribing to the poem *London*—and Samuel Johnson never ceased to be grateful. Into the circle around Dr. Johnson, now the Great Cham and the arbiter of English letters, the old soldier and colonial founder was received with enthusiasm. This is not so surprising as it sounds. Oglethorpe was much more than just a plain fighting man, for his family had a record of academic distinction and he had not been untouched by his sojourn in Eton College and Oxford. He had been elected a Fellow of the Royal Society and was not unworthy to associate on easy terms with such men as Edmund Burke, Goldsmith, Garrick, Reynolds, Boswell and Dr. Johnson himself.

To Boswell we are chiefly indebted for the record of Oglethorpe's meeting with the other members of the Johnson circle. Between the English soldier in his seventies and the Scots lawyer still in his thirties there was a relationship that was almost that of an affectionate and tolerant father and a son not lacking in respect. The friendship began with the older man's seeking out the younger one to congratulate him on his book, *An Account of Corsica,* eulogizing the Corsican patriot General Paoli.

Boswell at the time was in the emotional disequilibrium of his passion, if one may call it such, for the beautiful and talented Dutch bluestocking Isabella van Serooskerken van Tuyll, more conveniently spoken of as Zélide. The young woman, as it chanced, became engaged to a nephew of the general, who bade Boswell not marry until he had "first put the Corsicans in a proper situation." On one occasion Boswell records in his journal that he found his elderly friend "tedious but instructive" and we surmise that the complaint reflects the writer's annoyance at having to yield the floor to an equally determined talker whose age and position enforced respect. The tedium may have been due to the fact that the old general was much given to parentheses and sometimes got lost in them.

With Dr. Johnson the relation was more that of equals, for the disparity in age was less, about a dozen years as compared with the forty-four between Oglethorpe and Boswell. The general was one of the few friends whom Dr. Johnson could never beat down to a trembling acceptance of his pronouncements. There is an account in the *Life* of a dinner party at the general's house in London when Oglethorpe and his wife, "a good, civil old lady, with some affectation of wit," entertained Johnson and Goldsmith. The latter, not too tactfully, suggested for discussion the ethical aspect of duelling. Johnson's attitude was, of course, strictly on orthodox Christian lines, but "the brave old General at once fired at this, and said that undoubtedly a man had a right to defend his honour." Fortunately the talk switched to Oglethorpe's early experiences when serving under Prince Eugene, and the old warrior illustrated his narrative with a diagram of the siege of Belgrade drawn in wine on the tablecloth.

His own Spartan way of life and the habit of years of soldiering and colonizing was not allowed to cramp the general's style when he gave a party. His guests remembered with pleasure the "fine sack" and "rich Canary wine," which on one occasion at least prompted Goldsmith to sing, solo, a musical number composed for his box-office success, *She Stoops to Conquer.*

Oglethorpe was always kind and generous to young men struggling to find their feet in the hurly-burly of London. We see him visiting Goldsmith in his attic to help him when he had got into debt. At another time, when the young poet and dramatist was depressed by the savage newspaper criticism of the day, Oglethorpe invited him down to the country, "if a farm and a mere country scene will be a little refreshment from the smoke of London." He frequently invited Boswell to dinner and kept him talking far into the night so that the foolish young lecher should be more wholesomely employed than in the casual affairs with lights o' love that played havoc with his health and his conscience. There is further evidence of General Oglethorpe's goodness of heart in his holding directorships of both the Westminster Hospital and the Children's Hospital and in the enthusiastic support he gave to Granville Sharp, who was campaigning against the slave trade and was afterwards associated with Wilberforce in the abolition movement.

There is plenty of contemporary evidence that the energy James Oglethorpe had shown as a young officer and later

on as founder of Georgia stayed with him to the end. It is
amusing to read of a country squire in his late seventies issu-
ing a challenge to a neighbour for trespassing on his estate.
On another occasion, in his seventy-fourth year, the general's irascibility was aroused, with greater justification, when
he heard Sir Francis Bernard, a well-hated former governor
of Massachusetts and a notorious tyrant and snob, belittling
the character of the American colonists. The affair took
place in the Smyrna Coffee House, a fashionable London re-
sort of the time. The general called the ex-governor "a dirty,
factious scoundrel, who smelt cursed strong of the Hang-
man," and told him he had better quit the company of "gentlemen of Character." Then he saw him to the door, where
he asked him, "had he any Thing to reply." Sir Francis had
not; he "left the House like a guilty Coward" said a Boston,
Massachusetts, newspaper to which the tidbit had been re-
layed.

In 1780, when the general was eighty-four, he and his
aging but equally vivacious wife were still keenly interested in all that was going on in town. June, 1780, was the
time of the Gordon Riots, a terrifying orgy of violence and
destruction touched off by the fanatical bigotry of a mad
nobleman when the Catholic Emancipation Bill came before
Parliament. Johnson's friend, Mrs. Thrale, invited the old
general to ensure his safety by taking refuge with her household in Bath. He not only refused to do this, but went down
to Westminster to see things for himself.

The founder of Georgia had already become something
of a legend in the closing decade of the eighteenth century.
This was due in part to the error about his age which added
ten to his years. Even when we have made the correction,
we find the record of bodily and mental vigour surprising
enough. When he was eighty-seven and happy in a new

friendship, that of the poetess Hannah More, one of the literary ladies of his acquaintance writes that, "General Oglethorpe is very active and walks some miles every day, goes with his Waistcoat almost entirely unbuttoned in ye midst of Winter."

One of the books of anecdotal gossip popular in the era tells us of Oglethorpe, now eighty-eight, that, "as soon as he gets out of bed he throws himself upon the Floor, and exercises his Limbs for some time." A contemporary letter written by a Philadelphian then in London to Benjamin Franklin, who had once served as colonial agent for Georgia, and would be interested to hear of the old founder, gives a charming picture of the general. "He danced about the Room with gaiety, kissed and said pretty things to all the Ladies, and seemed to feel all he said as much as any young man could do. . . . This youthful old gentleman was General Oglethorpe whom I believe you know. He spoke of you with the strongest marks of esteem."

In his old age the general's sentiments tended to assume again the Jacobitism of his early formative years. This did not prevent him from being one of the small group of eminent Britons who could see the colonial side of the quarrel which lost the English crown its North American colonies. When his old friend Dr. Johnson, rabidly anti-American, brought out his treatise *Taxation no Tyranny*, against the "rebels," Oglethorpe and Boswell joined in expressing their sympathy with the colonists. In the course of the American War of Independence the general and his friend Sharp, both zealous opponents of all injustice, tried in vain to win the support of the elder Pitt, the Earl of Chatham, for what we should call a round table conference to settle the American problem in a way that would have satisfied the colonists. With Edmund Burke also a shared sentiment about America drew these two friends of Johnson closer together. Oglethorpe was outspoken in his scorn of the official attitude towards the Americans.

One of the penalties of longevity is to see one's old friends go to the grave first. When Oglethorpe had reached the age of seventy-eight he mourned the untimely death of Oliver Goldsmith in his forty-sixth year. Five years later another friend and fellow-member of the coterie, David Garrick, died at the age of sixty-three. Finally, in 1785, the Great Cham himself, Dr. Johnson, whom all loved and before whom all, except the Oglethorpes, trembled, passed away. It is good to know that Mrs. Oglethorpe was spared to save her husband from what would have been a great loneliness. The not so romantic marriage had long since blossomed into a genuine love match. Boswell tells us of a dinner table conversation on wives. Johnson, then a widower, lauded the qualities of his late wife, whom he reckoned as good as his friend the general's. We are not told if the latter was present; presumably the conversation took place when she had retired to leave the men in enjoyment of the host's good wine. Oglethorpe, "now thirty years married, professed subjection, and was glorying in it."

When he had passed his eighty-eighth birthday, he made the gesture which most unreservedly emphasised his sympathy with the Americans. In the summer of 1785 King George III officially welcomed John Adams as the first minister from the new-born United States of America to the Court of St. James. It was a sad blow for those who shared the late Dr. Johnson's feelings about the "rebels." A large section of the English press voiced their dismay. Three days after the king had received the new ambassador, the general called on Adams to pay his respects, express his affection and regard for America, his sorrow at the quarrel and his happiness to see its end. The visit was returned by Adams, who had a two-hour talk with the general and wrote to friends in Quincy, Massachusetts, that he found General Oglethorpe "very polite and complimentary." This was less than a month before Oglethorpe's death. There is a satisfying congruity about this last conspicuous action of James Oglethorpe.

Shortly after the meeting with John Adams the general was present at the four days' auction of Johnson's library at Christie's and we are told of his buying several lots of his dead friend's books. On this occasion the artist S. Ireland made the pen and ink sketch which depicts the general in extreme old age. He was tall and exceedingly thin, his skin like parchment, his chin seeming to incline towards his nose, the effect of loss of teeth. He was as lively as ever, said the future banker and poet, Samuel Rogers, and "amused us youngsters by telling of the alterations that had been made in London and of the great additions it had received within his recollection."

He was spared a long illness and he passed away at the end of June, 1785, attended in his last days by his Elizabeth and almost unnoticed by the English public, then excited about affairs in India, the new independent republic in America and the suspicion of something afoot in Louis XVI's France. Even the garrulous Boswell failed to make an entry in his journal at the time of his old friend's death, although years later on a visit to London he lamented the passing of old dinner companions and fellow talkers—"no General Paoli—no Sir Joshua Reynolds—no Sir John Pringle—no Squire Godfrey Bosville—no General Oglethorpe." The London literary ladies, who liked his conversation and his old-fashioned gallantry, were among the few who missed him at the time of his death. Mrs. Elizabeth Montagu, the

"Queen of the Blues," wrote to one of her bluestocking friends, "I was very sorry to part with my old Love the General, and heartily pity Mrs. Oglethorpe."

A poetaster, writing in a London periodical, spoke of the man who had

". . . founded Georgia, gave it laws and trade,
He saw it flourish and he saw it fade."

The "fading" was not, we think, viewed in a gloomy spirit by the Founder. Imperialist though he may have been in some sense in his earlier days, it is a fair assumption that he rejoiced to see his colony become a State in a voluntary federation.

INDEX